THE OTHER SIDE OF THE STORY

A Secret War In Hong Kong

NURY VITTACHI

YFL

HONG KONG

This edition first published in 2020 by YLF Hong Kong

ylf@youthlf.org

ISBN 978-988-8470-79-2

First published in Hong Kong in November 2020.

Reprinted December 2020.

"It's a scientific fact that the US has interfered in Hong Kong politics for years, sending millions to anti-China activists. Yet Western media hides that fact, and every time I bring it up, I get accused of being paid 50 cents by the Chinese Communist Party. Well, where's my 50 cents? They probably can't hear me asking through the walls of banknotes surrounding them."

Nury Vittachi, 2020

Contents

Author's Note And Dedication

Critics will say that this account misses event X or statement Y. They will be correct. This is nothing like a comprehensive record of political events in Hong Kong in 2019: that would require a text twenty times the length.

Some will say that this isn't a comprehensive journalistic probe like All The President's Men. That's also true. Nor is it an academic record, with every sentence footnoted and lists of sources and citations provided.

Rather, this book tells the story of a year in the life of a storm-hit community from the point of view of an old-school local newspaper "diary" columnist and his network of insider sources, consisting largely of Hong Kong moms and dads, plus others who have made the city their home. It's very different from the story told in the mainstream media.

You'll find misspellings aplenty, because I have not edited or corrected information which came to me via the Internet or as phone texts.

The media served the people of Hong Kong poorly, falsely splitting them into two opposing camps, one which they sanctified and one which they demonized. The truth is that the majority of members of the Hong Kong public were at neither extreme. They were and are hardworking, balanced, intelligent, law-abiding people, with an attitude to mainland China that is neither over-trustful nor irrationally hostile.

I know, because they sent me tens of thousands of messages over that tumultuous year making that clear. This book is dedicated to them.

Prologue

A Poor Choice Of Clothing

I'M RUNNING DOWN a street in Hong Kong. Darkness is falling.

There are gangsters behind me. Some of them are not nice people. Only last week, they responded to criticism by getting oversized baseball bats and hitting people.

I need to put some distance between them and myself. I'm allergic to having my brains beaten in: it gives me a headache.

An additional problem I'm trying not to think about is that I'm running away from one hostile group directly into the arms of another, possibly more dangerous group.

The ones in front of me are riot squad police officers. They too are armed with wooden sticks (different style, same brain-bashing capacity) but they also have guns with live ammunition.

They are also not likely to greet me like a long lost brother.

From their point of view, the problem is my poor choice of clothing. I am dressed in black from head to toe, the standard costume of the fashion-forward Hong Kong protester during the 2019 Fall Season.

By accident, black-clad me has been dropped out of heaven into the center of a gathering of "white shirts", the protesters' sworn enemy.

So it is clear that I need to be somewhere else, fast. But where? Fact is, there are A LOT of people dressed like me, all in black, not far from here —about a kilometer to the West, in the direction in which I am running.

But how to get there? There is a large cordon of riot police between me and the other Men In Black. And police officers, with very good reason, have developed a strong dislike of running males dressed as emos—especially one sprinting straight towards them.

If I somehow do get through the police lines and reach the rest of the Emo Army (the Eemy? The Armo?), I will face another problem. The black-shirts have an internet forum on which they recently distributed a photograph of me, identifying me as the enemy.

So basically I am a bad guy in the eyes of people on all three sides of this contretemps.

How did I get into this mess?

It's a long story. And it's not about me, not at all: I represent literally the least significant people in this debate, the journalists.

But my personal superpower is Not Shutting Up and so I have become a conduit for thousands of Hong Kong people who want something said but are unable to say it themselves for reasons of being far too intelligent to speak out when way too many people are holding baseball bats or batons.

A grander, more dramatic summary of the present situation in this city is one I heard this morning on the media: a clash of civilizations is taking place, and Hong Kong has been caught in the middle of it. I know that sounds melodramatic, but it may actually have more than a grain of truth in it. On one side is the United States, the richest, most powerful country in the world. On the other is—no, not China, which has stayed hands off, but the ordinary, non-radicalized, basically apolitical working community of Hong Kong.

It's certainly better than the standard interpretation. Most of the Western media has decided that one of the three elements, the black-clad protesters, are noble warriors fighting a crucial battle for Western-style freedom and democracy; and all the people who don't support them are cruel supporters of Nazi-like evil oppressors.

This is not the case. In some ways, it's the opposite of the truth.

Understanding what is really happening is not just important for anyone who wants to be well-informed, but gives us vital insights into the near future of our human planet, as the large but quiet East takes its place on the world stage alongside the small but dominant West.

It's a story worth telling. This book has a lot of ground to cover, so let's get going.

The world's first Monopoly theme park opens in Hong Kong tomorrow. Monopoly is a property-buying game where landlords make people pay ridiculous rents until they go bankrupt, or, as we call it in Hong Kong, "normal life".

CHAPTER 1

The Maddest Place On Earth

In Which We Introduce You To A Delightfully Eccentric Community—An Apolitical Majority—A Three-Piece Political Minority

WARNING. BY OPENING THIS BOOK, you will be entering Hong Kong, one of the world's maddest cities.

Only in Hong Kong does your car parking space cost twice as much as your Lexus.

Only in Hong Kong do bus stops have signs saying: "Octopus is Welcome."

Only in Hong Kong is your security guard eight times older than your building.

Only in Hong Kong do concrete towers carry names like "Lush Verdant Garden".

Only in Hong Kong are pizzas topped with octopus tentacles.

Only in Hong Kong does supermarket mince cost twice as much per kilo as pure copper on the precious metals market.

Only in Hong Kong is ownership of a lawn mower the ultimate status symbol.

Only in Hong Kong are the corridors larger than the apartments.

Only in Hong Kong are pro-business political parties allied with the communists.

Only in Hong Kong are pinko-leftie parties allied with violent anti-immigrant groups.

Only in Hong Kong do you find an eatery called "The Quite Good Chinese Restaurant".

Only in Hong Kong do you laugh your way through each day.

Laughs are particularly important now, at the beginning of 2019, since Hong Kong has been through a terrifying rough patch.

I refer, of course, to the way a massive swine flu epidemic has caused a huge rise in the price of pork, which is now catching up, centimeter for centimeter, with the cost of car park spaces. (actually true! Not a joke!).

This presents a serious conundrum for many Hong Kongers.

Do I feed my children or find a place to park my Lambo?

Decisions, decisions.

* * *

Yes, I'm being light-hearted, but I've spent much of my working life writing diary columns and humor pieces for newspapers and magazines under various names (Lai See, the Spice Trader, Mr Jam, Reliable Sauce and so on) and I like making lists, as you can see. Looking at things with a smile is what I do. I suck at covering funerals.

But the Universe sends all of us regular reminders that life is not all fun and games, and for this reporter, today is a case in point.

It is Tuesday, January 1, and I am on the street.

My spider-sense is detecting a small but growing puddle of darkness in this city of light. It's like finding a piece of salt beef in the middle of your Cantonese almond soup dessert (which actually did happen once, and may be the root cause of my PTSD).

As usual for this time of year, I am with the Hong Kong marchers—and we're madder than ever, in all three senses of that word (crazy, angry and a dark hue of red).

The People's Annual Start-The-Year Protest march is under way.

But I quickly note that the normal insanity level has been ratcheted up several degrees.

Just look who's here and listen to what they are complaining about.

A pro-independence group says it is marching to express fury that the government was DOOMING HONG KONG by flatly refusing to ABANDON the "one country, two systems" policy.

Behind it, a pro-democracy group says it is marching to express fury that the government was DOOMING HONG KONG by flatly refusing to UPHOLD the "one country, two systems" policy.

Further down the straggle of people there are two more groups of contradictory protestors.

Pushed to the fringe is the pro-Beijing group, who feels that Hong Kong should be FULLY REUNIFIED with China RIGHT NOW.

And just in front of them is a group demanding that Hong Kong be FULLY RE-UNIFIED with Britain RIGHT NOW. This second group has taken a leaf from Donald Trump, and is using the slogan: "Make Hong Kong Great Britain Again".

Aieeyah!

A thought strikes me about the political scene here.

What makes so many of us start campaigns we cannot possibly win?

Somewhere in the sky, Saint Thaddeus, the patron saint of lost causes, smiles. He has found his spiritual homeland.

As we reach Central (Hong Kong's creatively named central business district), I share a thought with the journalist next to me, who is new in town.

"These possibly aren't the weirdest groups to rally recently." I say. "That title should probably apply to a little gathering a couple of weeks ago."

I tell him that on December 22, a group of Hong Kong Filipinos marched in this city to enthusiastically celebrate the 50th anniversary of the Communist Party of the Philippines. Ah, communism, that peerless system of governance, and the Philippines, a lovely country full of lovely people that has been a, er, byword for governmental success for decades ... not.

Then we reach the end of the demo, and I hastily add that it is important to realize that not all the people of Hong Kong are like these marchers.

In fact, hardly any of them are. The vast, vast majority of residents are wisely avoiding this event. They are way too smart.

My family members all stopped coming with me to demonstrations several years ago. Even this reporter, an inveterate marcher, now considers himself a detached observer rather than a participant. The protest crowd has always been somewhat unfocused, but this year, they have left rationality behind completely, floating away on clouds of delusional thinking.

So why am I here? If I was 17, I would say "I'm here for the lols".

A long time ago, I swore I would never, never, never go back to seriously covering politics: it can be a very nasty game played by very nasty people—they are more powerful and more vicious than you think, and most of them stay in the shadows, never to be seen.

* * *

We sit down for a rest in Statue Square before heading to our next stops.

This may be a good moment to give the rookie correspondents at the march an overview (in the journalism business there are always new guys and happy amateurs).

As far as politics go, Hong Kong's people fall into three main segments.

1) The biggest group of Hong Kong people in numerical terms are the Apoliticals (Apols). They tend not to vote at all. Sometimes they register but don't turn up at the polling station, but mostly they don't even register.

Yet you absolutely cannot accuse them of being apathetic–they are incredibly busy, active individuals. They are the diametric opposite of apathetic. For many of them, ignoring politics is a conscious decision (and very wise).

These are in fact your typical Hong Kongers: busy business people, focused on making money, launching enterprises and making children, often all at the same time. They are healthily skeptical folk, and think that Western style liberal democracy is not about to dawn in this part of China. They are realists. They work for companies that operate in Hong Kong and outside the city, including in mainland China, because that's what smart people do, and Hong Kong people are smart.

One of the favorite phrases for the Apol group is "the actual situation on the ground", which they churn out like a mantra at frequent intervals.

So an idealistic young man with a band tied around his forehead will shout: "Vote for me and let's make Hong Kong an independent country by September."

And a quietly listening Apol will say: "Ah, yes, nice in theory. But that may not happen, considering the actual situation on the ground."

Judging from my mailbox, many of these folk are mothers, concentrating on raising offspring. But I know that statistically the majority must be business people of both sexes, and most cultures. It's just that women seem better at social media and talking about stuff in general.

Anyway, as I say, most Hong Kongers never join marches like this. They know it is unlikely to make a difference to the future of China or the world or (even Hong Kong) which local political party has more members in the Legislative Council of this city.

Of course some of the Apols can't vote at all, because they are here temporarily, or never got around to registering, or don't know (or care) if they are entitled to.

There are more than three million adults in the Apols category—plus more than a million youngsters and infants, because Hong Kong's children technically fit in the non-voting group. So in total, the non-voters number about four and half million out of Hong Kong's seven and half million people.

2) The second group, much smaller, is the Political People. They do try to vote at elections, but support various parties with slightly different themes.

Many journalists divide them into "pro-democracy" and "pro-Beijing" factions. This cackhanded definition, although widely used, is the root of so many problems, and should be strictly avoided if you care about this city.

In truth, the vast majority of people in Hong Kong are pro-democracy and pro-human rights, but they are also not over-hostile to China. (In my newspaper column I refer to some people as "Delaymocrats", because they say they are pro-democracy but nervously tend to delay its introduction, worried, quite reasonably, about the rowdiness and dodgy allegiances of some of the other political groups.)

The real main difference between the political parties is their level of approval or disapproval of mainland China.

Some reporters see them as the anti-China and pro-China sides. But that's also unhelpfully simplistic. It implies a level of extremism that simply isn't there in the vast majority of cases.

A more accurate description would be to say that there are many people who feel allied to the West, and have a negative feeling about China, which they often express rather stridently. And there are many who are less hostile and more accommodating or understanding of that country's ways of doing things, but are not necessarily naive about its failings.

It would be more truthful to call the two groups the dislikers and the understanders, perhaps, or the standoffish and the friendlies, or the fearful and the upbeat, or the pessimists and the optimists.

The China dislikers form themselves into little groups of activists, and get fed cash, discreetly or publicly, by a US unit set up by the CIA "to advance the cause of democracy". This is more than a little dodgy (other countries wouldn't allow it) but Hong Kong is extremely free and permissive, yes, even after the handover.

Adding both groups (the China-friendly and the China-unfriendly) together, we find there are between two and three million people in this category, the political folk. They are roughly equally divided, with numbers for each side hovering between 1.1 million and 1.7 million. In times of political strife, the people who dislike China tend to win elections, and in times of peace, the other team usually comes first. We have swing voters, just like in other places.

Now, on the negative side, among the stern-voiced critics of China, about 60,000 have a strong liking to gather and march regularly, but the number jumps up to about 200,000 during medium-grade periodic political upheavals, and 470,000 during major upheavals, when they manage to pull in all their active supporters. These numbers have been surprisingly consistent over the decades—and we'll come back to them later.

3) And finally, we have the radicals. They are, thankfully, a much, much smaller group of worryingly angry young people, mostly male, who are unfortunately prone to violence.

They've only really been around since about 2013 but announced themselves as a significant force in an incident in 2016 when a group of them set fire to things and injured more than 120 people on a single horrific night.

They tend to be openly anti-immigrant (that is, immigrants from China), and gravitate to parties using names like the Hong Kong Indigenous and the Hong Kong National Party, Civic Passion, the Hong Konger Front, Demosisto, the Hong Kong Autonomy Party, Hongkongese Priority and Hong Kong First.

Note how the words of some of them echo the names of anti-immigrant groups in the West, such as Britain First, America First, the National Front, and so on.

Many of these groups are so tiny that they disappear soon after they are announced. Sometimes they use the term "the localists" to differentiate them from people who were not born here. (Ironically, two of the more famous members, Nathan Law and Edward Leung, were actually born in mainland China, but that inconvenient fact tends to be omitted from feature interviews.) They think of themselves as leading a revolution and believe China can be persuaded to grant independence, full autonomy or self-determination to Hong Kong by marches. (St Thaddeus runs to the edge of his cloud and looks down happily. "My people!")

The radicals are often young and see things in black and white, like fax machines, dolphins, owl monkeys, and reporters who work for Fox News, CNN, MSNBC, and the Guardian.

There's some variety within this group. Some radicals are quite pleasant to chat with, but at the dark end of the gradient, many of them have lots of similarities with far right groups in the UK or Europe, and some members are not above simply assaulting mainland visitors on the street for speaking Mandarin.

The radicals love Trump (because Trump also hates China) and they like to use US right-wing signifiers like Pepe the Frog. Their newspaper is Apple Daily, a hard-nosed, gossipy, sometimes overtly racist newspaper (think of tabloids like The Sun in the UK). Apple popularized the term "locusts" for mainland immigrant visitors, and their readers' favorite website is an all-Chinese language discussion board called LIHKG.com which is a bit like 4Chan but with lower morals. Some people overseas think Apple Daily is a noble "pro-democracy" paper, but that's like saying a flame war on 4Chan is a polite debate.

* * *

So that's a rough political breakdown of our population. But to fully understand the pressures and undercurrents that power this place, we need to look at the cast list of active groups who make things happen in Hong Kong.

Let's start at the bottom with the press.

As I head home from the march on this opening day of the year, I use my phone to check the media coverage, and what I see makes me laugh—and then sigh.

The mainland Chinese media is often just awful, with too few exceptions. Most political happenings simply go uncovered. When they do report on something, it is often twisted to take a specific angle. They have been getting better, and occasionally you find a really good piece in there, but in general the political slant is clearly detectable.

The Western media these days is ... exactly the same. It presents a greater variety of views in the opinion pages, but the overall political slant of the news reports is often just as deliberate and heavy-handed as the Chinese media. The former spins the news to make China look good, and the latter spins it to make China look bad. There's surprisingly little difference.

The Western media is much, much more dangerous, because it has a sophisticated, suave, you-can-trust-me tone to it. No modern global intellectual with a brain cell can take a spitting, spluttering editorial in the People's Daily seriously, but the average person assumes the Financial Times and the Guardian are fundamentally trustworthy and unprejudiced. Some writers from those publications are. Yet so often these days, way too much of what they print is as crudely politicized as anything in the mainland China media. People constantly ask me to recommend balanced media, and I shake my head: there's no such thing. I tell them: read widely, talk to people, and make up your own minds about everything.

Over the past year or so, the two sides have become more alike in some ways. The Chinese media has definitely improved, with some colorful, critical writing, and some of the Western media has slumped into ridiculousness. For example, to a surprisingly large number of Western reporters, the Hong Kong government is a group of "puppets", as if they were Communist Party members dispatched from Beijing in 1997 to torment and oppress the people here. That is a common stance, although it's just silly and ill-informed.

The reality is that Hong Kong's ministers were nearly all born and raised here, and are about as communist as David Koch's big toe. The civil service people who ran Hong Kong when it had a white male leader before July 1997 are the exact same people who ran Hong Kong when it acquired an ethnic Chinese leader after that date.

They're painted as Beijing puppets, but many don't speak Mandarin and some are so Westernized that they are most comfortable speaking English rather than Cantonese. And until Starbucks arrived, almost everyone drank *lai cha* — the local name for British style milky tea.

* * *

And what does the press coverage of today's procession actually say? At the moment, I see nothing from the mainland China press at all.

But the international press is on the job. Foreign correspondents from many Western news organizations are presenting this tiny, totally incoherent march as further proof that the fiendish, tyrannical, communist elite from Beijing which runs Hong Kong has crushed all freedom in this city, while the people of Hong Kong are brave enough to defy the oppressors.

This is a big mistake that almost all the Western media people make. The minority of Hong Kongers who take the hostile "Western hawk" attitude to China—that means, about one in four of us—are presented as The People of Hong Kong. The majority of us don't exist, or are dismissed as "pro-Beijing" apparatchiks. We don't know it at this point, but this horrendous error was going to blight our city over the next year and a half.

Incidentally, not one of the Western press outlets reports the actual democracy-flavored statement the Hong Kong government has issued in response to the march: "The Government fully respects the right of Hong Kong people to take part in public processions and their freedom to express their views."

I know I am starting to sound like a crabby ancient reactionary, but (puts on high quivery voice) *in the old days reporters took time to dig a little deeper and tried a lot harder to avoid confirmation bias.*

Or maybe I'm wrong.

Probably my generation was just as bad. One can't be stubborn about these things, and we're all prone to confirmation bias, right?

Anyway, do you see how depressing this can be? You can see why I never write about politics. I find it much more worthwhile to write about other subjects, such as the history of Hong Kong, which is fascinating, and full of untold, amazing, even jaw-dropping stories, that most people don't know.

In fact, I believe this is a good time for a little history lesson.

Are you sitting comfortably?

CHAPTER 2

The Healthiest, Wealthiest Place In The World

In Which We Watch A Miracle Happening—
Expectations Of Doom In 1997—Health And Wealth Instead

IN THE BRIGHT, SUNNY spring of 1994, an extraordinary meeting was quietly held between police detectives from three very different but neighboring cities: British Hong Kong, Portuguese Macau, and Chinese Guangzhou.

The three groups of cops, each with different uniforms, badges and flags, talked about the possibilities of working jointly on cross-border crime.

It seemed a tall order. The future was full of political uncertainties.

Those were jittery times for everyone.

Hong Kong and Macau were just about to be handed over to the care of scary mainland China, the former in 1997, and the latter in 1999. There was a significant amount of distrust between the various sides, and more than that, there was genuine fear, too, particularly on the Hong Kong side.

We Hong Kongers felt that we had the most to lose. You see, the British settlement on the south coast of China was fiercely proud of its free, independent, capitalist way of life, which had made us one of the biggest financial centers on earth—and no one wanted to let that disappear into the terrifying maw of "the reds". They kill girl babies by the million, right?

Yet at the same time, we were, pretty much all of us, strongly in favor of the transfer of sovereignty, even the political people who strongly disliked China, a group which included this author at the time. (I was one of the biggest fans of its leader, Martin Lee Chu-ming.)

That sounds crazy, but think of it like this: What do you think of the notion that it's okay for a community of one ethnicity to be governed indefinitely by a handful of people of another ethnicity? Should whites lord it over blacks, or blacks lord it over whites, or Asians lord it over Europeans, or Europeans lord it over Asians?

Clearly not. All those scenarios feel wrong in principle. Both Western and Eastern ways of thinking agree on that. Indeed, I had often thought that the first miracle of Hong Kong was the way the majority population had allowed that ludicrous situation to continue for so long.

So there was no real dispute that the handover of this community to China was the right way to go. It had to happen.

And it wasn't just the ethnicity issue—there was geography, too. Any child looking at a map could see that Hong Kong was a natural part of China, not the UK. This coastal city wasn't Bournemouth.

Our Eastern culture was another factor. Fully 92 percent of the residents of Hong Kong were ethnically Chinese, and many of the others, including me, had roots in other parts of Asia. White folks were thin on the ground and pretty much limited to the top of the ladder.

So you can see why we all agreed that that had to change.

But on that spring day in 1994, and from the point of view of police chiefs, the proposed meeting was important mainly for practical reasons. The existence of a hard border meant there were daily opportunities for fleeing criminals to take advantage of the fact that divided legal and economic systems existed side by side.

Criminals were thoroughly enjoying this—as were business people, who were building swanky offices on the Hong Kong side (to give buyers the impression that they were high-class operations that deserved trust) and cheap factories on the China side (to take advantage of the extremely low cost of labor).

The recipe worked brilliantly, making our community rich at extraordinary speed.

Robbers took advantage of the border in a more straightforward way. They could steal as much as they liked from Hong Kong people and then simply slip over the border to Guangdong—or vice versa.

It was way past the time for the police on the different sides to start working together too, just as business people did.

But what would happen as the transfer of sovereignty took place? Would Hong Kong's world-class legal system survive the transition to rule by our feared Beijing overlords?

The proposed British-Chinese scheme, known as "one country, two systems" (or 1C2S), had never been tried before, and seemed, frankly speaking, an unworkable pipe dream.

At that time, in 1994, activists and reporters painted images of doom and gloom, and there seemed to be a one-in-a-million chance of success. One Western publication summed up the general feeling in a stark headline:

"The Death of Hong Kong".

And that was just one of many similar cover stories and even entire books carrying the exact same message. Commentators nodded grimly. But as is so often the case, we in the media got things completely wrong.

Time passes. Roll stock footage of pages flying off a calendar.

A quarter of a century later, in 2019, what we had painted to be the least likely scenario had come to pass.

Hong Kong had blossomed into an extraordinary miracle: a city in China with a world-class legal system, a lively free press, and an entirely capitalistic, free-wheeling economic model—the one country, two systems scheme had been spectacularly successful. It had worked better than even the most starry-eyed among us had dared to hope. Even Martin Lee, head of the party most hostile to China, admitted to being pleasantly surprised.

Hong Kong felt more like a democracy than the vast majority of democracies on the planet, as visitors often remarked. And more than that, our community felt like a *successful* democracy in a way that many Western countries didn't.

We'd become one of the richest cities in the world and we lived and worked in literally the world's most expensive buildings. The average poky little apartment in Hong Kong was worth more than the average house in London. A shop in New York's swanky Fifth Avenue was significantly cheaper to rent than the same size shop in Hong Kong's Causeway Bay.

In terms of performance, our financial workers regularly beat their equivalents in London, New York, and Tokyo, and we were the world's undisputed number one go-to-destination for multinational companies that wanted to launch themselves onto international share markets.

In business terms, we were "Masters of the Universe" in English, or "Heavenly Kings" in the Chinese turn of phrase.

And it wasn't just money that we were good at. We're not totally crass. We were also the world's healthiest people—literally.

Despite the pollution we often complained about, we were doing astonishingly well in terms of health indexes. Our longevity was now the world's best, having overtaken Japan's legendarily high levels.

We also had the best levels of health across social groups, planet-wide. Many societies have long-living rich people. Ours had long-living poor people, too. And we achieved that against huge odds.

You see, a downside of living close to factories in Guangdong was the smoky, particle-filled air. Yet that too was a problem that was being actively fixed by our community. By 2019, the major air pollutants in Hong Kong had dropped dramatically. They had fallen between 34 and 80 percent over the past 20 years.

Our once filthy harbor was now clean enough to swim in. To be honest, "Hong Kongers ruling Hong Kong" (another slogan) had done a superb job. And they WERE Hong Kongers. Our civil servants come from here, and were not particularly fond of Beijing, although no amount of persuasion would ever convince some Western correspondents of this.

We who lived in this Miracle City had other things to be proud of, too. In particular, our legal system was not just good, it was world-class—and arguably a major part of the secret of our success.

Hong Kong had repeatedly been rated number one for judicial independence in Asia by the Global Competitiveness Report of the World Economic Forum. In the World Justice Project's Rule of Law Index, Hong Kong was ranked 16th out of 126 countries and territories for its overall rule of law performance—higher than many Western countries.

In the "absence of corruption" category, Hong Kong was rated an impressive ninth in the world, ahead of the vast majority of Western countries.

Back in the colonial days, in 1996, British colonial Hong Kong scored an impressive 69.9 for rule of law in the World Bank's Worldwide Governance Indicators project. In recent years Hong Kong score's has been well into the 90s.

By 2019, Hong Kong had become, quite literally, one of the best-governed, most law-abiding places in the world.

Why such high scores on the legal front? The secret: our judges rocked. Hong Kong's judiciary was fully independent of the government, and regularly produced judgments which annoyed ministers (something not common elsewhere in Asia, and increasingly rare in some Western countries).

And compared to the rest of the world? I would say that Hong Kong's judiciary was not as good as our Western equivalents: I would say it was better. Seriously.

The city has a unique international system: as well as many excellent home-grown judges, the top bench had judges from the United Kingdom, Canada and Australia. This system is disliked by some people from Beijing, but they have to suck it up. "Even the UK doesn't have that," a senior Law Society member told me.

There's another thing: Hong Kong's anti-corruption agency, known as the ICAC, which is short for Independent Commission Against Corruption, had been so successful it now trained counterparts in more than 40 countries—including mainland China. We're not just clean, but we spread cleanliness in all directions. It's really important to understand this.

Still, I don't want to overdo it. I'm not saying that this was a utopia. Oh, no. Far from it.

Successful business people and happy flat owners are good to see, but coins always have two sides. Pollution and over-priced property were heavy burdens. I had a semi-permanent tickle in my throat, as do many Hong

Kongers. Viruses tended to blow from north to south and we often suffered. Usually it was small things, like colds and flus, but occasionally there was a big one, like SARS in 2003.

People in Hong Kong start coughing at certain periods of the year and explain it by saying things like "it's the change of weather". They mean it literally. The wind changes direction, the flavor of the air changes, and smoke and pathogens arrive from factories and farms to the north.

Property was also a big issue. I wanted to faint when I paid rent or mortgage bills every month. We'll talk more about Hong Kong's challenges on that front later.

Yet still, considering what had been predicted for us 25 years ago, we had plenty of reasons to be cheerful in 2019.

Go back for a moment to the lack of confidence about Hong Kong's future at that first cross-border police officers' meeting in 1994—and then consider the city today.

Hong Kong had not only maintained its freedoms, but it had built on them—and was creating an increasingly powerful relationship with the legal sector of mainland China, which was itself growing in positive ways.

* * *

And so we come back to the present day, or at least the present day of this report. In April of 2019, in Guangzhou, the top CID officers of Chinese Hong Kong, Chinese Macau and mainland city Guangdong met for their 25th anniversary celebration of their annual confab, marking a long and impressive record of successful joint crime-busting operations: a quarter of a century of co-operation.

Media coverage? As far as I know, there wasn't any, bar a short item in my newspaper column in The Standard newspaper.

That meeting didn't fit the media narrative of that moment, so went entirely unreported by the mainstream media, which was pushing a very different story in the first half of 2019.

Now we've covered the historical context, we need to get back to the main plot line. And we'll do that after one more thing – briefly introducing your guide.

* * *

Your narrator of this book is a Sri Lanka-born writer who has been living in Hong Kong since 1987. I love the people of this town so much I adopted three of them. No nobility in that—my wife and I felt it a privilege to become a permanent part of this community in this way. Hong Kongers in the main are amazing people: warm, intelligent, patient, calm—and able to create and power through delicious 12-course banquets with astonishing regularity.

The city this community has built really is one of the best places to live in the world, with an astonishingly low crime rate, very little unemployment, glorious scenery, and multiple cultural groups working well together.

Even better, it was on the border of China, physically and metaphorically—a particularly good place to be any kind of observer of the world as it evolves, so it was perfect for a writer of books and news columns such as myself. The future was right here.

As a columnist, I started off by mainly doing the usual obnoxious bully-pulpit thing of poking fun at the elite and generally being trivial and snarky. (In the early 1980s, I'd worked for the so-called "Fleet Street" papers in London.)

But in Asia, I quickly stumbled on a group of people who were far wiser, funnier, more observant, and better connected than I was: the readers. So my columns evolved, often becoming more like lightly edited letters pages, with a huge diversity of views, and a lot of humor.

I worked for the South China Morning Post, Reader's Digest Asia, the Far Eastern Economic Review (writing the Travelers' Tales page), and my work appeared in hundreds of papers through syndication.

I was no celebrity, but a reasonably well-known working writer with a good network. On the Western front, my essays had appeared in everything from the New York Times to Time magazine. I'd appeared hundreds of times on TV and radio, including CNN, Bloomberg and the BBC. I was also proud of the fact that I could also be found in huge numbers of Asian newspapers, too — not so famous as the Western ones, but often with far bigger circulations.

In my spare time, I wrote novels and non-fiction books, and was fortunate enough to have some of them printed by the world's biggest publishing houses, including Penguin Random House, Scholastic, St Martin's Press, World Scientific, Oxford University Press, John Wiley and so on. That part of my work triggered an interesting spin-off. For about 17 years, I'd had a side job teaching "The Power of Stories" in the Media Department of Hong Kong Polytechnic University, the largest center of tertiary education in the city. In the Bachelors' class, I taught students how stories shaped the way we saw the world, and in the Master of Science class, we looked at the way stories used multiple parts of the brain to infuse information with emotion.

But recently, on the reporting side, I had begun to become uncomfortable with the way the international voice of journalism told Asia's story. The lens through which everything was seen was very, very Western—and not just that, but frequently actively hostile to fundamental Asian mores and often starkly, openly anti-Chinese.

As I said earlier, pretty much everyone knows that much of what you read in the mainland Chinese media is politically spun, while too few people realize that this can be even more true for much of what one reads in the international (as in, Western) media.

Between those two harmful extremes, the nuanced, complex stories of real people in real communities were largely being left untold. There was a serious need for journalists to listen to the Asian community and write down what we actually say and think. And that means all of us, not just the hostile-to-China people beloved by Western journalists. After all, Asians make up more of humanity than all the other cultural clusters put together. Don't our mores count for something?

The simple truth was that sometimes even the mainland Chinese government did good things, as did the Hong Kong government—and those events deserved to be reported without the sour distorting lens of the international media.

For me, the answer was to strictly avoid politics, and just write the news as it was, with just enough snark to make readers smile.

And sometimes that meant forcing myself to occasionally print positive news items about the government.

> **Secretary for Security John Lee reported on Saturday that Hong Kong's crime rate had plummeted to its lowest level in 49 years.**
>
> **Our 35,000 police officers are going to have to start arresting each other just to have something to do.**

CHAPTER 3

The Importance Of Being Critical

In Which We Observe The Free Press—
Criticizing Leaders—An East-West Civil Service—A Mother's Plea

Wednesday, January 2

Your unesteemed narrator is sitting at his desk, juggling multiple sources. Some are on the phone, while others are on Whatsapp, WeChat, Facebook, email, Twitter, Messenger—or just shouting at me from across the coffee shop.

In the great scheme of things, this reporter is an unimportant person doing an unimportant job, filling a newspaper "diary" column of snippets: but I invite you to be my shadow at work for a while, because watching the flow of news may be the quickest way to get a feel for the free and easy way Hong Kong operates.

I usually maintain a few "offices", all of which tend to be coffee shops. (If they were good enough for news gatherers in London in the 1700s, they're good enough for me.)

This year I have chosen one near the Stock Exchange in Central so I can chat with business people, one at Hong Kong's biggest university because I lecture there and like to keep in touch with young people, and one at a technology hub called Cyberport so I can be in the loop with tech developments.

Today I am at my Kowloon office, a popular glass-walled Starbucks on the campus of Hong Kong Polytechnic University. The buildings of the university are arranged alphabetically, and this is the Block X coffee shop.

It's the second day of the year and a critic of China has just sent me a report about Our Great Leader, China's President Xi Jinping.

"Chinese don't attack Chinese," the great man said in a "special message" to Taiwan today.

(Mr Xi seems to have conveniently forgotten 2,600 years of feudal history.)

But in the case of people who want Taiwanese independence, he would make a special exception: "We make no promise to renounce the use of force."

How charming. Mainland officials are the gift that keeps on giving to Asian humorists. With a distinctively grandiose tone that cries out to be parodied, they make themselves an irresistible target.

Also today, Chinese officials announced that they had sent a rocket to the moon.

The moon? Really?

It was time to mix up these news items and deliver this piece of news in fantasy form as a piece of Private Eye-type humor, for the newspaper or the Internet or both.

XI CALLS FOR "FULL REUNIFICATION" BY 2050

Unification between China and the Moon is "inevitable" and will take place within 30 years, China's President Xi Jinping said in a landmark speech this morning.

"We believe in peaceful resumption of land that belonged to us 4.5 billion years ago before it broke away."

"However, if moon-dwelling aliens try to prevent full reunification, we reserve the right to use force."

As a result of this tiny piece of mockery aimed at China's leader, goons from the Hong Kong government arrive at my coffee shop just 58 minutes later.

They kick down the door, and kill me, shooting six bullets into my head.

SIX BULLETS. Right into my head.

My cappuccino flies off the table in 60 frames per second slow motion.

Seconds later, I am lying on the floor, motionless, as the other diners get out their smartphones and start recording, their fingers splayed across their amazed faces as they dream of the number of social media hits they are going to get.

No, they don't.

None of that happens.

That's the point. You see, the truth is that nobody official reacts in any way. People in Hong Kong are used to me and other humorists doing this sort of thing. We're entirely free to do that stuff. This city operates like a modern democracy, only without the crime.

The Hong Kong government doesn't respond, Beijing doesn't respond, and nobody does anything bad to me at all. I've been doing the exact same thing since the 1980s.

The only difference is that things today are rather less censored than they were in the past, in the British era: that's the truth of it. When I point this out, people always say: "You have freedom of the press today, but tomorrow it'll be gone."

"Yeah," I reply. "And people have been saying that to me every week for the past 30 years too."

"But this time it's true."

"And people have been saying THAT to me every week for the past 30 years too."

Ding! Technology tells me I have a message.

With perfect timing, a reader sends me more evidence of the harm done to Hong Kong's image as painted by fantasizing foreign correspondents.

A shocked man named Guru Bhat has just used Twitter to lament the way Hong Kong had been crushed by an "iron-fist dictatorship" and wishing that "Hong Kong can be a city state like Singapore and free".

FREE LIKE SINGAPORE?!

My blood is instantly boiling.

Aieeyah! I would just like to point out that Singapore, on the journalists' freedom of information index, is behind South Sudan.

Hong Kong's press, in contrast, is possibly the freest IN THE WORLD.

Not only can journalists print anything we like about our leaders, we can also print lies, slander and gross misinformation with gay abandon, and we frequently do, to be perfectly honest.

You can't print blatant lies in Western newspapers, can you?

Well, unless you work for the Inquirer, of course.

Or the Daily Express.

Or the Daily Mail.

Or Fox News.

Or CNN.

Or the New York Times.

Or the BBC.

Okay, whatever.

* * *

Monday, January 7

Several days (and dozens of diary items and columns) have come and gone; today this author is not poking fun at mainland China officials.

Local humorists have another juicy target close at hand: Hong Kong's own government apparatchiks. Mwa ha ha ha ha. (Rubs hands together, grinning.)

Like civil servants anywhere, some of ours are wonderful, others are a waste of space, some achieve miracles, while others steadfastly prevent miracles from occurring.

Now if I was forced at gunpoint to be perfectly straight, I would begrudgingly admit that I probably wouldn't swap our civil service sector for their counterparts anywhere else in Asia. Our lot, at best, can be breathtakingly cool and efficient.

Even so, it's a commentator's duty to keep them on their toes by sniping at them, right?

So, for example, our commerce minister Eddie Yau recently highlighted the fact that the huge majority (47 million out of 60 million) of this city's visitors were "mainland visitors coming to Hong Kong looking for some non-mainland experience".

In my newspaper diary I suggest an item of "non-mainland experience":

"So, Eddie, we could open a bookshop in Causeway Bay selling books banned on the mainland? That would count, right?"

Heh-heh-heh. They won't like that.

Tuesday, January 8

Again today I find myself writing about the glorious Hong Kong government.

In some ways, our apparatchiks are very Western, probably the most Westernized civil servants in Asia. Pop into their offices and you see a group of quiet, bespectacled people drinking milky tea, eating wholewheat biscuits, and organizing official government campaigns to raise awareness of transgender rights. (Literally. That's one of the government projects this year.) It could be The Guardian readers' club in Islington.

Most importantly, from my point of view, Hong Kong civil servants take the mockery on the chin, like Westerners, and decidedly not like Asians. In most other Asian countries if you mock government people, they arrest you, bankrupt you, or kill you. That's not a joke or an exaggeration: that's what happens. My father was a journalist too, and he was followed by people with guns after he criticized the rulers of the place in which he was living.

But here in Hong Kong, civil servants put up with all sorts of absurd allegations fired in their direction by columnists, cartoonists and broadcast hosts. I've made a good living out of it.

Yet again, I don't want to over-egg this pie. Our leaders can be very Western. But in other ways, Hong Kong civil servants are very Eastern. For a start, a Western-style sense of what is currently politically correct can occasionally be glaringly absent, reminding us that we are in Asia.

Case in point: today, the Hong Kong government's film archive team has just announced it has organized a film festival with a theme of funny fat people.

Viewers will see "six films featuring figurative AND LITERAL comedy heavyweights" on February 7 and 9 at the Hong Kong Film Archive cinema in Sai Wan Ho.

The festival is called "A Big Fat Happy New Year".

It has been organized, the official press release says, "to mark the Year of the Pig". (I am not making this up.)

One featured movie is a 1956 black and white movie in which big girl Tam Lan-hing "plays a marriage-hungry woman who provides a feast of laughter" called "Fatso Married Skinny".

So in this instance, maybe the government is not like the Guardian readers' club in Islington.

Wednesday, January 16

Another cast member who must be included in any attempt to understand this city's mindset is the Hong Kong police officer, of course. They are among the most beloved and respected police forces in the world, with public approval rates off the charts. But there are critics.

Today, I receive two announcements about these uniformed ladies and gentlemen, forwarded by a reader named Tin Sin-chong, who is not a fan.

The first one reveals that Hong Kong's police force has organized a series of 175th anniversary events.

The second is a separate notice from statisticians who confirm that Hong Kong crime rates have fallen to record lows. Across almost all categories of crime, the figures have plummeted to extraordinarily small numbers.

"Was this coincidence or collusion?" asks Tin.

The timing does seem suspiciously neat. Perhaps cops had a word with robbers?

Police: "Excuse us, folks, but could you lay off committing crimes for several years before our big anniversary party in January? Thanks."

Friday, February 8

And of course Hong Kong's own leader must be on our cast list for this story.

The rules of independent journalism require that reporters and columnists make snarky comments about whoever leads their country (worshipful US reporters during the Obama years being the embarrassing exception).

So all Hong Kong humorists look for opportunities to make digs at our city's supremo, Carrie Lam. If you want to follow the general media portrayal of her as a robotic Communist Puppet sent from Beijing, go right ahead. We have a free press here, and some people feel the need to report that, despite it being untrue.

Yet if one gets to know her, being hostile becomes tricky. Yes, she's an iron lady in many ways, but she likes young people, and has a disarming soft side which differentiates her from her less smiley predecessor, a surveyor named Leung Chun-ying (generally known as C.Y.).

Also, many property developers hate her (she keeps trying to tax them) so that also puts her in the good books of journalists who follow Hong Kong affairs closely.

Her deputy, a man named Matthew Cheung, also has a likeable side. He keeps turning up in person at charity events to help Hong Kong ethnic minority people. It's not just talk, either: he and his boss keep hiving off chunks of cash to set up social aid projects for us.

In the last week of January, Mrs Lam slipped away from global leaders at Davos, Switzerland, to spend time with Sally Begbie, an inspiring Hong Kong woman whose Christian charity organization, Crossroads, is seen as a world-class model for the way rich places can help poor ones. Mrs. Lam is a massive fan, as indeed all thinking human beings should be.

Later, Hong Kong's leader returned to the main halls of Davos—and took her turn at the microphone.

While other leaders boasted about their GDPs, Mrs. Lam told the audience that what she was really proud of was her community's welfare sector. Hong Kong's public sector is only 20 percent of GDP (unusually small), but fully 60 percent of that cash is spent on social services (unusually large).

So, contrary to common belief, the Hong Kong government has rather a soft soul, as those figures show. Nobody believes me when I say this, which is why I include the numbers. You can't really argue with numbers.

Yet when I do that, I get labeled "government suck-up", but whatever. You have to be balanced and give the facts, whatever people say, right? And if you spend year after year sniping at the government, you've earned the right to occasionally send them a bouquet instead of a brickbat, right?

Looking back at the notes above, I find myself worrying that I have been too nice to the Hong Kong police.

True, they probably do deserve the title of "Asia's Finest", but if you know what police in this region have been like over recent decades, you'll know that phrase is the ultimate example of "damned with faint praise".

In much of Asia in the past 50 years, the police and the villains have been the same type of people—the officers were just a better-dressed, better-financed criminal gang.

Furthermore, I personally have had some rather negative experiences in my dealings with the force in Hong Kong.

Yet truth be told, I would still probably prefer being detained in Hong Kong than in any other place in Asia—and perhaps the world, with the possible exception of the UK, which also has nice police officers. In Hong Kong as in the UK, the police corruption level is low, the efficiency level is high, and they have an excellent relationship with the general public.

This doesn't mean the Hong Kong police are perfect, and there are some bad ones among them. In other words, they are no different to any other any large group of people. (There are about 29,000 officers, plus some 5,000 auxiliaries.)

The police also get needled in my columns.

Shortly before writing this, The Standard, the newspaper which carries my diary column, reported that police officers arrested a bar manager after viewing "lewd activities" in Tsim Sha Tsui.

The officers visited the bar disguised as regular punters multiple times, staying for about four hours on each visit.

"Officers' testimony showed they only touched the women's breasts for work," the report said (those were the actual words). Yeah, right. And just remind me, how much do they get paid for this "work"?

Monday, February 18

But the main cast member of this story is Hong Kong itself—as a community and as an extraordinary piece of geography. It's a wonderful place to live, I have to say.

BUT.

There's a *YUUGE* "but" here.

Hong Kong has an image problem. If you are reading this from outside the city, I need to advise you to separate the place you see in gangster movies and particularly in video games from reality.

For some unfathomable reason, game designers limit themselves to portraying Hong Kong as a horrendously dark, ultra-violent city ruled by gangsters.

A week before writing this, the world's video game players were ecstatic as a new extremely gory title was released—with mass murder in Hong Kong as its theme.

In The Hong Kong Massacre, the player becomes a detective running through buildings shooting people, leaving walls and floors splattered with blood.

It has "over-the-top gore!" enthused Sherif Saed on game review site VG247. In fact, every video game review site I looked at reported gleefully that the game, developed in Sweden, is extremely violent and thus excellent.

You can hear the drool dripping when you read the previews, all written by men. (This is strong evidence for euthanizing the entire cohort of human males, if only women would realize it. I know we're all supposed to be Western style ultra-liberals these days but this sort of "entertainment" makes me want to take my family and move somewhere deeply conservative like Malaysia or North Korea.)

And another thing! The Swedish company that makes this game describes Hong Kong as "a moody, crime-riddled city".

What!? The simple truth is that crime rates in Sweden are climbing steadily (look 'em up), while Hong Kong remains pretty much the safest major city on the planet.

Tuesday, February 19

Aieeyah! This reporter is looking at this screen, his brow furrowed.

Another letter saying the same thing. That's the fourth in ten days. In among the regular mail and messages from readers, I am receiving regular notes about a dastardly plan from Beijing.

The writers, who are expats or antsy young people, say the mainland authorities are changing the laws in Hong Kong so that they can snatch anyone they like to whisk over the border—and dissidents, pro-democracy campaigners, and irritatingly critical journalists are going to be top of the list.

That would be me.

And not just people like me, but the general public too is in danger. The new law introduces a kind of mass deportation policy.

I shoot off a few emails to gather information and soon find that not all the people on my network are saying that.

Other writers, older ones, who tend to be better connected, comment that the dark allegations going around town have the story almost exactly backwards.

They say that government lawyers in Hong Kong have proposed a new law, not people in Beijing—and it is a good and necessary thing, designed to upgrade our legal infrastructure.

I remind the panicky people raising this issue that I strictly avoid heavy political issues—there are more than enough over-politicized pontificators in Hong Kong, as indeed there are the world in general. They almost always amplify problems, not solve them.

But when a mother for whom I have a lot of respect tells me that her 22-year-old son is becoming quite "radicalized" about the "Evil Law" I reluctantly promise to check it out.

"He's going to meetings about it," she writes. "And they are planning marches and things."

I reassure her that marches are fine—they are a sign of Hong Kong's freedom, and I have been participating myself for more than 30 years.

"Peaceful marches are good things, and keep us ahead of Singapore," I tell her.

She is the archetypal Hong Konger, but hates the media so I should perhaps refer to her only as Mrs. Ho, or by her nickname, which is Mother of Five (Two Children and Three Enterprises, or MoF-2C3E.)

But for a moment I pause and think back to the march on January 1, and the feeling I had that the spinning top of Hong Kong politics is slowly slipping off the edge of the table.

The behind-the-scenes stirrers are up to something. I know it.

This reporter sits at the Block X coffee shop at the university, contemplating.

Chapter 4

The Truth Behind The New Law

In Which We Learn About Extradition—A Financier's Insights—A History Lesson About Independence—The Western Media Is Unhelpful

NO CHOICE-LAH. Have to get up and get out there. Check things out for Mother of Five and the rest of my audience. I reluctantly leave my comfortable seat at the coffee shop and go to my other office, a branch of Starbucks in Exchange Square, Central, to meet people.

First, a civil servant briefs me off the record.

It's interesting. The government's legal policy wonks are pretty happy with themselves. It is now 22 years after the handover, and Hong Kong has developed into a healthy, wealthy city with a world-class legal system, as mentioned earlier.

Not only that, but it is now on the global map as a major legal center for certain specialist interest areas, such as arbitration. Loads of international conferences choose this city for their annual legal confabs. Law was one of the things Hong Kong did best.

But there was one obvious problem needing to be fixed: Hong Kong was being criticized by international law experts as being weak on extradition treaties, and thus deficient in international cooperation against crime.

The G7's Financial Action Task Force (known as G7-FATF) had recommended that we fix this so we could play a bigger role in the fight against money laundering and terrorist financing.

"We couldn't join in because we didn't have the right laws," she said. "The SAR's deficit in the extradition area was 'undermining collaboration'."

Think about it this way, she said. "You could commit the most horrendous of crimes, bankrupting a country or murdering large numbers of innocent people, and literally swan around Hong Kong in plain sight, and you'd be completely untouchable," the source told me. "This was terrible for a Western-style city which aimed to be a global model for the rule of law."

Furthermore, Hong Kong had signed a United Nations pledge to "significantly reduce illicit financial and arms flows, strengthen the recovery and return of stolen assets and combat all forms of organized crime" by a deadline of 2030. Were we on track to succeed? No.

Critics pointed to Article 1 of the UN Model Treaty on Extradition which made it clear that in the interest of social justice, states had an obligation to promote extradition treaties.

Hong Kong did have a functioning extradition law—but it was extremely limited, applying to only 20 countries out of the almost 200 on this planet. In the entire 22-year history of Hong Kong, China, only 100 people had been extradited. Most went through lengthy court processes and then were simply put on planes to the United States.

Hong Kong needed a proper, grown-up, Western-style extradition law to lift our game to global standards, as the G7 had been recommending for several years.

So Hong Kong civil servants had gone to work.

I looked at some of the literature they had reviewed. Jurisdictions which claim to uphold social justice and the rule of law needed to have extradition treaties, said the writers of an influential 2011 UK report on the subject.

It was a surprisingly interesting read. Extradition must NOT be limited to places with similar legal systems, it said. Otherwise only the top handful of economies would have agreements with each other. The opposite had to be true. By definition, extradition pacts had to bridge the gaps between very different legal systems, reaching outwards and downwards.

"States have increasingly recognized that effective extradition should operate on the basis of mutual trust and confidence (not suspicion and disrespect)," the document said.

In other words, successful extradition pacts totally depended on communities setting aside mistrust and taking that all-important step of faith.

This was worth doing, and not just because it was vital for justice, allowing criminals to be punished and victims compensated; but because extradition agreements, in a very real sense, export higher standards to places which needed them. They forced others to follow rule-of-law procedures in handling fugitives.

A separate international law document said that extradition treaties were particularly necessary for places with shared borders, such as "neighboring states". Otherwise the most dangerous people on the planet could simply slip through a fence and escape—exactly as Hong Kong, Guangzhou and Macau police had noted back in 1994.

Britain had signed extradition treaties with numerous countries with utterly abysmal human rights records, such as Iraq and Zimbabwe.

America had signed deals with the Congo, Myanmar and El Salvador, among others. So, in Hong Kong, the Department of Justice staff prepared to follow the leads of Western countries in this area. It was clearly the right thing to do. Simple, right?

Yes—until unnamed rumormongers had somehow turned "the upgrading of our extradition laws to Western standards" into "the introduction of a new law from Beijing that allows instant deportation of Hong Kong dissidents in large numbers to mainland China jails".

That was clearly factually wrong—yet that was the tale the young people were being told and were spreading far and wide. Who was spreading this wildly inaccurate story? It was hard to track the rumor down to its roots: it just seemed to have emerged from opposition political groups, some of which we knew were funded by the United States.

But was the official story from the Hong Kong government a fair summary of the situation? I didn't know enough to make the judgment. I needed another, completely unrelated source to give an alternative view (this is a classic old-school journalism technique). I soon found several, some under my feet and others above my head.

Below the coffee shop in which I sat was the Hong Kong Stock Exchange. Above it was a skyscraper that housed many of the city's top business people and investment bankers. These people have to know what's going on. Their bonuses depend on it.

* * *

Two cappuccinos later, one of my top financial sources had given me an expanded view on the proposed law. Here's what he told me.

Behind locked doors in Beijing, the internal enemies of Premier Xi Jinping were slamming him hard on two fronts, said the exquisitely tailored man, whose name I have to keep secret on pain of a very, very slow and agonizing death. "One was the China-US trade war, which was now causing easily detectable damage to their country's economic indicators," he said. "And the other was the rise in illegal capital outflows, often through underground banks to Hong Kong, where it has been distorting the property markets."

This rang true. I had already been hearing numerous reports of a sharp rise in capital outflow from China in recent months. Underground banks were moving corrupt cash from the mainland to Hong Kong. "A China state newspaper recently exposed a list of corrupt individuals sending money out of the country for storage, often in the form of Hong Kong apartments or as international crypto-currency deposits," he said.

Evidence? If this was true, Hong Kong property prices would defy gravity and logic. They would simultaneously crash (this is the natural point in the cycle) and boom (as the hot money arrives in waves).

And you know what? That was exactly what we were seeing at that moment.

On a single day we could see reports of people walking away from their multi-million dollar deposits, confident of a crash, and people paying record prices for property, confident of a boom.

> The most gripping real-life mystery in Hong Kong at the moment is the property market. People are abandoning multi-million dollar deposits and running away—a sure sign of a crash. And people are running to queue up to buy new flats—a sure sign of a boom. Property brokers haven't the faintest idea what's happening. So, no change there.
>
> * * *

I had often commented on this in my columns.

"Another clue that people are missing is the fact that a PAIR of Hong Kong laws are being amended at the same time," my source added.

The first concerned extradition, the return of wanted criminals hiding in Hong Kong, and the second was the Mutual Legal Assistance in Criminal Matters Ordinance—which was all about recovering stolen assets across borders for return to their rightful owners.

The first was being speculated upon ad nauseum but the second had gone virtually unnoticed.

I had a question: what about the Hong Kong government's version of the story? That the G7's FATF group was recommending it?

"That's actually true," he says. "There's definitely a need for such a law. It's long overdue, and it does raise us to international standards in dealing with cross border crime. But the halting of the leaky money tap is an important bonus. The Hong Kong government is solving two major problems at once. Everybody wins."

But why do it now? Both these issues had been around for several years. Why would this Hong Kong administration do this at this time? Had there been instructions from Xi Jinping?

"Who knows?" he shrugged. "Maybe. But not necessarily." He explained that there was a direct advantage for Mrs. Lam to follow through with this. One of the most under-reported stories in Hong Kong was the local government's spiky relationship with property tycoons. While previous governments were seen to work with developers, Mrs Lam's government was implementing regulatory changes designed to hit developers' bottom lines and bring property prices down—and it had been succeeding until the hot money from China started to turn into a flood.

The extradition law, if it stopped the flow of illicit capital flowing out of China and into Hong Kong, would help her achieve a major pledge, lowering property prices for ordinary people.

In short, the new amendments might be a negative for some business people with a guilty conscience, but was a positive for Hong Kong as a rule-of-law community in general.

Financiers in Exchange Square could see all this—although did not want to say too much in public. In fact, most people didn't want to say anything in public. There was already a feeling that this whole topic was a bit of a minefield.

Many people were happy to talk to me, but nobody wanted their names in print. There was just too much hostility around. Somebody was stirring things up much more energetically than usual. They were also labeling the issue as a "freedom and democracy" issue.

This was bad news. It was always people with an intemperately hostile view of China who linked debates to Hong Kong's road to greater democracy—a tale that had been grossly misinterpreted by the media over recent years, me included.

Time for another short, sharp history lesson.

To understand how Hong Kong reached the point in its relationship with China at which it stood in the first half of 2019, we need to slip beneath the surface.

Here are four incidents on specific dates which are helpful.

1) A Kind Of Unwritten Rule

On December 26, 2013, a group of people hostile to China illegally broke into the Hong Kong headquarters of the People's Liberation Army carrying a British colonial flag.

They were widely condemned as *gang du*. This is a term for independence campaigners, or "separatists" to use the mainland term.

Shortly afterwards, an unwritten law emerged, miasma-like, from the regular closed-door meetings between Hong Kong's rulers and their mainland Chinese overlords. The actual wording was a puzzling edict about the primary importance of loving Hong Kong and loving China. We were "required" to love both, it said.

Western reporters rolled their eyes. Representatives must love Hong Kong and love China? How can you regulate "love"? To them, it was idiotic. But people with long experience of China's terminology knew exactly what it meant. Get your filial loyalties straight, because we are cousins. It was easy to see the essence of it: "Be free, but be family."

In plain English, it meant this: "Hong Kong can have all the freedoms it wants, AS LONG AS NO ONE PROMOTES SEPARATISM. China does NOT LIKE separatism."

This had always been forbidden in Hong Kong: we all knew this so well that it had never needed to be said in so many words. It was a national security issue, and thus covered by mainland China, according to the Basic Law, which promised autonomy only up to a degree. Country-level issues were excluded. National security issues were country-level issues, and thus the prerogative of Beijing.

But now the topic was being openly discussed in Hong Kong. Denunciations of tiny, unsupported independence campaigns suddenly became a regular theme for Hong Kong's then leader, Chief Executive C.Y. Leung.

The newly enunciated version of the rule was a very big carrot (all the freedoms you want!) and a very small stick (except for one little one!).

It was actually an excellent deal, since Hong Kong people did not want to be a separate country, but we did greatly value freedom of press, freedom of information, and so on. Not one of our major political parties favored independence: all assumed the continuation of the present successful "one country, two systems" relationship.

This is worth taking a moment to clarify, at the risk of being repetitive: foreign correspondents from the West nearly always arrive in this city with the assumption that Hong Kongers hate and fear our neighbors to the north.

This is absolutely not so. We have a love-hate relationship with China as a place and as a concept. We simultaneously hold "positive and negative emotive affiliation toward national identity" as academic Chan Chi-kit said in a well-known academic paper.

Hong Kongers' favorite holiday destination is mainland China. When there are disputes over islands in the sea, Hong Kongers passionately support China's claims, some of our citizens even sailing out there to wave the flag. Importantly, these crews include people from the political parties most hostile to China.

In a thousand different business sectors across our city, Hong Kong people want more integration with mainland China, not less.

Hong Kong pretends to be a global tourism hub, but the reality is that we know that four-fifths of the tourists on whom our economy depends are cousins from mainland China. We're basically China's holiday resort.

But was it legal to ban the promotion of "separatism"? Technically, yes.

Hong Kong has no formal constitution in practice, but follows a small book of articles called the Basic Law, as mentioned. It guarantees Hong Kong "a high degree of autonomy". Get that? Not "autonomy" but "a high degree of autonomy"—in other words, partial self-determination but not full self-determination.

In practice, we have a fabulous deal: Beijing gives Hong Kong full autonomy on almost everything except matters to do with national security. That's the same everywhere. In any country in the world, if people in one area want to break away and form an independent country, that would be seen as a national-level issue, not a local one.

2) Hitting A Wall

After that development, our wide freedoms continued unabated, but the second part of the newly discussed rule eventually caused a stumble on August 31, 2014.

Hong Kong's civil service revealed that we could have universal suffrage, as promised, but of course there was that vague and annoying proviso that the candidates would needed to be checked for suitability first—to see if they "loved Hong Kong and loved China". So this would be added to the jobs of an (already-existing) electoral committee.

Outrageous! Media pundits (including this present writer) interpreted this as an unacceptable vetting procedure that would only allow pro-Beijing candidates to stand. I summarized the proposal as "Choose Your Own Puppet" in a meme that went viral.

Let's all march!

This reporter joined thousands in protesting against it as part of what became known as the Umbrella Movement. I was a huge supporter and wrote editorials for the New York Times about it, and even made a music video that was viewed 50,000 times.

But looking back, many of us feel that perhaps we got it wrong.

Rechecking the details of that proposal, we now know that Hong Kong people were being offered full universal suffrage, a one-man, one-vote system, with the simple proviso that we could have anyone EXCEPT an independence activist, since China felt that would spoil the present positive relationship.

And while pro-establishment politicians were not separatists, NEITHER were any of the pro-democracy leaders of the time, such as Anson Chan, Martin Lee, and Audrey Eu.

A major university research survey of the public at that time suggested that about 55 percent were in favor of the scheme IF the vetting committee had a sufficient range of people on it. So the fact was that most Hong Kong people were in favor of the scheme, which would bring full democracy, yes, universal suffrage, yes, one-person-one-vote, for our community—as long as we promised not to elect an independence campaigner, which was irrelevant, as Hong Kong people did not favor them, and none of the popular parties offered them.

That was the key moment when Hong Kong could have moved towards being a Western-style democracy.

But we missed it.

CRASH!

It slipped from our hands and shattered on the floor.

The entire scheme was rejected lock, stock and barrel by those so-called pro-democracy politicians, their voices amplified by columnists like me, causing an unfortunate return to the universally disliked electoral college system known locally as "the small circle election".

Many people now feel that was a mistake, said Daniel Vukovich, an East Asian studies scholar in Hong Kong who has written several acclaimed books on Chinese politics. It's possible that what we were offered wasn't 100 percent pure Western democracy but it was extremely close, and very likely the closest thing possible in Chinese territory. Most other places around the world also have vetting committees or "electoral colleges" of one sort or another, so it wouldn't have been a stretch at all to accept the proposal.

Actually, democracy can be a touchy subject to discuss in Asia generally. Statistical evidence shows powerfully that Asian "illiberal" democracy (Hong Kong, Singapore, China) can speedily rescue people from abject poverty and give them health and wealth in a single generation. To hundreds of millions of women, children, and men, this is of towering importance. It was the World Bank which reported that the Beijing leadership had lifted 850 million people out of poverty in an extraordinarily short time, just 50 years.

Unfortunately, the purest form of Western liberal democracy is the only societal management model acceptable to the international media—which is a shame, since it can make development progress tragically slow in Asia (see India or the Philippines for obvious examples). From the point of view of people who live in this region, this wasn't about political models or GDP charts. This was about human beings, our cousins and neighbors, getting enough to eat. In his book, Vukovich warned against the "the arrogance or presumptuousness" of assuming the existence of "supposedly universal norms and political forms".

3) Stumbles

There were several moments when we saw slight stumbles in our system. Here's one example: On October 11, 2017, a British Conservative Party member named Benedict Rogers, then a friend of this present writer, was denied entry into Hong Kong. Many in the media, this author included, expressed dismay.

But there was a story behind it. Before leaving the UK, Rogers had been warned by a contact at the Chinese embassy in London that he may be denied entry into Hong Kong.

He had regularly spoken and written about people wanting more freedom in China's restive edges, and this had led to him being labeled as a separatist.

Rogers was irrationally angry about this, and that fury would become a serious problem for Hong Kong, as he started a "human rights group" which specialized in spreading negative Twitter allegations about this city.

4) Promoting Independence

On October 7, 2018, a Financial Times editor, Victor Mallet, received a shorter-than-expected visa for his stay Hong Kong, a move seen as an expulsion.

Many interpreted this as an attack on the freedom of the press.

But the truth was that he'd never complained of the Hong Kong government censoring his work in any way.

The trouble came purely from Mallet's decision to host a high profile speech for a Hong Kong independence campaigner—and thus break the unwritten rule that all knowledgeable journalists knew our "high degree of autonomy" depended on. Why would he do such a thing?

Before this event, Mallet had already decided to leave Hong Kong and had made arrangements to move to Paris. I know this is true, because he told me himself.

Global press coverage of the event portrayed it as the shocking expulsion of a Hong Kong journalist, and every single report I saw omitted the fact that he had organized the platform for the independence campaigner in full knowledge that he was planning to leave shortly (and indeed had been house-hunting in France).

CHAPTER 5

The Activist Cycle

*In Which The Network Is Annoyed—The Activist Cycle—
Mr. Lee Goes On a Speaking Tour—What The Extradition Law Says*

Thursday, February 27

Today this reporter is holding court at Office Number One, the Block X coffee shop at Hong Kong Polytechnic University.

The network of Hong Kong mothers who write to me all the time are even more annoyed than ever.

"The international media continues to track down and shine their spotlights on Hong Kong's most extreme radicals, despite the fact that they really, really don't represent the views of the Hong Kong people," says one.

She's right. We all agree that it's fine for the international media to focus on the people who are hostile to China. As mentioned, these people, known as "the pan-democrats" or just "pandems", and their supporters, make up about one in four or one in five Hong Kong people, a sizable cluster.

But the radicals who want independence are tiny and ill-supported groups who appear to represent no one but their own youthful selves. The support they attract is tiny. No one likes them. The pandems like them least of all.

Yet Western media people are going out of their way to track them down and put them on platforms. The result is that this breaks the national security rule and harms our community.

The cause of today's unhappiness in my network of parents is a report from Canada's Globe and Mail newspaper which describes how an independence activist spends his hours.

(Note: As mentioned, Hong Kongers with an accommodating attitude to China call such people "separatists" while folk nervous about China prefer "independence activist". I tend to go with the second option for the simple reason that the first group are long-suffering people who rarely complain while the second group is easily offended and over-reacts instantly and vociferously.)

From the Canadian article, you can see the independence activist's movements.

6.00 pm: Independence activist attends Hong Kong independence rally.

8.00 pm: Independence activist has dinner at McDonald's.

10.20 pm: Independence activist goes to a bar.

1.00 am: Independence activist goes to McDonald's for a late supper, then returns to bar.

Still 1.00 am: Independent activist's female friend vomits.

4.00 am: Independence activist goes to McDonald's for breakfast.

The guy had THREE MEALS at McDonald's in eight hours.

Never mind the politics: He must be stopped for the sake of his cholesterol levels.

But to be serious, the Hong Kong mothers felt it was a real shame that Western journalists were obsessed with giving public profile to any radical who made the ridiculous claim that he could persuade Xi Jinping to grant independence to Hong Kong. The inevitable friction that results was great for Western journalists' careers, but did undeserved harm to the Hong Kong people of all political leanings or none.

Informed Western journalists knew this was our community's sensitive point, and yet the ones with ambition for themselves kept scratching at it. And, like any scratched sore, it became likely to erupt into something far more harmful for our community.

Thursday, March 19

Today I laugh out loud when I hear about two groups of arch-enemies talking behind the scenes in the Legislative Council.

The pandems and the business lobby have realized that if they unite, they can use their joint votes to veto the planned extradition agreement between Hong Kong and China.

This is amazing! These guys usually hate each other.

The anti-China folk don't want it because they fear they will be arrested for fake crimes—and bribe-paying business people don't want it in case they are arrested for real ones!

Friday, March 20

It's the third week of March, and except for passing jokey comments, this reporter has taken very little part in print regarding the discussion over the extradition amendment.

I write privately to the Hong Kong mothers and tell them what I have found out about the law from my well-placed sources, but add that I still feel loath to cover the story and write public articles about the topic. It was too political.

This writer used to be a fervent supporter of the pandems, the biggest cluster of China critics.

But many of us had distanced ourselves from them in recent years. The group's loudest voices had swung from being pro-Hong Kong to being anti-China—an important and unwelcome change.

My generation's pro-democracy hero, Martin Lee Chu-ming, came across as a sincere, Christian man in his day. But the present generation of featured voices, like localist Edward Leung and independence activist Joshua Wong, often displayed a callous disregard of Hong Kong people's opinions and a hostile attitude to mainlanders that was nastiness bordering on bigotry.

When Chinese leaders had pointed out in 2014 that the protests would lead to fewer mainland Chinese families being allowed to visit Hong Kong on holiday, Joshua Wong tweeted: "And they call that a punishment?"

Other radical leaders simply assaulted their perceived enemies. Edward Leung earned a six-year jail sentence for riot and assault, convicted by a jury of Hong Kong people. He was an unashamed fighter for an independent state. His slogan was "Free Hong Kong, revolution now".

* * *

But as I say, these were not the sort of issues I discussed in my writing.

The majority of Hong Kong people had better things to do than listen to radicalized young men telling us on Western-run news platforms how they were going to turn this city into an independent nation against the wishes of the majority of residents.

Yet an increasing number of people in my network, the most worried ones being parents, were asking me to "bring some sense" into the discussion about the extradition law.

No, sorry, I'm a humorist, I replied. I'm not qualified to bring sense to any discussion.

But this wasn't really true. I had been on the Legislative Council beat for some years in the 1990s.

Thinking this through, I realized that there was at least one important insight I could share with the Western media. An important piece of information that we need to know to understand Hong Kong is the existence of a process we sometimes call The Activist Cycle.

* * *

The Hong Kong civil servants' proposal for the lengthening of the extradition countries list had been filed in February of 2019.

At that point, the job was under the remit of Hong Kong justice minister Teresa Cheng and security minister John Lee.

An illustration for the need for the new law had emerged from the news cycle. A young man from Hong Kong had confessed to a murder in Taiwan, but could not be arrested for it. The body of Amber Poon Hui-wing, 20, was found in bushes in February of 2018—and her boyfriend Chan Tong-kai, 19, was the only suspect for the crime.

But Hong Kong found its hands tied. We could not even call for his return, let alone lock him up for his crime.

The incident wasn't just dangerous, worrying, and embarrassing—but it made real the glaring hole in Hong Kong's ability to manage international crime. G7 FATF had been right.

Clearly, that case showed that an expansion of extradition treaties to cover greater China was needed to maintain the Western-style rule of law that had made Hong Kong what it was, exactly as the civil servants had said.

But the folk hostile to China were upset—and were agitating about the disaster they said the new amendment would trigger.

Western journalists and younger local reporters were now running to give them air-time. But older ones would hold back. Why?

It's important to recognize that panicking in this way was standard practice for local activists. Just two years earlier, a decision to allow co-operation between Chinese and Hong Kong immigration channels at a railway station in Kowloon had caused similar expressions of horror.

Journalists and civil servants saw this as "the activist cycle" and were very familiar with it. We'd been watching it for more than 30 years, and it followed predictable lines almost every time.

The Activist Cycle

Stage 1) A practical step is proposed which involves a mutually helpful element of co-operation with our counterparts from mainland China (such as the combining of mainland Chinese and Hong Kong processing facilities at the high-speed train station in Kowloon at our end of the line).

Stage 2) The pandems and the radicals make dire predictions of doom. "This is a dagger in the heart of Hong Kong which will kill us all" was a line used. We in the media duly trumpet such claims to the world, and the tale gets picked up by Western media hungry for stories that put Hong Kong in a bad light now that it is associated with China.

Stage 3) Hong Kong's planners and engineers respond with puzzlement, saying: "No. There's no negative political story here. This is simply a massive convenience for travelers." But nobody takes them seriously and few journalists bother to even quote them.

Stage 4) The planners and engineers sigh, but suck up the abuse and go ahead in the face of hysterical bleating by the news media (and columnists such as me).

Stage 5) A couple of years pass and it becomes obvious to everyone that the planners and engineers had been right. Hong Kong has not been killed by a dagger in its heart. The result, and the ONLY result, had been a massive convenience for travelers, as they said all along.

Stage 6) The long-suffering engineers and planners are NOT congratulated for getting it right. The activists and the media do NOT apologize for getting it wrong. It's just the system. We're all used to it. It sells newspapers and wins clicks.

Stage 7) Rinse and repeat every couple of years.

Indeed, this process has been repeated so often in Hong Kong over the past decades, on large scales and smaller scales, that the civil service knows that the wise thing to do is to nod and smile politely at the whining of activists and the media—and go ahead anyway.

They've done it with bridges, with train stations, with the Hong Kong international airport, and with the 1997 handover itself.

In every case, sure-fire doom was confidently predicted, but the results were ultimately the opposite: the bridge was widely used, the handover had gone smoothly, our train system was among the world's best, as was our airport. Yet it was slightly different this time. There was a feeling among government people that the harbingers of doom at stages one and two of the above Activist Cycle were louder and were attracting more ears than normal as they attacked the extradition amendment.

Something else was afoot. Rumors were being very efficiently circulated which created fear and mistrust. Also, the international media seemed to have grown more hostile to Hong Kong, and had decided to join the activists more overtly, causing the normal successful process to become unbalanced. Some foreign journalists appeared to be ferociously anti-government in a way that we hadn't seen before.

This felt as if we were seeing the work of behind-the-scenes organizers, in the same way that we eventually found them behind the Umbrella Movement. After that event, journalists had discovered that there had been a secret committee with lots of input from Western protest consultants, there was printed material for pre-training protest marshals, and so on. Was that same team involved here? At that time, it was impossible to say.

But there was certainly a disproportionate amount of hostility to the new extradition amendment. Worse still, the ultra-hostile anti-mainlander radicalism of groups such as the localists was increasingly spreading upwards into the pandems.

This left the older members of the pro-democracy lobby in a quandary. There were stark differences between them and the radicals, particularly over the issue of independence and the use of violence.

But the angry young separatists fighting for independence had energy and drive. They also had the international media in the palms of their hands—the Western press scrambled to give them platforms, at high cost to the average Hong Kong parent's peace of mind.

It was clear from the ensuing silence that the pandems were choosing not to condemn the radicals, even for their most extreme statements, but to increasingly draw closer to them. They knew this could be played to their advantage.

A perfect storm was beginning to build.

* * *

Instead of just doggedly pressing on to stages three and four of the activist cycle (that is, to ignore the misinformed bleating and bring in the Western-style extradition law that the G7 had recommended), the current leaders decided to be a bit more responsive—they had also detected unusual undercurrents in society.

They decided that they would try to do a better job of backing the civil servants who were doing the work. In this case, it wasn't planners or engineers who needed help, as in the case of the railway station, but Department of Justice officials.

So Chief Executive Carrie Lam encouraged security minister John Lee to explain the extradition amendment better and more often to more people. He went on tour, making speeches to numerous groups. Color brochures were printed in Chinese and English making the process easier to understand with diagrams. They were distributed physically and on the Internet.

Hong Kong's extradition law, based on the UN model used in the West, was simple at heart, Lee told his audiences. It targeted fugitives hiding in Hong Kong who were suspected of one or more of a very limited list of serious crimes, including murder and rape and major financial fraud.

After a lengthy series of court hearings, with many safeguards, these fugitives could be sent back to the requesting territory. The caseload was expected to be very, very small.

The amendment was not about sending Hong Kong dissidents of any kind to mainland China, he explained, and indeed specifically excluded that possibility.

Furthermore, any offenders accused of crimes related to politics and religion anywhere would automatically be untouchable. Tax-related matters were added to the exemptions list. Importantly, ALL decisions would be made by Hong Kong's legal community under Hong Kong law, none by the requesting territory.

He actually did explain it well, to give him due credit.

But people in the media had stopped listening. His speeches were not quoted. Instead, reporters latched on to the entirely fictional versions of the story which implied mass deportation of Hong Kongers, interviewing activists denouncing the amendment as a law which allowed mainland police free reign to arrest dissidents and critics in this city in large numbers.

There was an astonishingly large gulf between the two versions of the law being bandied around—they couldn't be the same thing. One or other had to be a lie. But which was it?

* * *

As the debate became louder and harsher, the number of people who contacted me to speak out for them grew rapidly, until my inboxes were overflowing.

Most heart-rending were the Hong Kong parents whose teenage or young adult children were becoming infected by tales from human rights activists and NGOs and anti-government websites saying that the civil service was arranging for huge numbers of us to be sent to mainland jails. We had "just weeks" of freedom left before all being sent to gulags in China,

"When I mention you, they say you'll be arrested too," one mother of a college-age man told me. "For all your jokes about Xi Jinping."

A visit to social media (such as Facebook or Twitter or local site LIHKG or Reddit's Hong Kong page) was frightening, giving a horror-film interpretation of what was going on.

Yet few people dared to try to set the record straight.

If you did try to correct the errors, you were (at best) labeled a Communist Party puppet or (at worst) had your face, address, phone number and family tree published on the Internet for purposes of abuse by a fast-growing group of angry, panicking, violent people.

A few brave souls, such as Ronny Tong, one of the city's most respected lawyers, did try to tell the other side of the story—but was immediately labeled a pro-China stooge.

This was terribly unfair. Ronny Tong, if anything, leaned the other way, being one of the founders of the Civic Party. He was and is a good representative of Hong Kong people: Strongly pro-democracy and pro-human rights, but not missing the fact that making the best of our relationship with China isn't something we have a choice about.

I could see that he very much represented the Hong Kong majority, who were not at either extreme of the political spectrum, but just took an intelligent, informed, realistic stance in the center.

Yet his pleas for rationality led to him being painted as a Beijing lackey in a media-led uproar.

By April it was obvious that the pandems had made their decision. They had chosen to side firmly with the radicals and jointly went on the attack against "the Evil Law" in the strongest terms. Chinese newspapers such as Apple Daily and Ming Bao led the charge. Even the previously pro-government South China Morning Post enthusiastically joined the parade of anti-government critics denouncing the legal amendment.

By the end of April, I was getting scores of messages from Hong Kong people, asking me to use my platform to bring some rationality into the discussion. After the attacks on Ronny Tong, almost no one was speaking out to give the other side of the story.

Aieeyah! What to do?

The last thing I wanted to do was join such an acrimonious argument. Yet I felt guilty that we in the media were so thoroughly misrepresenting the real situation.

In my discussions and interviews, I began asking anti-extradition people a simple question:

Have you read the draft law?

"No."

"Nope."

"Not the actual law, no."

"No, but I know what it says."

"Ain't nobody got time for that."

"No, I haven't read it myself."

"No, I haven't, but I know what it says—I've read what it says in the [Apple Daily/ SCMP/ Ming Bao] about it."

The number of people who said "no" was 100 percent—literally everyone I asked.

I asked my colleagues in the media the same question, and got precisely the same answer. Not one of them had read it—not even the ones writing lengthy columns condemning it.

There was no choice.

It was time to risk death by boredom and devote a day or two to painstakingly going through the text and getting lawyer friends to talk me through the difficult bits. The things we do for love.

The bad news: It was every bit as ghastly as I expected, an extraordinarily turgid document in heavy legalese.

You know the sort of text where you have to read some sentences several times over just to get the basic meaning, even if you are entirely fluent in English?

It was one of those.

The good news was that I eventually got through it, and, with the help of legal friends, managed to summarize it in a manner that could be understood by humans.

There were basically 20 stages (although that depends on how you divide up the steps).

Importantly, you could easily see precisely how it worked in practice by cross-referencing it to actual cases in the courts. This is because it had been used for two decades in Hong Kong—the amendment simply widened the remit of an already existing system.

Hong Kong's Extradition Process In Simple English

1. A fugitive hiding in Hong Kong is identified by an international crime agency.

2. The agency sends a request to the Hong Kong Department of Justice.

3. Justice staff study the request to determine whether multiple conditions are met. They REJECT the request:

a) UNLESS the crime is one of 37 listed categories of serious crimes; and

b) UNLESS the crime is a serious one, punishable by seven years or more in prison.

Furthermore, they ONLY consider accepting the request:

a) IF the offence in question is a crime in both Hong Kong and the requesting jurisdiction;

b) IF the offence in question is not of a political character; and

c) IF the offence is not punishable by death.

4. There are several other exemptions: the person is not arrested if it involves religion, tax disputes, and so on.

5. If the Hong Kong justice department determines that the above conditions and limitations are met, they then forward the request to Hong Kong's Chief Executive.

6. She or he reads it and is offered the chance to veto it at this point.

7. If she or he decides not to, the suspect can then apply for a judicial review, with a right to appeal to Hong Kong's highest court.

8. That review then goes ahead. If the highest court decides to reject the appeal and proceed with the extradition request, an arrest warrant is issued, after which the subject is immediately barred from leaving Hong Kong.

9. The case moves back to the courts, where a preliminary hearing is held.

10. The court considers the question of whether there is a political motive behind the request. If there is not, it will proceed.

11. The court will further decide whether there is sufficient prima facie evidence. If it decides that there is a possible case, it can then make an order of committal.

12. At this point, the suspect can file an appeal.

13. With the first stage of the judicial process over, the request goes back to the Chief Executive, who can again decide to deny the extradition request and release the arrested person on humanitarian grounds.

14. The suspect can petition the Chief Executive to oppose extradition at this point.

15. After considering the petition, the Chief Executive may decide not to proceed with the extradition at this point.

16. But if she or he decides to proceed, an extradition order is filed.

17. At this stage, the suspect can again appeal to the courts to stop the extradition.

18. This new appeal is then heard in the courts.

19. If the latest appeal is unsuccessful, the suspect is cleared for extradition.

20. The individual is then transported to the requesting country. (Most often, the individual is put on a plane to the United States.)

* * *

Okay, that's it. Boring but necessary.

When I click my fingers you will all wake up.

Click.

For those of you who glazed over during that passage, let me just summarize it in three key takeaways.

1. This entire painstaking process deals with one individual at a time and typically takes years. There is no possible interpretation of it that supports allegations that groups of people can be snatched off the street and whisked over any border.

2. At no point in the process does the place requesting extradition have ANY part in the decision-making process. It is all done by the place receiving the request, and fully under the legal system of that place, and that place only.

3. It gives specific and clear protection to many groups. For example, any request even remotely associated with political dissent or religious activities of any faith is automatically rejected. Death penalty cases are also specifically excluded.

The facts were clear, in print, in black and white.

But many reporters, for reasons of their own, preferred a completely different story, which was now spreading around the world.

CHAPTER 6

An Explosion Of Conspiracy Theories

In Which The Pandems Cause An Uproar—Fearmongers Win the Day—Too Scared to Speak—Financiers Build On Their Story

BY THE FINAL days of April, the unholy alliance of pro-independence radicals, pandems and the anti-government media had spontaneously developed a very clever strategy. Small clusters of pandem supporters in various groups, such as the legal sector, the restaurant sector, the health sector, and so on, would present themselves to the media as if they spoke for the entire sector.

Sometimes they would form new unions or alliances specifically for this purpose. Other times they would organize small marches of their members within professions.

Complicit (or just lazy) journalists would present the views of these small clusters in print as if they spoke for the whole sector.

So, for example, pandem supporters in the legal sector sent out a message that they should get as many legal people as they can to march through

Central, all in black suits. At the end of the parade, the media was told that 3,000 lawyers were present. In truth, my network members counted about 800 people present, and quite a few were very young, apparently interns or law students.

If you followed media reports in April, you would think that all the lawyers in Hong Kong, plus all the business people, plus all of the unions, plus pretty much everyone else, were completely united in dropped-jaw horror at the "Beijing-imposed" law that would allow "the communists" to "snatch" huge numbers of Hong Kong dissidents off the street to secret gulags from which they would never emerge.

But anyone who took the time to contact senior people in those sectors quickly learned that this was most certainly not the case.

Lawyers, in particular, were a key focus, and presented as being united against the law. There are about 13,000 lawyers in Hong Kong. One small group, the Bar Association, was known in legal circles for its leadership's open support for the pandems and hostility to the government. A few members of the association identified what they felt were weaknesses in the wording of the law and commented on them. This was not unusual for new laws or amendments.

But the columnists of Apple Daily and other newspapers (not to mention Twitter, LIHKG and other social media sites) were immediately beside themselves with excitement—if the "legal sector" of Hong Kong criticized the law, that proved the radicals were right! We ARE going to be snatched over the border in a series of mass deportations, probably "within days" of the law being passed!

It was logical nonsense to assume that the fact that some barristers had criticized aspects of the wording could be taken as proof that Hong Kong's legal community as a whole supported the mass deportation story.

Yet the media failed to differentiate between the leaders of the barristers—a handful of people who led a group of only about 1,500 individuals—and the wider legal community, a group which included an additional 11,000-plus lawyers, many of whom didn't share the anti-government position and had a much wider range of opinions. (There were also many barristers who opposed the stance taken by the leaders of their group, as did many foreign lawyers working for overseas firms.)

At Hong Kong's Department of Justice, there was a measure of bafflement at the sheer level of hostility. A Western-style extradition law was clearly a positive step in terms of Hong Kong's prized adherence to the highest standards of international law—and at least part of the main impetus for the change had come from the West, from the G7.

From the civil servants' point of view, it was horribly unfair.

Little did they know that it was about to get worse.

* * *

On May 1, obsessive China critic Gordon C. Chang (a right-wing former Baker McKenzie lawyer in Hong Kong, known for his spectacularly ill-timed 2001 book The Coming Collapse of China) wrote a widely circulated essay claiming that Beijing was behind the amendment as part of an operation to crush Hong Kong.

"Beijing, with methodical ruthlessness, is trying to bring Hong Kong to heel," he wrote. "Many believe new rules facilitating the sending of suspects to China would effectively allow Beijing to grab people at will and thereby completely control the city."

Grab people at will?

The piece was banal and ridiculous. It read as it if were written by someone who had no understanding of the fundamental fact that extradition laws "returned" fugitives to crime scenes, rather than grabbed citizens and "sent" them over borders to other jurisdictions. Nor was there any understanding of the fact that extradition cases in Hong Kong took years.

A frustrated Hong Kong lawyer, parent of two, after forwarding Chang's rant to me, said: "If this was true, tourists could not visit UK without being in danger of being snatched by Zimbabwe and tourists visiting the United States could be snatched by the Congolese government, but who could believe that for one second?"

At that time, I felt it was impossible to believe that such a ludicrously wrong-headed summary of what extradition meant could be accepted by anyone.

I was wrong.

His version of the tale was widely accepted and spread fast. It almost felt as if there were people behind the scenes pushing inane stories in all directions while deleting voices telling the simple truth.

Within a week, the main narrative for the majority of the Western media was that desperately evil communists running the puppet Hong Kong government were following Beijing's secret orders to destroy the city's rule of law so they could snatch dissidents in huge numbers for mass incarceration in mainland jails.

In just days, special secret trains would be arranged to send the populace of Hong Kong to concentration camps being readied in secret locations.

But noble youngsters like Joshua Wong were fighting this in a desperate bid to save Hong Kong.

Typical was Vox's headline: "The Fight to Save Hong Kong".

Time magazine had: "Hong Kong's Extradition Law Would be a Victory for Authoritarianism Everywhere".

Quartz had: "Hong Kong is in the Fight of Its Life".

This writer found himself in the extraordinary position of being begged by my readers of all ages and cultures to defend a government I had spent 30 years criticizing. AIEEYAH!

* * *

When Hong Kong's final British colonial leader, Chris Patten, apparently swallowed the dissident-grab tale lock, stock and barrel, my network was buzzing with comments on every channel.

"The whole story of China using the law to grab dissidents is just so obviously untrue," said Sarah Ching. "Why would he do such a thing?"

"The West cannot bear to see a rising China, eager to rule the world without a single shot fired," said Glenn Rogers.

I told my readers that I was disappointed with Patten. "In general, I've always been a big fan of Chris Patten, but he really loves to stick the knife into post-British Hong Kong," I said. "I mean how can you sign extradition deals with Iraq and Mugabe etc and then claim to hold the moral high ground?"

Paul French, author of Midnight in Peking, said: "It's worth remembering that nobody in the UK has voted for Chris Patten for anything since 1992 when he was kicked out as MP for Bath—since then it has been one Establishment appointment after another—HK, Northern Ireland, EU, Oxford".

"He has taken sides with one political group against the majority of the Hong Kong people, who do not want independence," said Sunita Chau. "It's unkind".

While the barristers' leadership was hostile to China, some members saw the illogicality of the complainers.

"The exact same Mr. Patten is perfectly happy to see his own country sign extradition treaties with Zimbabwe, Ecuador, Sierra Leone, Cuba,

Uganda, El Salvador, etc., etc.," said one barrister who did not wish to have his name in print. "Oh, and the UK has also signed extradition deals with both Iraq and Brunei, so I guess his values include lopping off limbs and stoning people."

* * *

Days pass. The weather gods flip a switch and spring turns into summer. The humidity returns with the force of a city-sized sauna, dropped from the sky. We all race from one air-conditioned building to another to avoid bursting into flames. I spend hours chatting with specialist lawyers and other people in the coffee shops.

One lawyer tells me that the main roots of this grotesque misunderstanding was the issue of scale—both in terms of time periods, and in terms of the range of people the law would affect.

The Western media version was completely wrong, he said.

There was no question of groups of people being grabbed off the street and whisked across the border. A single Hong Kong extradition case involved one individual at a time, and typically rolled on for a year or two, he said.

And it was equally silly to suggest that "every single person in Hong Kong" was at risk, as the localists and pandems were saying. Hong Kong's existing extradition arrangements only handled four or five cases a year. Even if the amendment caused the number to double or triple, it would still be a tiny number.

Yet these activists were informing the world that the entire population, PLUS any number of "visiting tourists"(!), were in imminent danger of being dragged off the street and sped over the border to mainland jails: a genuinely terrifying prospect.

"Hong Kong's end game: why the extradition bill is an 'infinity stone' that could decimate half of society", said a headline in the rabidly anti-government website called Hong Kong Free Press over an article by Canadian lawyer-activist Jason Y. Ng, a vocal supporter of Joshua Wong.

That one was so melodramatically over the top that when it popped up on our screens, it made us laugh out loud.

* * *

Towards the end of May, the debate had become entirely detached from reality. Hong Kong leader Carrie Lam took the ball from security minister John Lee's court and headed north, with a view to conveying news about the concerns in Hong Kong.

Mrs. Lam periodically reports to Zhongnanhai in Beijing in the same way that Hong Kong's British leaders periodically reported to Whitehall in London.

She told Central People's Government representatives that some Hong Kong people had significant anxieties about the extradition amendment that the city's own Department of Justice was trying to introduce.

But she said that she felt it was worth continuing. A significant portion of society was in in favor of the amendment, although their positive declarations went largely unreported.

This point was fair. News articles continued to blithely imply that businesses, diplomats and lawyers were all united against the law, but that was absolutely not the case.

The outbursts from the barristers and wild stories from the media had created widespread misgivings, naturally—but many senior lawyers who had read the draft amendment saw that extradition laws were not only a positive thing, but were, as the United Nations had said, necessary for communities which believed in social justice.

"It was a good law," an American lawyer said to me. "But you only knew that if you read it, and nobody had."

After Mrs. Lam's return, John Lee's tireless education process continued, and gradually, the tide began to turn. Education turned out to be the right answer.

All five of Hong Kong's biggest business organizations moved to a position of being in favor of the law. The Hong Kong General Chamber of Commerce, The Chinese General Chamber of Commerce, The Chinese Manufacturers' Association of Hong Kong, The Federation of Hong Kong Industries, and The Hong Kong Chinese Importers' and Exporters' Association, all publicly declared themselves in favor of the legislation, and most urged the government to pass it as soon as possible. Another plus was a series of quiet conversations civil service people had with individual senior business people. They normally supported the government, but many had backed off. It turned out that most of them had a single, shared specific fear: Their staff would almost certainly have paid bribes on the mainland at various times in the past before (or in between) the mainland's anti-corruption drives. That might make them or their companies liable to problems in the future.

But once the business leaders were assured that the law was focused on a limited list of large scale crimes, like murder, they relaxed and came on board.

The majority of Hong Kong's foreign consular officials, after a detailed briefing on the amendment, came on side too, recognizing the positive intentions and extremely close similarity to their own extradition laws.

But most media simply did not report these declarations of support. The absurd narrative of the law as "legalized kidnapping" by Beijing still ruled the front pages of newspapers, as well as the majority of discussions on the Internet.

In coffee shop and on-line discussions, members of my networks were increasingly shocked by the huge gulf between what was being reported by the world's media and the actual extracts from the law that I was sharing.

"Interesting," said Laurel West, a mother of two. "From what I have read, Hong Kong's courts will play no role in deciding who gets extradited and who does not. This will be a decision of the Beijing-appointed chief executive. Is this not true?"

"That is so totally wrong," replied Mark Pinkstone. "The whole extradition process hinges on the Hong Kong Judiciary, which the World Economic Forum's Global Competitiveness Report ranks Hong Kong first in Asia for judicial independence. Every person facing extradition will appear before Hong Kong's courts first. Fourteen eminent overseas judges from the United Kingdom, Australia and Canada currently sit on our Court of Final Appeal as non-permanent judges, which in itself is a testimony to the integrity of Hong Kong's rule of law and independent judiciary."

Mandy Ho said she had read the "instant mass deportation" stories so often and in so many media that she felt that there was a campaign to hide the boring truth that the law will only affect a handful of people, those being criminal fugitives who needed to be brought to justice.

A reader named Ting agreed. "The foreign reporters' hatred of China is causing them to highlight only the most extreme and unlikely interpretations of the law," she said. "This helps nobody in our community, and simply sows discord and unhappiness."

A tsunami of disinformation was washing over the city. It was hard to tell whether it had appeared spontaneously from nervous people or whether people were deliberately generating it. Almost certainly both were true.

* * *

Later that day, this reporter went back to the coffee shop above the stock exchange for a catch-up on the views of analysts and investment bankers, many of whom appeared far better informed than reporters.

I wanted to follow up the buzz I'd heard earlier about Beijing wanting to stop corrupt officials taking money out.

It was still obvious that money was continuing to pour into Hong Kong from mainland China. As well as property, the hot money was buying up entire local companies, and also huge amounts of stocks and shares.

None of the business or professional sources to whom I spoke believed that Hong Kong's proposed extradition law had anything to do with snatching violent radicals or pro-democracy activists.

"They're minnows," said one. "It's nothing to do with them."

"But they're smart," said another. "Fear is the best way to raise support, as Donald Trump has proved."

Several pointed out that it was an open secret that Hong Kong's activist groups and websites received funding and training from political groups in the West. A portion of these actually appeared listed in the accounts of the CIA unit known as the National Endowment for Democracy, or NED. They sent at least HK$5 million (US$640,000) a year on the record, and probably far more through underground channels.

The fear was irrational. Financial sources still insisted that the dual purpose of the law was to bring Hong Kong in line with Western nations on international legal co-operation—and to help to halt the capital outflow problem, removing hot money from the local property market.

"Look for yuan exchange rate volatility to confirm the concern about the cash outflow from China," said the first speaker. "And regarding extradition: China has said that there are 300 people in Hong Kong they would like to have a word with. If you really think these are student democracy activists, you are naïve. We're talking about [mainland] Chinese adults with serious money."

The G7 proposed law was actually nothing to do with Hong Kong people, from Beijing's point of view. For them, they'd like to use it to catch specific mainland criminal individuals.

But there was so much money, energy and support behind the "mass kidnapping" narrative, that the mundane truth was being drowned.

CHAPTER 7

Europe Attacks

In Which Europeans Show Their Hypocrisy—
Grim Memories Of A Violent Night

THE *DING-DING-DING* of my phone receiving a slew of messages all at once indicated that something newsworthy had happened.

What fresh hell was this?

A flurry of news reports said executives from the European Union had just attacked the proposed fugitive offenders amendment. I know very little about European international criminal law, so headed to town to talk to someone who did. (I'd often wondered what people who studied "international affairs" do when they graduated. Now I found they did have a use.)

The source who (of course) did not want her name printed in connection with this story said that the European officials' view was "extraordinarily hypocritical".

"The truth is, Europe itself has always been keen to extradite fugitives back to China, and has no reason to deny that privilege to Hong Kong", she explained. "They send back huge numbers. The consuls know this."

Many European countries, including big ones like France and Spain, have full extradition arrangements with China, of exactly the type that Hong Kong wants to implement. Other European nations use domestic immigration laws, Interpol operations or straightforward deportation policies to achieve the exact same end in a sharper, more brutal way.

"Chinese fugitives know they shouldn't head for Europe because they will be arrested and sent back at high speed," she explains.

I ask: If the EU returns criminals to China all the time, why does it want to stop Hong Kong doing the same?

"Because mainland Chinese criminals avoid Europe," she says. "European officials would prefer poor Hong Kong to be stuck with them."

It's bizarre. If you read the editorials in the Western newspapers, it seems that only the most heartless monsters would even think of interacting with China on legal matters, particularly with the transfer of human beings.

Yet Western governments do it all the time.

Later that day, a reader forwarded me a report about a leaked 2015 document which revealed that the United States was pressuring the Chinese government to provide documentation for nearly 39,000 people it wanted to deport from the United States to China. Yes, 39,000—that's not a misprint.

So America wanted to return tens of thousands of lawbreakers back to China with no due process, but was condemning Hong Kong for wanting to send single individual fugitives back with full legal protections that are so thorough they take a year or two to go through.

That made no sense. There was something very wrong here. This whole story was about something else—it wasn't about extradition at all, I knew for sure, now. I know what you are thinking: That I was becoming a conspiracy theorist. But the opposite was true. I am a natural-born skeptic.

I worked for 11 years for the Far Eastern Economic Review, a magazine whose best known editor, Derek Davies, was long rumored to be an intelligence agent for the West. In fact, most people (including this staff member) dismissed that allegation for years—but Derek admitted that he had come into journalism from a job working for the British Secret Intelligence Service, also known as MI6—yes, the same outfit that James Bond works for in the books and movies.

During my coverage of the Umbrella Movement protests between 2014 and 2016, I had also noticed that close examination led observers to identify multiple layers of activity. On top were the high profile participants—Benny Tai and his team. Below that were large numbers of young people, many of whom were university students.

But below both of them were shadowy groups who did extraordinary amounts of training and briefing, and who even supplied cash—but always insisted on staying out of the spotlight. The training came from Europeans, specializing in over-throwing governments while the cash came from the United States.

It was a secret when the protests started in September of 2014, but all good reporters knew about it by the end of that year.

* * *

But back to 2019. A few hours later, the international affairs expert sent me a link to an article that explained that the real irony was that there was one huge difference between Hong Kong's choice, legal extradition, and methods such as deportation used by Hong Kong's critics in Europe and the United States.

Hong Kong's law was better for all concerned. A person extradited from Hong Kong would get all the legal safeguards of the city's world-class Western-style legal system.

Deportation, in contrast, "deprives the deportee of the rights to which he would be entitled if he were an extraditee," wrote Ivan Shearer, one of the world's top experts on international extradition.

"The more important of these are his right not to be returned to a demanding State for a political offence, and his right to be tried after surrender only in respect of the offence or offences for which his return was demanded (the principle of specialty). The deported alien finds himself in a singularly unprotected situation."

In other words, the proposed extradition treaty would not only be good for the free people of Hong Kong, and good for the victims in China seeking justice, but it would also be good for the mainland fugitives being returned. Literally all sides win if the amendment is passed, including the person in the dock.

* * *

The next day, May 21, Hong Kongers heard even more bad news from the West.

It said that two violent criminals, fugitives from the city's justice system, had been given refugee status in Germany, after claiming that they were innocent "pro-democracy" activists who their hometown civil servants wanted captured and whisked off to mainland jails for God knows what punishment.

Local coffee shops were filled with amazed chatter about the case.

We knew these guys' names. Ray Wong Toi-yeung and Alan Li Tung-shing were two of the most violent rioters ever to have darkened Hong Kong's jail cells.

The European country had made a horrendous mistake.

Some Hong Kong people reacted with hollow laughter.

"Normally you have to invest at least 100,000 euros to get a European

Community passport," a risk analyst (parent of one) said to me. "Instead I can just attack Chinese immigrants, buy a business class flight to Frankfurt, and tell the Germans that the Hong Kong civil service is trying to kill me."

Europe's gullibility levels were approaching America's, one reader tells me.

"That would be bad," replies SC Ho, father of two. "But you may be right."

A lawyer suggested organizing a class action application for all seven million Hong Kong people to claim German refugee status. "After all, we've probably all got a Winnie-the-Pooh item somewhere in our homes," he says.

That makes me laugh. (I have a whole set of Winnie-The-Pooh merchandise, thanks to having three children.)

* * *

On May 29, I expressed the feelings that Hong Kong people had shared with me by writing an open letter to Germany.

It was entitled "One Night in Hong Kong".

DEAR GERMANS,

You think Hong Kong is a terrible place that citizens need to be "refugeed" out of. Here are 10 things you need to know about what happened one night in Hong Kong.

1) Pro-democracy campaigners immediately realized there was something seriously wrong with the protest that broke out in the Mong Kok area of Kowloon after dark on February 8, 2016. Reports of violence, arson and vandalism made it seem wildly out-of-kilter with their policy of peaceful, non-violent protest.

2) Witnesses said the rioters arrived with vans of equipment, including shields, sharpened wooden sticks, goggles, helmets and gloves. Many had matching facemasks to cover their features, and some wore "uniforms".

3) At about 10 pm, protestors grabbed a hawker's food cart filled with boiling oil and pushed it at food safety inspectors. The first police officers on the scene, unarmed traffic cops, tried to intervene but were attacked.

Journalists started to broadcast the scenes live, and horrified Hong Kongers watched as members of the gang surrounded and attacked an injured police officer who had fallen to the ground.

4) The rioters said they were defending the hawkers from arrest, but hawkers quickly disassociated themselves from the gang.

Street salesman Leo Chan told a South China Morning Post reporter that there was no conflict between the hawkers and the police, who had good relationships–the trouble came from the radical protestors.

5) The leader of the rioters was a thin young man who climbed on top of a smashed taxi to call for the mayhem to escalate. Members sent messages on phones to friends: "Come join the riot, it's fun!" was one of the texts. Dustbins, bricks, paving slabs and glass bottles were thrown at police officers.

At least six fires were started. The gang attacked a van containing police. Officers said they feared for their lives.

Some 124 people were injured, including 80 police officers. Streams of ambulances ferried the wounded to hospitals.

6) The Democratic Party said it totally condemned violence and acts of arson, and expressed sympathy for the injured. Pro-democracy campaigners strongly disassociated themselves from the people causing the violence. These attackers were not protesters, but criminal thugs of the worst sort.

7) Other than two warning shots to clear individuals away from a wounded officer, police officers followed instructions to use no guns, rubber bullets or tear gas. They were told not to make mass arrests but only to identify and stop violent people causing injury to individuals.

8) At one stage, the attackers changed the story that they were helping hawkers and told reporters they were making a political statement. The main gang was identified as Hong Kong Indigenous, a group which opposes the legal position of the city as a semi-autonomous democratic administrative region, and instead demands full independence from China.

9) Afterwards, police gathered more than 200 witnesses to help create an accurate picture of what happened. Two members of the gang police identified as causing criminal levels of violence were Ray Wong Toi-yeung and Alan Li Tung-shing. (Wong was the young man standing on top of the taxi in a famous image of that night.)

10) Riot leader Wong pledged to stay in Hong Kong with a HK$100,000 cash bail payment and a surety of HK$100,000 paid by his mother.

But he and Li jumped bail and escaped to Europe, where they told Germans, who are very nice people, that the two of them were "pro-democracy activists" in danger from Hong Kong's brutal and corrupt civil service.

A German refugee agency swallowed the line and recently awarded them Wong and Li "refugee status".

Germany's acting consul general in Hong Kong, David Schmidt, is distancing himself from the agency's decision.

Dear German refugee activist friends—now you know why.

Digging up all the reports on that awful night in 2016 left me with dark memories. Arson is a terrible crime in this tightly packed city—and especially in Mong Kok, one of the most densely populated urban districts on the planet.

Hong Kong people respect fire: They know it belongs to one of the Immortals, a man named Tchu Yoong, who tamed it for the use of all mankind.

But that night the radicals seemed to have a primal need to light fires in the middle of roads, so that their mayhem was lit by an orange-red glare.

China is the only part of the world in which one of the most important divine beings is a welder (not a joke—he features in some of the children's books I've written).

When we see lightning flickering in the storm clouds, we say that Tchu Yoong, the Celestial Welder, is working in the sky.

* * *

My network, too, was anxious to highlight the difference between peaceful protesters and the violent black-clad radicals. To people who live here (but apparently not to foreign correspondents), there was a clear difference between the participants in the Umbrella Movement and the anti-mainland-immigrant lobby.

"I'm with you," said a teacher from Lamma. "I applaud the Umbrella Movement. It was the most wonderful non-violent movement I've ever experienced. The Mong Kok rioters spoilt it all in my honest opinion. The violence spoilt it all."

"These guys are criminals, not political asylum seekers," said Terry Greene.

The granting of refugee status in Europe was "such a sad irony", said Alan Cai.

"They were criminals the moment they skipped bail," said Peter Beilby-King.

"The world's gone mad," said Jenny Tam.

"Yep," said Anette Guang. "That is the bigotry of the EU."

But it wasn't just the European refugee agency that swallowed the thugs' fantasy tale. Their line was also adopted wholesale by many journalists, who wrote about these violent individuals as if they were heroic victims.

People in Hong Kong were asking: Why are so many foreign reporters getting it wrong? People who were born here, or had worked here a long time, supported the theories that there were people in background working to destabilize Hong Kong.

Fingers were naturally pointed at the United States. Consulates and their equivalents in Hong Kong tended to be quite small, with the largest probably being the office representing China, known as the Liaison Office, with about 200 staff.

In contrast, the United States consulate in Hong Kong had more than 1,100 staff. This was an inexplicably large number, and it was generally assumed that some of the CIA's China operation was based in the building.

CHAPTER 8

A Peaceful March With A Shocking End

In Which A Large Demonstration Takes Place—The Radicals Return—Author's Pledge Abandoned—A Stormy Day Leads To A Dark Night

IT'S NOW THE second week of June, and fanciful interpretations of what the draft extradition law "really" means, ie, the total loss of all freedom in Hong Kong, have been proliferating through Twitter and other social media.

This led, on Sunday, June 9, to a march of hundreds of thousands of people (but not a million–no self-respecting journalist presents "the organizer's claim" as a fact)

It was mostly peaceful—and for this reporter, brought back memories.

The march was similar to the May 1989 and the July 2003 marches, large and high-spirited but generally good-natured. I've always enjoyed Hong Kong marches. They often have a carnival atmosphere. But less so, this time.

On the downside, most people to whom I spoke on the march itself had been at least partly motivated by the version of the tale jointly pushed by a coalition made up of the pandems, the radicals, and Western commentators like Gordon C. Chang—they had to Fight the Evil Law which would enable instant mass deportations of Hong Kong people.

The Christians had a slightly edited version, telling me that they had been told that the Evil Law was specifically designed by Beijing to enable instant mass deportations of Hong Kong religious people so that they could be "disappeared" in mainland jails.

What I wanted to reply (but didn't): If you can read the whole Bible, you can spend a few hours reading the actual law!

In a few instances, I asked marchers what they thought of the law's section five—which specifically gives Hong Kong's independent legal sector the power to exclude any case related to politics or religion. Nobody to whom I spoke had read the law, or believed that such exemptions existed. If they did, the media would have told them, they replied. (Hah!)

If I actually showed them the passage on my phone, they often responded by saying something like: "The Chinese don't follow any laws anyway."

It was a telling reply: When you are defeated on rational grounds, just retreat into generalized prejudice.

The fact was that many marchers weren't really interested in reading the law or finding out the details. The march wasn't really about the bill at all. It was just an expression of deep-rooted mistrust of China from the significant number of Hong Kongers who felt hostile to it—and in that sense, was actually simply a continuation of the marches of the past 30 years.

Unseen hands were amplifying our natural fears, the media had fanned the flames, and the pandems had pulled in their usual hundreds of thousands of supporters, as they had had for decades, including myself and many of my friends and colleagues.

I still felt a lot of sympathy for the marchers, and even solidarity. These people had been told frightening tales about what was about to happen to them and were responding in an entirely reasonable way. You can't blame a listener for the work of a storyteller.

Was the media really at fault? We were partly to blame, for sure. We were lazy, we failed to go back to the source material, we failed to talk to a wide enough range of people, and we allowed ourselves to be used by whoever was energetically ratcheting up the fake news.

But there was something else behind this, I felt. A subconscious distrust of China was one element. Yet there was a curious amount of co-ordination behind all this.

I hated the whole "foreign agitators" argument, but realized that I had to keep my mind open. They were here. We just had to find them.

* * *

And the response from the authorities? Hong Kong's puppet government released a statement vehemently denouncing the marches as being against the law and demanding that the people show full obedience to Beijing's dictates or face mass arrest. All further marches were strictly forbidden with a threat of life imprisonment for organizers.

No, of course it didn't. Nothing like that happened.

The office of Hong Kong leader Carrie Lam released a statement recognizing that the demonstration that had just taken place was a good thing, a positive sign of a free society: *"As a free, open and pluralistic society, we acknowledge and respect that people have different views on a wide range of issues. The procession today is an example of Hong Kong people exercising their freedom of expression within their rights as enshrined in the Basic Law and the Hong Kong Bill of Rights Ordinance."*

This totally didn't fit the media's chosen narrative, so as far as I can tell, not one major news outlet published it.

After the march, many journalists, including the present writer, confidently speculated in print that Carrie Lam would have spent the evening in deep consultation with her ultimate boss Xi Jinping over what to do next.

I couldn't help picturing the scene by making a meme of the two of them having a panicked conversation.

In fact, I later learned that we had got it wrong.

Xi Jinping was not called; there was no consultation that day between Mrs. Lam and Beijing. She and her team were busy monitoring events in Hong Kong, and discussing how to respond. They found no time for interplay with Chinese officials.

Late that night, journalists' phones began to ring.

After most of us had gone home, a body of a few hundred people, mostly stick-thin young men dressed in black, had stayed behind and gathered outside the Legislative Council Complex.

There, they had screamed abuse at the police who were standing in front of it.

At about 10.20 pm, a group of young men lifted the protective metal dividers, known as mills barriers, and started hurling them at officers. This was followed by a shower of bricks and other items. A sharp steel pole was thrown, hitting one officer in the head. He was carried away, blood pouring from a head wound, by a colleague.

Other thugs physically attacked police officers, leading to scuffles and fights.

The police looked as shocked at the outbreak of unfettered violence as the rest of us. Some backed away, their eyes wide, totally caught off guard.

Other members of the group of black-clad attackers attempted to block roads and build barriers to stop cars moving.

All told, eight police officers were injured, two seriously enough to be hospitalized. One was kicked in the head by a protester, badly damaging his eye socket.

The police struggled to keep control. On their side they were only equipped with aerosol cans containing pepper spray, plus wooden batons—little use against flying bricks, rods and metal barriers.

Despite being outnumbered, police managed to eventually take control of the situation. They arrested 19 people, mostly in their late teens or twenties. They found that the group had arrived at the protest with scissors, box-cutters, blades, multi-purpose knives and plastic ropes.

Those of us who had long followed Hong Kong news in detail were horrified. I slowed down the video taken by an Apple Daily reporter and looked at the way the attackers were dressed. They were mostly youths clad in ninja-style black, with their hair and faces covered, bricks and sticks in their hands.

I recognized them immediately.

This was a move-for-move repeat of the radicals' violent riot in Mong Kok on the night of February 8, 2016.

These were not peaceful protesters or even pandems, but members of the Hong Kong Indigenous or other localists or related groups: This city's equivalent of Britain's National Front or the US's far right anti-immigrant groups or France's National Rally.

The scariest sector of the Hong Kong radicals was back in action.

Like many Hong Kong people, I was profoundly shocked.

The next morning, I sent an apologetic message to Mrs. Ho, mother of two children and three enterprises.

"You know, you're right. I should be covering the protests. Send me your views. Get your friends and colleagues to do the same. Anything that needs to be said, but you're too scared to say, send it to me. I'll get it in print."

It was a turning point for this journalist.

I had to stop sitting on the sidelines, making trivial jokes about Xi Jinping and Carrie Lam, and start doing my job.

* * *

That next day, Monday, June 10, the organizers claimed that "a million people" marched. This was clearly untrue, and you didn't even have to count participants to know this. March organizers of all political colors have exaggerated their support since the beginning of time, and always will.

As I said earlier, no self-respecting journalist accepts their conclusions as fact. (They do have different exaggeration factors, though—in Hong Kong, they multiply by at least a factor of three. We'll take a scientific look at this question later.)

But on this occasion, journalists simply presented the lie as truth.

"Mrs. Lam, the demands of one million protesters were very clear—they want the bill withdrawn, they want you to step down," a reporter said at a press conference that morning.

Mrs. Lam patiently explained that there were a great many misunderstandings about the extradition law, in which decisions were made by the Hong Kong legal system, and specifically *not* the Chinese legal system.

But the reporter was not listening to her, just hearing what he wanted to hear. The "million" marchers "have expressed a lack of trust and confidence in the Chinese legal system," he replied.

"This bill is not initiated by the Central People's Government. I have not received any instruction or mandate from Beijing to do this bill," Mrs. Lam patiently replied. "We were doing it and we are still doing it out of our clear conscience and our commitment to Hong Kong."

Until now, I have not been a fan of the Hong Kong government, but in this case, I felt truly sorry for her. From my discussions with ordinary working civil servants and business people, she was clearly telling the truth.

But no one in that room was listening. They were in their own worlds caught up in a planted story of evil northerners snatching innocent southerners and whisking them over the border to disappear into gulags that appear on no maps.

* * *

The next day, Tuesday, June 11, Mrs. Lam showed another side of her personality—and revealed some fascinating statistics about the post-British era of Hong Kong people ruling Hong Kong.

She was the speaker at the Asian University for Women Gala Dinner and updated an enthusiastic audience about Hong Kong's achievements in regards to equal opportunities.

In the British era, men held two-thirds of professional jobs such as accountant and solicitor. In today's Hong Kong, women took up almost half those positions and their presence was growing steadily: they would soon be the majority. Two decades ago, 80 percent of managerial positions were taken up by men. Today, women have more than a third of them, and again, numbers were rising at speed.

"Those percentages are very much similar to those in our government," she said. "Today, more than one-third of Hong Kong civil servants at the directorate level, that is the most senior level, are women." In the British era, it had never risen above 15 percent.

* * *

The next day seemed to dawn late, and felt ominous. Dark, heavy clouds filled the heavens. It's a wet Wednesday, June 12. I'm sitting on the 25 bus flipping through the messages on my phone, glancing up at the lowering sky.

Tchu Yoong, the Celestial Welder, is expected to visit. The morning feels like evening and a lightning storm is predicted. You can see black clouds and occasional sparks already. He's checking the flints with which to light his heavenly oxy-acetylene torch.

The international media is reporting that Hong Kong as a whole has ground to a complete halt as the populace go on a "general strike" in continuation of Sunday's protests of "more than a million people".

None of this is true. My bus ride through town shows that shops and offices are open as usual, and everything is moving normally on the roads except for the area around the Legislative Council Complex in Admiralty.

I get off the bus. There is a big crowd present and a dark undercurrent in the small crowd that is nothing like the largely positive atmosphere of Sunday's march.

Who are these individuals clustering on the streets? Some look like the violent radicals from Sunday night, but many others seem to be curious young hangers-on, general pandem people, and gawkers (I guess I count as one of the last group).

Some activists are clearly middle class, with some owning cars, which they park diagonally in the middle of the main highway to prevent buses moving along Queensway, a main thoroughfare. Many of the protesters are well-heeled.

Younger people on foot, many of them male, are blocking nearby Harcourt Road and Lung Wo Road with any materials they can find, such as garbage bins and items from building sites. Some have damaged cars and police vehicles.

I'm told that police are not stopping the crowds of youths, but allowing them to surge around, while leaving narrow paths open for everyone's safety and medical access.

In fact, if you watch for a few minutes, you quickly realize that the police are actually working to help the demonstrators by diverting buses and finding new routes for trapped motorists. It seems their leaders have decided they should not stop the protests, but enable them to proceed, as the best way to avoid further violence. It's a good example of how Hong Kong operates like a crime-free version of a Western democracy.

But the people putting barriers in the road to cause blockages are taking advantage of the police's soft-handed approach.

At this moment, it looks like the whole of Admiralty may seize up, in the way it did during the Umbrella Movement gathering of September 2014.

But the Celestial Welder has other ideas.

Suddenly the heavens open and a heavy rainstorm descends. Within minutes, it has cleared the streets. It's like a monsoon. Everyone runs for shelter.

Five Vignettes From June 12, Morning

I run for cover too. As a huge rainstorm batters a coffee shop window, I sit down and jot down five observations from what I see in front of me and from reports I hear from others.

1) At least 10 death threats have just been made against Hong Kong leader Carrie Lam and justice minister Teresa Cheng—and police are taking some of them seriously.

One said that Mrs Lam's husband or one of her children would be killed within 24 hours.

These are horrible, violent messages, and again remind me that an unusually dark side of the anti-government movement is in the ascendency here, and dominating the debate in a way that is completely alien to the positive atmosphere of traditional Hong Kong marches.

2) I also note a huge and growing campaign of disinformation on Twitter, Facebook and the other social media websites.

Many Christians are saying that they have had clear confirmation that the new law is all about them, and calling for all believers to join the protests; activists are telling everyone that it specifically targets political activists, who will be deported en masse; and both groups, plus others, say that it is a clever way to introduce the death penalty to Hong Kong.

This is all malicious disinformation, but there is an ocean of it, and it is quite unstoppable. These allegations are everywhere on social media—and people who try to correct them are quickly labeled "Communist Party puppet" and un-friended.

You can see it happening in real time. Every time the truth is input into an Internet discussion, it is quickly declared a lie and overtaken by repetition of the false narrative.

It surprises me that opposition politicians and the media are declining to set people right on even the most obvious pieces of misinformation. On the contrary, many are instead forwarding allegations that they surely know to be untrue.

Activists are using Twitter, LIHKG, Signal and the Telegram anonymous communications app to call for protestors to keep up the pressure and surround the Legislative Council Complex non-stop for a week.

3) I get a call from my conference-watching source in Wan Chai, where most conventions take place. He tells me that Secretary for Justice Teresa Cheng has just finished attending an international criminal law conference.

Speaker after speaker talked about the vital need to work together as cross-border crime soars—which is, of course, what the entire extradition bill process was about.

My source says: "I'm surprised she didn't storm out and drag the Admiralty protesters inside and say: 'LISTEN TO THIS, PUNKS'."

4) Again, my phone lights up. "The event this afternoon is postponed indefinitely," says the message on the screen. Polytechnic University events (I was due to be Master of Ceremonies at one this afternoon) are being cancelled at high speed, given the febrile atmosphere.

Most events are being rescheduled for next week.

At the moment, no one is expecting this to turn into a lengthy shutdown as happened in 2014.

I also check with my business contacts. The Hong Kong stock market is falling and one of the biggest property deals of the year has been cancelled.

5) As the rainstorm takes a break, I go back out on the street and start tracking down people to whom to talk.

As well as chatting with protestors, your narrator speaks to former and current senior government people, long-term Legislative Council members, well-connected business people and police officers.

Everyone comes across as wary, unsure of what is happening and unclear as to what attitude they should take. There's a general feeling in the air that things are all spinning out of control.

The most insightful comment I get is this from an old businessman, watching from a shopping center terrace: "The tragedy is that none of this is about what people are saying it's about."

CHAPTER 9

Setting Up The Police

In Which June 12, A Stormy Day, Leads To A Dark Night—Attack On The Legislative Council Complex—Protesters Have Many Smart Strategies

IN THE AFTERNOON, violent young men return to the Legislative Council Complex and a group of them again attack the police officers guarding it. The formation is similar to Sunday night—a group of frightening, abuse-shouting young people in black at the front, plus a large contingent of less directly involved protesters behind them. At each side is a group of press photographers, trying to get the front line of angry men and the police officers into a single shot.

And, just like Sunday, it spins out of control.

I get the full story in detail later, not from police, but from a contractor who is inside the building, watching horrified through the windows.

In among the crowd, just behind the front layer, are masked young people with bricks and steel rods. The metal poles have been carefully pre-sharpened to turn them into lethal weapons.

They have a clear strategy—they locate building sites nearby and steal as much throwable stuff as they can from them. Many have bricks. One group has large numbers of planks.

These armed people are spread out in at least three separate clusters, slightly behind the front row of protesters.

At some kind of pre-arranged signal, all three start throwing their missiles. The air is suddenly filled with flying objects heading straight for the police.

The throwers then split into two groups, and run to each side, joining the press photographers and intermingling with them.

Some of the police are hit by missiles and go into defensive mode, covering their heads, while others follow the attackers and try to target them with batons or pepper spray—but of course what happens is that these police officers end up charging towards the press, behind whom the missile-throwers are now hiding.

"It was a really clever strategy," said the contractor. Whoever organized it knew what they were doing and had almost definitely done this sort of thing before.

By mingling with the press, attackers drew the police to spray reporters and photographers—who were instantly infuriated. And that was the point —to create anti-police anger among journalists.

At the back, some young men run to the building site to collect more bricks to throw. By this time, the front line is a full scale riot.

The huge mob behind can hear the fighting in front, but cannot see exactly what is happening—and just contributes roars of anger at the police and cheers to front line protesters.

There's the tell-tale smell of smoke, too. Some of the attackers are lighting fires in the road. The violent anti-immigrant group is back in action.

* * *

As the afternoon wears on, a new and distressing pattern emerges.

Young, male police officers, many looking nervous, are positioned in front of the Legislative Council Complex.

A large mob of protesters charges them, throwing objects that can cause harm. The police call for the crowd to disperse and use pepper spray to try to create a space.

The crowd retreats for a while, and then at some sort of signal charges forward again.

After a while, the strategy changes. The "safety gap" between the police and the crowd is left to stand for a while—and then a single protester will defy police orders and go and stand or sit in that space. He will ignore all shouted orders to leave it.

At first, observers are baffled by this strategy. It achieves nothing except to annoy police officers and spoil the temporary peace.

Using loudhailers, the police repeatedly ask the person to vacate the safety gap or be arrested, but he continues to ignore orders.

Then a small group of police officers is dispatched to arrest him.

As soon as they reach him, a thousand cameras start shooting—and the purpose of the strategy becomes clear.

What people present at the scene see is a small company of besieged police officers, armed only with items from their non-lethal cabinet. They have pepper spray cans and batons, hand-thrown tear gas balls, and guns which fire bean-bag rounds and rubber bullets: All unpleasant dispersal tools, but nothing designed to cause lasting damage.

On the other side is a huge, shouting crowd with primitive but potentially harmful weapons: Metal spears, bricks, planks, and mills barriers.

But what people who are not present at the scene will eventually see is something very different.

The clips are cropped to show ONLY the moment when a single protester is grabbed by multiple police officers. After watching a few clips, you feel that innocent members of the public are apparently sitting or standing peacefully, and are suddenly being set upon by roaming groups of police in riot gear.

The carefully chosen still shots being transmitted are even more damning.

It's a brilliant strategy, making the police, who are very much the underdogs, look like the aggressors. The trick is done repeatedly, with various refinements. The "sacrificed" protester is urged to struggle as much as he can, so that it takes up to six police officers to hold him down. Of course, the police succeed in restraining him in the end—but at enormous cost to their reputation.

The protesters are very, very clever. At that time, I had absolutely no idea whether these skillful techniques had been spontaneously generated, or whether they come from strategic meetings with people who specialize in this, such as a well known group from Serbia, or certain US groups which train people with similar techniques.

But whoever taught them to do it, it is working superbly.

A video later distributed by Amnesty International would later collate many of these edited videos, creating a damning impression of the Hong Kong police.

* * *

Hours pass, and this reporter hears that one group of protesters has taken over an underpass, Lung Wo Road, near the Legislative Council Complex.

This is a repeat of the road-occupation techniques used during the Umbrella Movement protests—but these individuals are much harder people than "we" Umbrella protesters were. Police leaders are distressed to be informed that the protesters have taken hostages this time.

They have blocked both sides of the underpass and are refusing to allow vehicles or the people in them to drive out or reverse. Ordinary workers, business people in sharp suits, families with young people—all are trapped

Police negotiators are dispatched to the scene, but the hostage-takers are totally intransigent, despite the obvious distress of the Hong Kong people trapped in the cars and vans. It takes eight hours of negotiations to free the trapped people.

By the evening, sporadic fighting has taken place, with more than 80 people listed as having suffered injuries, including 22 police officers. Eleven people have been arrested for disorderly conduct in public place, unlawful assembly, assaulting police officers and other riot-related offenses.

Officers are told that a full review of today's activities will be made, and any necessary adjustments will be made the following day. The radicals are extraordinarily well organized, that's for sure—and the police know they will need to step up their game.

* * *

In the evening, Carrie Lam releases a statement. "Fellow citizens, throughout the day, you could all see the distressing scenes in the Admiralty area. These acts of rioting, which damage social peace and disregard the law, are intolerable in any civilised society that respects the rule of law. Clearly, this is no longer a peaceful assembly but a blatant, organised riot, and in no way an act of loving Hong Kong."

Mrs. Lam reveals that she believes, as do most members of the civil service and the legal profession, that the extradition bill is not the real issue—it is being used as a tool.

"The fact is that since the return to the Motherland, issues involving the

Central Government and the Hong Kong Special Administrative Region, the mainland and Hong Kong, will be used by some people to stir up controversies and disputes," she says.

This, I realize, is an important point. She could ditch the extradition bill tomorrow and it would have absolutely zero effect. Instigators behind the scenes, wanting to cause trouble, have tapped into an entirely genuine malaise and unhappiness among the pandems and the radicals to foment an unusually violent re-assertion of the presence of anti-China feeling.

"Hong Kong is a free, open and pluralistic society that values different opinions on everything," Mrs. Lam continues. But in Hong Kong, violence is never the answer. "I hope that society will return to order as soon as possible and I don't want any more people to get injured in the riot. I appeal to all citizens who love this place to stay away from violence. I believe that any problem can still be resolved in Hong Kong, a civilised society, in a peaceful, rational and law-abiding manner for the overall interests of Hong Kong."

She's not a charismatic speaker, but the sentiment expressed does sum up the feeling of many Hong Kong adults. The violence feels alien to this low-crime society.

But many of the mothers and fathers on my network are angry with Carrie Lam, who they think is being too soft-handed. Violent protesters should be arrested promptly, they say. Hong Kong people are peaceful.

* * *

I spend the evening of June 12 chatting with a group of Hong Kong adults, mostly parents, and then decide to go back to the Admiralty area to see whether things have quietened down. By the time I arrive, it's late: past 11.30 pm.

The violence has dissipated. The rain has paused, and the inky streets are still full of young people. I'm walking along a road in Admiralty, the heart of my beloved hometown, which now looks like a war zone: The street is all barricades and rubble. The ground floor Starbucks at Pacific Place is closed, of course, but could have done good business—there are many people on the street, and causing mayhem is thirsty work.

As midnight approaches, I hear shouting.

I follow the sound of the raised voices and see that a team of police officers has emerged on foot from nearby police headquarters to clear blocked roads.

But they are instantly surrounded by a crowd, shouting and screaming foul abuse at them, some using megaphones.

The young man next to me starts throwing objects at them—anything at hand, including other people's water bottles. Some of them are extra-large bottles, still full, and are clearly heavy—they could easily break bones.

Other protestors charge towards the junction where I stand watching, and the mob quickly grows to form a huge group, surrounding the small group of officers. I can see how easily it could turn into a mob lynching, but the police, thank God, just take the abuse without responding, except with shouts at people to keep their distance. The crowd surges around them without further attacks, except for occasional thrown items.

Three immediate thoughts: I feel much more scared for the officers, many of whom are worried-looking young men trying to do their jobs, than for the protestors, who greatly outnumber them.

Second, I feel scared for myself: You can easily see how this scene can turn into a battle and I am in the middle of it trying to take pictures in the dark with an entirely inadequate phone.

Third, I feel scared for Hong Kong: This entire episode is entirely unnecessary, flames fanned by distrust and opportunism and huge amounts of inaccurate, agenda-driven reporting and deliberate misinformation.

I eventually give up trying to take pictures in the dark, but just talk to people. Later, I retreat from the fray and sit on a step to assemble my thoughts.

Five Thoughts From The Evening Of June 12

1) Hong Kong's protesters in general are actually mostly good people, non-violent and reasonable: What the British call "salt of the earth". But there are some very bad folk around. By no means all the late-night crowd are dangerous, but a significant proportion of them definitely are.

The pandems' disapproval of China and antagonism towards the Hong Kong government is understandable: it's an old and familiar story—but what happened on Sunday night and was happening again today was something quite different. To some extent, it is the return of the hostility, bigotry and violence we associate with the young radicals behind the 2016 Mong Kok attack. But it also much more carefully organized.

Scanning reports, I see that reporters are talking about Hong Kong looking like a "war zone" (as I just did) but the truth is that it only looks like that in a few corners.

We're exaggerating, as usual. This is not a war. We need to keep perspective—we're NOT talking bullets or bombs. The police are mostly being very restrained, sticking to aerosol sprays and batons.

On the other side, I see a distressing number of radical protestors carrying knives, masks, body armor, and sharpened sticks, which is worrying. Some have sharpened steel rods, which could kill someone easily.

Who would have thought that spear-throwing would be a serious threat in a modern city in this day and age?

2) In the media, the Hong Kong police are being painted as instigators of the trouble, but that's plainly wrong. "Riot police fired tear gas and rubber bullets in downtown Hong Kong" is the headline or opening paragraph of most reports.

But the truth is that you can easily see that officers respond rather than attack, and have followed that guideline in every instance I have seen. For all their lack of experience at large scale mob attacks, they are doing surprisingly well.

As for the protesters, while some are just random clusters of individuals, milling around, others seem to be following orders, and if you look carefully, you can see leaders in the crowds, discreetly marshaling and controlling them.

3) Again, I asked the young individuals in the street this evening about the "Evil Law" and found that none had read it or even had much interest in it. They had seen on Twitter or LIHKG that it allowed Beijing to deport Hong Kong people in large numbers "at will" and that was enough.

Besides, they hated China. This was a good excuse to show that.

The irony, of course, was that extradition laws in practice focus on people who commit crimes in the requesting country.

Many of the pandem politicians make it a point never to go to China, while others have been so hostile that they are unlikely ever to receive visas to visit—so that would make them literally the one group that can never be "returned" by the extradition law.

The ones making the biggest noise are the ones who are quite literally immune to the law.

4) As for the young protesters, I found myself admiring their honesty to some extent. They were more straightforward than the political activists or media columnists of this world, who are pontificating at length about a law they had never read.

These young people admit they have little interest in the extradition law. They hate China, and want to assert Hong Kong identity, and are grateful for the opportunity to be able to demonstrate this.

Also, there was an oddly infectious joy about the young people—we have conquered our city, we rule the streets, they seemed to be saying. And they had. They had taken over Admiralty, and were blocking the routes to Pacific Place, one of the most expensive shopping malls in the world.

Some young men seemed drunk on power: You could see it in the way they walked. They held bricks or rods in their right hands and affected a sort of swagger. In psychological terms, it was fascinating.

5) As mentioned, I had also spent time talking with older Hong Kong Chinese families this evening, discussing the situation, and their words also stayed with me.

It was interesting that they shared a distrust of the mainland legal system—but they were all strongly in favor of the extradition law.

Hong Kong and China definitely needed to work together to maintain the rule of law, and a Western-style law, from a United Nations template, seemed the wisest way forward, they said.

But they had trouble trying to explain this, even to their own children.

Among the Hong Kong adults to whom I spoke, I noticed that the ones who had spent most time in China were the ones most strongly in favor of the amendment: that was interesting.

"To maintain the rule of law, we need more cross-border co-operation, not less," said one, a man who ran a small manufacturing company over the border in a Guangdong city. A co-operative legal relationship between the two places didn't just benefit both sides, but was absolutely crucial for the future, the Hong Kong parents believed.

CHAPTER 10

Listening To Hong Kong Voices

In Which We Hear What People Are Saying—
The Rise Of Doxxing—Westerners Drift Apart From Hong Kong People

THERE ARE FASCINATING discussions among members of my social and other networks the next morning. I put the quote from June 12 morning on the Internet to see what people think: "The tragedy is that none of this is about what people are saying it's about."

"Spot on," says Gary Cheng. "It's always about something else."

"Then what do you think it is really about?" asks Mark Leung, father of one.

I reply: "Mark, good question, and I don't know enough to give you a confident answer. Still need to talk to more people. There are things which puzzle me."

There are clearly people in the shadows here, pulling strings and making things happen, while staying out of sight.

The public is more insightful than the newspaper columnists.

Paul Midler says: "This is not only about extradition laws. To be frank,

I don't even think it's MOSTLY about the extradition possibility."

Some have spotted mysterious individuals among the protest crowds.

Doreen Jaeger-Soong has a warning: "Friends of mine working in Admiralty and surrounding buildings thinks many are 'fake' protestors there just to rough people up. One of my friends got shoved by one when she was trying to walk through to her office. Possibly triads? Or Fifth Columnists?"

René Sequeira agrees that there is a violent element present: "There's plenty of young triads among the protesters who seem to be there to stir up trouble. We had a few ask us to join the protest or go back to Kowloon."

"I love Hong Kong protests, which are 90 percent family friendly," I write. "But the police collected lots of 'prepared weapons' from the gang that attacked on Sunday night, and some of the ones this morning have that 'waiting for violence' look about them. I have horrible memories of all the people hurt when Ray Wong and his gang went crazy and started lighting fires and throwing bricks in Mong Kok that time."

"I do not disagree, but it seemed that there were people there who are really trying to discredit the 'real' protestors," Doreen responds. "My office was in Hutchison House during the Umbrella movement and I remember walking past young and rough looking men, in the underpass by Bank of America and Fairmont House who were most definitely not students but were tattooed and wearing masks so they looked like triads to me. They were gathering wooden pallets and plastic barriers but I did not hang around to watch what they were doing. I think the same could be happening now."

Philip McBrayer, who has lived in Hong Kong since 1991 and knows the city well, says: "I hate to do this but I really side with the government on this. This has moved beyond protest and transitioned into a riot."

He is speaking good sense, and everyone agrees that peaceful protests are fine, but this type of riot, in which protesters intentionally cause harm to people and property, is not.

"No government is going to sit back and let a mob overthrow it, if that government can prevent it," says Philip. "It is better stop this before it gets further out of hand and 1000s of people get hurt or killed."

Many of us have little sympathy for the overseas commentators who are blaming the government for the violence.

Philip relates this point expressively: "It is easy for people who do not live in HK or who have a citizenship elsewhere to say *Protest, keep protesting, it's the PRC and they're evil. Evil, I tell you!* Because when the tanks roll down the street you'll put your white rear-end on a plane and leave. What about the people who cannot do that? The PRC has a long record of putting down this type of thing in a brutal fashion and the end is worse than the beginning. These people are tempting the PRC to intervene brutally. That intervention would mean a fall in the quality of life for most of the people that actually MUST live here and can't bug out to Canada/UK/Australia/US/NZ. It would also mean the end to the Basic Law (Hong Kong's Constitution) and one country, two systems."

His prediction that the ultimate result would be an unwanted crackdown from Beijing rings true.

The media is falsely saying that people are agitating because Hong Kong's freedoms have been crushed.

We all know that they have not been crushed—but some people are desperately trying to goad China into doing exactly that. They want China to step in, to send in troops, to arrive in tanks, to remove the legislature, to ditch our legal system, to stomp on us.

But why would anyone want to do anything to destroy the "one country, two systems" arrangement that has served Hong Kong so well?

There's an untold story here: That much is obvious.

That morning, Thursday June 13, I scanned the papers with bleary eyes after having been up very late the previous night.

Most of the coverage was wide-eyed reporting about the range of protests and the amount of disruption caused, with the police, being painted, ridiculously, as the root of the problem.

But there was one dull little political story that most people probably ignored, but it caught my eye. The report in the Standard newspaper quoted a Beijing official criticizing the media coverage of the moves to introduce the amendment.

The media "portrayed the story as [if] the Hong Kong government made this amendment [as a result of the] instruction of the Beijing government," Chinese official Liu Xiaoming had said the previous day. "As a matter of fact, Beijing central government gave no instruction, no order about making amendment. This amendment was initiated by the Hong Kong government."

This was very probably God's own truth, according to all the sources I had spoken to who actually knew insider details about this issue.

But people are so brainwashed against China, that no one was going to believe the words of a Beijing official. The extradition amendment didn't come from the North, but from the West.

* * *

Later, I see a new issue being raised by a reader. Yanyan Ip writes: "I'd like to tell you something that you don't know. Some shops supported the amendment are being suffered from bullying. Many fake booking. Many annoying call. Many fake worst comments."

There's a whole separate civil disobedience campaign taking place, at huge scale, and that's where the real trouble is. "No one can believe that suppression of the freedom of speech is not imposed by China, but the protesters," she continues. "Many policemen, their supporters and those families' details are uploaded to different forum, let the protesters to create nuisance to them. Some teachers also said they will take revenge on policemen's children."

Yanyan and other readers are soon highlighting a dark undercurrent that is being missed by the mainstream media so far.

There is a large scale angry campaign of deliberate troublemaking going on, with police officers and anyone who highlights the violence of the protesters being turned into targets.

This trend was dubbed "doxxing", a word derived from the slang term "dropping dox", meaning finding and distributing documents giving personal details of individuals, who can then be harassed.

Johnny Ku agrees. "The pictures of two British officers who did their duty during the riot were named and posted with harassing comments," he writes. "Lots of propaganda posts before, during and after the riot. Sad for Hong Kong."

* * *

The next morning, I head to the Block X coffee shop and am approached by a source as soon as I enter.

"Hong Kong leader Carrie Lam has friends in high places," says Sin-Chong, my police critic friend.

"Really? You mean ...?" I point heavenward.

"No, not God. And not Mr. Xi Jinpooh."

Tin is talking about the weather angels.

It's Friday, June 14, and activist Tin is expressing deep suspicion about the astonishingly well-timed downpours in recent days.

Protestors planned to meet three days ago, on the evening of Tuesday, 11 June, to set up an overnight camp outside the government headquarters—but there was a huge rainstorm, forcing them to go home for dry clothes.

At midday on Wednesday, 12 June, they had decided to set up camp for the whole week—and the heavens opened again, sending them home again.

He and his friends decided to start the week-long sit-in yesterday morning, Thursday, and, yes, there was another massive downpour.

The sit-in was postponed to 2.30 pm, by which time they hoped that the rain would have stopped.

At 2 pm, the Hong Kong Observatory app on his phone pinged. "Thunderstorm warning. Stay indoors," it said.

At 2.30 pm, it pinged again: "Amber rainstorm".

The final proof came when he showed me the official weather forecast for the next nine days: Rain and thunderstorms EVERY DAY.

"How does she do it?" he asked.

I tapped the side of my nose and closed one eye. (I have no idea what that means, but that's what Westerners do in movies at moments like this.)

But what I'm thinking: Tchu Yoong, god of lightning, Celestial Welder, is trying to dampen a metaphorical conflagration.

* * *

Western foreign correspondents are filling their newspapers with absurd stories in which they try to make China the sole bad guy in what is happening in this city (although it has had minimal involvement—in fact, quite possibly zero involvement. If there is a superpower involved in this, it doesn't seem to be China).

I eventually toss the papers aside and go and talk to Hong Kong people instead—who have a much more nuanced, detailed understanding of what's happening. By simply giving this city's own population a voice in the media, I'm receiving literally hundreds of letters. It's extraordinary.

Serina Cheung writes: "Nury, thank you for giving us both sides of the story. It's truly astounding how people complain about media censorship in China, and the one sided view of everything there—yet the media and the public are doing precisely the same thing here. 'Where's your photos and evidence? Don't you have a phone? For real?"

She continues: "A scroll through all the latest images and they're all of police. The media is all on the populist side—they would never publish a counter story that would attract fewer viewers. Where are the photos of protestors collecting bricks, hiding knives? 'Oh wait who cares cuz the authorities are using tear gas! They're the villains!' Seriously–life isn't so black and white. It's easy to argue that 'only a small number of protestors were violent'–but it's okay to generalise and say that the entire police force is 'corrupt and brutal?' It's like once they don their uniforms, everyone can treat them as anything but human."

She ends by writing: "The hypocrisy is shocking. I stand against the extradition bill, but I will not stand for the blatant violence that is giving China even more reason to tighten its grip. Thank you, Nury, for speaking up against the populist wave."

At this time, I notice a curious divergence in the comments that pour in.

The majority of Westerners who write to me are firmly on the anti-China side of the debate, their positions strongly blaming Beijing for everything, their views apparently influenced by the English language media.

But the Hong Kong Chinese voices are very different. They have a much broader view, and are more inclined to look for balance.

"Let's remind everyone to be civilised and respect others regards of the differing viewpoints," says Steven Mok.

Hamton Cheung writes: "Nury Vittachi, Thank you and support for your sharing! You are telling something that most of the public are missed from another true side of the incident."

"The groupthink and confirmation bias is so strong that otherwise intellectual people just blindly justify and whitewash rioters and violence while demonizing the entire police force in a way that is getting scary!" says Lauren Chan.

In contrast, Anthony Lavery is quick to attack me, convinced that I am a paid spy: "Mainland Financed 5th Columnist Causing Trouble. Endgame: They Can Call In The PLA."

Juan Barcelo has a simple harsh comment for me: "You've lost it, mate. Move to Beijing."

There are exceptions, but in many cases, the gulf between Westerners and Hong Kong people on this is growing wide. Many Westerners see China as a cartoonish Evil Empire, while the local Hong Kong people have a wider and more sophisticated range of views, being more aware of the layers beneath the surface.

CHAPTER 11

A Seriously Big March

In Which The Law Is Cancelled—
Another Big March—Birth Of A Marching Culture

BIG NEWS. IT'S SATURDAY, 15 June, and Carrie Lam has just shelved the extradition law.

It's over, the media is saying.

The plan has been dropped. The amendments, both of them, have been suspended and the teams preparing them have been told to stand down. The proposals will not be revived, and, like any abandoned bill, will automatically vanish like bathwater down a plughole at the end of the Legislative Council term.

Mrs. Lam explains that the huge marches and outpourings of fear about the bill have forced her to make this concession to the activists, as has the increasing danger to life and limb for innocent people: Ordinary Hong Kongers and police. (Some people on Twitter and LIHKG paraphrase this as a declaration that "we only listen to violence" but that's extreme cynicism.)

And how does she deliver her speech? She condemns everyone and wags her finger at the camera to scold participants.

No, she doesn't. She *thanks* everyone who participated—and not just those who supported her, but all the peaceful protesters too.

"I would like to thank all the pro-establishment legislators and members of the public for their support all along for our legislative exercise, as well as the people and organizations that have expressed their views in a peaceful and rational manner, even if they do not support the bill," she says. "As a free, open and pluralistic society, Hong Kong needs such a spirit of mutual respect and harmony in diversity."

She also makes an apology: "I want to stress that the original purposes of the exercise stem from my and my team's passion for Hong Kong and our empathy for Hong Kong people. I feel deep sorrow and regret that the deficiencies in our work and various other factors have stirred up substantial controversies and dispute in society following the relatively calm periods of the past two years, disappointing many people. We will adopt the most sincere and humble attitude to accept criticisms and make improvements so that we can continue to connect with the people of Hong Kong."

The news of the cancellation of the bill annoys the people who realize that the law would have been a positive addition, but most of the ones who write to me say that they understand the decision. With the world's media claiming that it is a mass deportation law which is about to send Hong Kong dissidents to mainland jails, the few rational voices pointing out the truth have been drowned out.

The news causes the many anti-extradition commentators in the media to rejoice. They've got what they wanted. They've "won".

But my group knows immediately that these media commentators are quite, quite wrong.

It's not over at all.

They don't understand what the protests are really about.

The protests are not about the extradition amendment at all.

The truth is that several hundred thousand good, honest, non-violent people who are understandably nervous about China, which is, after all, more than a little authoritarian, have joined forces with a couple of thousand violent, immigrant-hating radical Hong Kong nationalists, powered by unseen hands, and are on the march to express their fears. Their shared emotion is an entirely understandable one about the need to preserve Hong Kong's unique identity, and its corollary, the fear that the tough mainland Chinese leadership will destroy it.

But although their motivation is fundamentally good, a huge compaign of disinformation has amplified and exploited their fears.

One parent says to me that the people stirring up anger have shown excellent timing. The China accommodators have ruled Hong Kong for several peaceful years, and this year is the turn for the China fearers to assert themselves—this is the period of the political cycle for the opposition to rise. Pendulums swing.

It's over? No. The real story is too nuanced for the media to see, but all we have to do is wait. They'll see soon enough. They are saying it's over, but it's clearly just beginning.

* * *

Twenty-four hours speed by. It's now the evening of Sunday, June 16, and today there has been another huge march against the anti-extradition law—as if Mrs. Lam's announcement yesterday had never been made.

The international media is baffled.

The government again releases a statement expressing a highly positive, even warm view of the peaceful protesters, expressing thankfulness for the marches:

"Over the past two Sundays, a large number of people have expressed their views during public processions. The Government understands that these views have been made out of love and care for Hong Kong. The Chief Executive clearly heard the views expressed in a peaceful and rational manner. She acknowledged that this embodied the spirit of Hong Kong as a civilised, free, open and pluralistic society that values mutual respect, harmony and diversity. The Government also respects and treasures these core values of Hong Kong."

My correspondents from overseas are puzzled when I show them the statement.

This sounds so unlike the Beijing puppets that they have been told are now dominating the Hong Kong civil service.

None of the foreign correspondents quotes the above government statement in their report. It simply does not fit into the stark good-guy, bad-guy, narrative they are pushing.

Why is the Hong Kong government expressing such a positive reaction to the huge march?

We need to talk about this.

* * *

Hong Kongers march. That's what we do. We're proud of it. It's important.

And it's not just Hong Kongers: mainland Chinese people in general are habitual protest marchers, or at least were until the Communist Party decided that the only processions on the mainland could be ones which favored them.

Evidence? Consider the national anthem of China. It's a marching song, written for a 1935 movie in which the "common people" marched, yes, for "freedom".

The song is called The March of the Volunteers, and ends with an echoing line: "March on, march on, march on".

I approve of marching, and have been donating my shoe leather to demonstrations since I was a teenager. It's important for people to be able to take to the streets to express their dissatisfaction with policies of their governments.

Sadly, that point is missing in today's heavy-handed mainland China.

But it's different in free Hong Kong. We march all the time, or have done for the past 30 years.

In fact, I believe it may be that a forgotten stormy day in Hong Kong in May, 1989, is a key to understanding one of the most astonishing series of street protests in modern history—and one which isn't over.

But first, a popular mystery. I'm writing this on Wednesday, June 19, and last week, it seems that every major media outlet in the world reported that "a million" people marched in Hong Kong because they wanted the government to shelve the new extradition law. (It wasn't actually a million people, but it was a lot.)

The government suspended the new extradition law on Saturday, June 15.

Success? No.

The day after that, EVEN MORE Hong Kong people marched. The media said it was two million.

Why march after you get what you want? I can't blame them for being puzzled. Which is why I say that a forgotten episode in Hong Kong's history may help us understand.

You see, the people of this community started an extraordinary, record-breaking march on Sunday, May 21, 1989, thirty years ago, and that march has never stopped.

I believe all major demonstrations since that date can be seen as direct continuations of that one—and it's the shared underlying message that gets huge numbers of Hong Kong people out on the street.

And it's not about democracy or freedom or extradition or any of the things that we think it is about.

* * *

On a hot, wet Sunday in May, three long decades ago, huge numbers of people spilled out onto the streets of Hong Kong Island's North Point, blocking King's Road. This was the late 1980s, with Michael Jackson newly named "the King of Pop" and Russia's leader Mikhail Gorbachev visiting China.

In Hong Kong, we ran up onto the ramps leading to a new raised expressway that ran along the waterside on the eastern side of the island, and started marching towards Causeway Bay and ultimately to the Chinese government's office in Happy Valley.

The atmosphere was electric—literally. Typhoon Brenda had slammed into the region, and everyone on the streets was suffering from the results: Electrical storms, gale-force winds and periods of torrential rain. Brenda shredded my umbrella.

The celestial welder, Tchu Yoong, was on overdrive—strange flashes lit up the black clouds floating over the waterfront of Hong Kong Island.

The gusts of wind were sudden and unexpected. It was if the air was slapping our faces to keep us hyper-alert.

It quickly became obvious that this was no ordinary protest march. It was HUGE. Realistically, there were hundreds of thousands of people there—perhaps 300,000 to 400,000.

But of course organizers did their usual thing and claimed "between a million and 1.5 million". The international media rounded the figure to "a million people" and reported it to be one of the biggest marches in recorded history anywhere on the planet. Maybe it wasn't that, but it was big, trust me.

The demonstration's route went past the tiny three-bedroom apartment in Tin Hau, bordering Victoria Park, that my wife of two years and I had just bought in anticipation of having children. We raced upstairs to take photographs from our living room window. It was a sea of umbrellas.

The march had been called to show Hong Kong's solidarity with students demonstrating in Beijing. But we were a community shortly to be placed in China's care, so of course there was a deep, personal fear too.

Several things made that 1989 march astonishing. First, it was a new experience for many. Fully 90 percent of marchers told reporters that it was the first time they had done such a thing. One analyst said he was amazed, as Hong Kong was "not a place where people take to the streets with their politics". (Then, as now, the dominant political stance of the Hong Kong populace was to be apolitical.)

Second, the march unified an astonishing range of people, Easterners and Westerners, folk who loved China and folk who were suspicious of it, government officials and road sweepers. Mainland China officials in Hong Kong were part of it too–people find that hard to believe, but it's absolutely true: I saw it myself.

Mainland officials in Hong Kong raised up their own supportive banner, saying: "Chinese Give Support to Besieged Brethren". Acknowledging their presence is absolutely essential to understand the complexity of Hong Kong and to escape from the false "good versus evil" narrative.

We were all supporting the students in Beijing, who repeatedly said they were campaigning for purer, better communism—so it was completely natural for staff at the Xinhua offices in Hong Kong to join in the protest. They wanted exactly the same thing. The song most often sung by the students in Tiananmen Square that spring was The March of the Volunteers, China's national anthem. "March on, march on, march on." We marched out of love for China, not hate.

Third, something changed that day in Hong Kong. The concept of mass peaceful protest became an integral part of this community's DNA. (It was probably already there, but had not been activated since 1967, more than 20 years earlier.)

We all spontaneously agreed to meet again the next day. In fact, people marched again the next day, and the next, and extra-large marches were repeated the next two Sundays.

The gatherings finally started to shrink and eventually died down, but they didn't stop. They simply became periodic items on the calendar.

We'd march on particular holiday dates, such as January 1 and July 1. We did so every year. Like clockwork, we would all suddenly appear out of nowhere. True, there were fewer of us every year, but the loyal ones hated to miss it. I was definitely among the loyalists.

* * *

Eight years passed from the time of that first march, in 1989.

In 1997, the flags changed on July 1—but a huge number of Hong Kong people were involved in the latest leg of the Great March. By then, it had become a regular reunion.

By this time, our underlying message had been refined to become more of an assertion of identity, and it was something like this: "We are Hong Kong. Flags may change, but we're still us. Thank you."

(Hong Kong protestors are very polite, in the main, and in those days we were not anti-China, nor overly critical of the Hong Kong government, and certainly never violent.)

By the early 2000s, the core group of us were holding what we called a "patriotic democratic" march every year on July 1 while others joined on special occasions. It was always called a "patriotic democratic" march because it was vital to understand that we were all pro-China. We were patriots, and proud to be called that. Yes, we criticized China, but not because we wanted to be American or British or anything else. We were marching not against China, but in favor of China being its best self.

I dragged my growing family along if extra numbers were needed and they were willing.

When a law was proposed that banned subversion in 2003, panic spread quickly, and certain activist groups organized the latest episode of the Great March. Numbers swelled to 470,000 and the international media were back with their cameras.

By this time, my wife and I had adopted three Hong Kong Chinese children, and we brought them with us, the youngest in a stroller, to express our fears about Article 23.

In 2014, an election system which our activist leaders dubbed "undemocratic" was proposed, and we were all back out on the street in huge numbers.

We soon had a new nickname ("the Umbrella Movement") and there were plenty of new faces, but the main elements of the 1989 marches were present: The nervousness about China, the desire to retain Hong Kong's uniqueness, and the good-natured, peaceful atmosphere.

That protest had a special charm during its opening weeks, but quickly turned sour for a number of reasons. There were at least three layers of people trying to manage it—two public, one (at least) secret—and they increasingly disagreed about strategy. At first, the Western element in the protest was kept extremely well hidden, but by the end it was obvious and very awkward.

By 2016, critics complained that Hong Kong's activist community members (the locally generated elements and the US-sponsored elements) were over-sensitive, marching on the streets for every perceived problem about our mainland Chinese masters.

The critics were right. We totally need to plead guilty about that.

Sometimes we got things spectacularly wrong, like the incident I mentioned earlier about the railway station. To recap, in 2016-2017 we protested loudly that a joint mainland China-Hong Kong passenger processing facility at a railway station in Kowloon would lead to the death of this city. It patently didn't. The aforementioned Activist Cycle caused us to complain about everything—and wise heads in the civil service did the smart thing and went ahead and ignored us, building a new airport, new infrastructure, new stations and so on.

By 2019, only greying Hong Kong adults like me remembered the 1989 march, the first year of what had become three decades of regular marching. To some extent, I was quietly pleased that the marching spirit was as strong as ever.

Yet at the same time, the 2019 protests were different.

Every single news report said that it was about the extradition bill. But they were wrong. The bill was irrelevant. The marchers hadn't read the bill, and the local and international media had grotesquely misrepresented it, some out of laziness, and some deliberately, as an anti-China strategy.

I think many people at the two peaceful marches, June 9 and June 16, were simply asserting their identity as a community. We were 28 years away from being subsumed into China, and marchers were worried. The message of the peaceful people on the march was the same as it had always been: "We are Hong Kong. Flags may change, but we're still us and want to stay that way. Thank you."

As the days of that wet and stormy June passed, I saw that every major news outlet in the world was reporting that two million people, almost a third of our adult population, joined a single protest.

It's an astonishing thought that should have filled an enthusiastic old marcher like me with pride.

But instead it dismayed me.

I knew it was untrue. And truth is important, especially when the march is carrying a political label. It was deeply unfair to the people of Hong Kong, particularly the nine out of ten of them who had not been on the march for whatever reason. How can almost third of the population be at a march when nine out of ten weren't there?

Social media users are terrible at estimating crowd sizes, which is why you have to go to the professionals and use proper scientific methods.

Do the math. A 70-feet wide march of two million people would fill a street that was 58 kilometers long, starting at Victoria Park in Hong Kong and ending in Tanglangshan Country Park in Guangdong, mainland China, according to one standard crowd estimation technique. If the two million of us stood in a single file queue, we'd stretch much, much further, of course, some 914 kilometers (568 miles), from Victoria Park to Thailand.

Even if all of us marched in an organized regiment 25 people abreast, our troop would stretch right off the island of Hong Kong, onto Kowloon, and then a long way towards the Chinese border. Even if we were 50 or 75 people abreast, we'd still have spilled off Hong Kong Island.

Yes, there was a very large number of us at that march. But getting key facts so obviously wrong helps nobody. This is something we should discuss, in fairness to the 75 percent to 90 percent of Hong Kong's population who joined neither of the great marches of June, 2019.

CHAPTER 12

A Brief History Of Lies

In Which We Consider Scientific Ways to Count Crowds—A Brief History of Lies—Police Estimates—A Plea For Balance

WE HAVE NOW reached the end of June, 2019, and for the past week, Hong Kong parents have been repeatedly asking me to find out "the real number" of people at the recent mass rallies in this city.

They can't believe the huge numbers claimed. The media assertion that it was one in three of all adults in the city implies that Hong Kong is a monolithic community sharing the opinion of the radicals and the pandems.

At the time, I declined for an obvious reason: There were a large number of us. What did it matter whether it was hundreds of thousands or a million? To me, that wasn't important.

But my critics pointed out that the term "two million" was right at the top of almost every report about the marches. Clearly it WAS important.

In fact, I noticed that my journalistic counterparts who were the most insistent that the inaccuracy of the "two million" claim was not important were the ones most likely to put it in their headlines and opening paragraphs.

So I decided to do some research, get on the phone, and look at the topic. If you're interested, the data and analysis is below. If not, skip this chapter. The takeaway is that nowhere near two million marched (or even one million). In fact, all claims of numbers of marchers, whatever their politics, were wild exaggerations.

The Science

Scientists use density checks, crowd-flow data and impact assessments, and work in this area has been done by Hong Kong Polytechnic University (Hong Kong PolyU), Hong Kong University of Science and Technology, University of Hong Kong, and Hong Kong Baptist University.

Density

Figures gathered in the past by Hong Kong Polytechnic specialists using satellite photo analysis found a density level of one square meter per marcher. I know from experience that Hong Kong marches feature long periods of looser spacing (one square meter or one and half per person, walking) and shorter periods of tight spacing (about half a square meter per person, mostly standing).

Joiners

For accuracy, we include people who join halfway. In the past, a Hong Kong University analysis using visual counting methods cross-referenced with one-on-one interviews indicated that peak attendance estimates should be boosted by 12 percent to accurately reflect late joiners or non-peak extras.

Speed

A Hong Kong Baptist University survey earlier found an average passing rate of 4,000 marchers every ten minutes. This measure is useful in that it highlights when a claim is impossible—such as for example when the total claimed figure could only have been achieved if everyone had sprinted the entire distance.

Distance Times Density

We know the walking distance between Victoria Park and Tamar Park is 2.9 kilometers. Although there was overspill, the bulk of the marchers went along Hennessy Road in Wan Chai, which is about 25 meters (or 82 feet) wide, with looser crowds on parallel roads.

Steve Doig, a specialist in crowd analysis approached by the Columbia Journalism Review, analyzed an image of Hong Kong marchers to find a density level of 7,000 people in a 210-meter space. Although he emphasized that crowd estimates were never an exact science, that figure meant that if there had been ONE million Hong Kong marchers present, they would have needed a street 18.6 miles long—which is 29 kilometers, or ten times the actual distance of the march.

Extrapolating these figures for the June 16 claim of two million marchers, you'd need a street 58 kilometers long.

But remember, the actual route was not even three kilometers long. In short, the organizers' claims that have been widely accepted and printed were simply impossible.

Could this problem be explained away by the turnover rate of Hong Kong marchers, which likely allowed the main route to be filled more than once?

The answer is yes, to some extent. But the crowd would have to be moving very, very fast to refill the space ten times over in a single afternoon and evening. We would have had to have been sprinting. We weren't.

While I can walk the distance from Victoria Park to Tamar in 41 minutes on a quiet holiday afternoon, doing the same thing during a march takes hours.

More believable: There was a huge number of us, hundreds of thousands, on June 9 and on June 16, but not a million on either occasion (and certainly nowhere near two million).

A Brief History Of Lies

Yet the figures, one million for June 9 and two million for June 16, are printed everywhere, and presented as fact. Where did it all go wrong?

I'll tell you. (Age comes with some advantages.) In 2003, as mentioned earlier, a very large number of us walked from Victoria Park to Central to express fears about Article 23. My family provided five of those individuals, four marching and one in a stroller.

The next day, newspapers gave several estimates of crowd size.

The differences were relatively small. Academics using scientific counting methods said it was 350,000 at the minimum. The police, using similar methods, counted 466,000.

The organizers, a group called the Civil Rights Front, rounded it up to a neat total of 500,000.

No controversy there—all three groups of counters agreed that the final tally was in the same range, so probably about 400,000 to 450,000.

But there was trouble ahead.

At a repeat march the following year, 2004, it was obvious to all of us that our numbers were far, far lower that the previous year. Fewer than half of us turned up. You could easily see that, even from inside the march. As a committed, veteran marcher, I was disappointed.

The scientists and police independently produced figures which matched closely. The first group said 194,000 and the police said 200,000, so they were closely in line with each other, with the police offering a slightly higher estimate.

But the Civil Rights Front insisted that there were MORE than the previous year's march: 530,000 people.

This was clearly a bald-faced lie. They'd almost tripled the real number!

The organizers lost credibility even with us, their own supporters. (To this day, we all quote the 2003 figure as the high point of that period, ignoring their 2004 invention.)

The following year, 2005, several organizations, with different political allegiances, decided to serve us better, with detailed, scientific counts. They came from a range of political positions, and happily produced similar results.

On that occasion the march was smaller again, just a fraction of the size of the earlier demonstrations. Even from within the march, we could see that there were fewer than half the 200,000 of last year, so not even 100,000.

And the results? The scientists said the headcount was between 60,000 and 80,000 and the police, using similar scientific methods, said 63,000. Separate accounts by other independent groups agreed that it was below 100,000. So a fair summary would have said the number was in the region of 70,000 people.

But the organizers? The Civil Rights Front came out with the awkward claim that it was 250,000! Yes. A quarter of a million.

This was almost four times the real figure.

Ouch. No one was happy.

But then came a twist that none of us expected.

Western media chose to present ONLY the organizer's fantasy number—the number that all of us, on all sides of the political spectrum, knew was FAKE.

"Dressed in black and chanting 'one man, one vote', a quarter of a million people marched through Hong Kong yesterday", said the revered Times of

London in 2005.

"A quarter of a million protesters marched through Hong Kong yesterday to demand full democracy from their rulers in Beijing", reported the UK's The Independent, a London broadsheet.

What was happening?

It became obvious that international media outlets were committed to emphasizing whichever claim made the Hong Kong government (which they chose to see as an extension of China) look as bad as possible, even if everybody on the ground knew that it was patently untrue.

The Western media is still doing that.

At universities in Hong Kong (including PolyU, where I work), there were passionate discussions in 2005 about the decision to lie about the numbers as a deliberate strategy, with the international media in mind.

Anyone who actually wanted the truth would choose a middle point as the "real" number: Thus it was worth inflating the organizers' "count" to a level as high as possible, making the median figure misleadingly high. (The police, whose count tended to roughly match the scientists' count, sometimes slightly higher, sometimes slightly lower, could be presented as evil, corrupt puppets of Beijing who were deliberately low-balling their estimates.)

Once the inflated figure was established in the Western media, it would become the generally accepted figure in all publications, on the Internet, and in history in general. If The Times of London said that 70,000 people was a quarter of a million, then their version became the accepted story, the historical "fact" that ended up on Wikipedia, despite being untrue.

This prediction was bang on target. For example, in 2011, scientific crowd-counts showed that between 63,000 and 95,000 of us marched. Our delightfully imaginative organizers MULTIPLIED BY FOUR to claim there were 400,000 of us—and that was the ONLY figure the international media printed.

In 2012, scientists and police produced headcounts very similar to the previous year: Between 66,000 (scientists) and 97,000 (police). But the organizers claimed that it was 430,000, an obvious untruth printed as fact.

Old-school journalists who can count and do occasionally make a feeble attempt to be honest (we exist! Really!) were soon working out a formula to try to derive the real number from the organizers'/media's claims.

At that time, we worked out that the Hong Kong exaggeration factor had grown to about six (70,000 times six is 420,000) for very big marches. But it occasionally rose to being a ten-fold exaggeration. If the march was very small—just a few hundred, or a thousand people—the exaggeration factor was brought down to about three, so 490 would become 1,500 and 950 would become 3,000.

* * *

Now back to the 2019 march: how many of us were out on the street during recent marches during that hot, uncomfortable June?

An academic study put the June 9 rally at 199,500. Police said the peak was 240,000. Some people said the numbers should be raised or even doubled to reflect late joiners or people walking on parallel roads.

Taking the most generous view, which is a 100 percent boost, this gave us total estimates of 400,000 to 480,000.

But the organizers, God bless them, claimed that 1.03 million marched: this was four times the researchers' conservative view and more than double the generous view.

The addition of the ".03m" caused a bit of mirth among social scientists. Even an academic writing in the wildly pro-activist Hong Kong Free Press struggled to accept it. "Undoubtedly, the anti-amendment group added the extra .03 onto the exact one million figure in order to give their estimate a veneer of accuracy," wrote Paul Stapleton.

But here's the rub. The vast majority of international media and social media printed ONLY the organizers' eyebrow-raising claim of a million plus for June 9—and their version soon fed back into the system and because the "accepted" number. (Some mentioned other estimates in their initial report to cover their bottoms and then dropped them.)

The same process was repeated for the following Sunday, June 16, when the organizers' impossible claim of "nearly two million" was taken as gospel in the majority of international media.

"Two million people in Hong Kong protest China's growing influence," reported Fox News.

"A record two million people–over a quarter of the city's population" joined the protest, said The Guardian.

"Hong Kong leader apologizes as TWO MILLION take to the streets," said the Sun newspaper in the UK.

Even the newspapers who one would hope would value the truth happily presented the lie as a straight out fact, including The Financial Times and The Economist.

The New York Times hilariously stole the form of words from discount shop windows and said "up to two million"! (Imagine how hard they would come down on Trump if he used the same trick: "Up to two million people attended my inauguration! Tremendous! Everyone agrees!")

Friends, colleagues, fellow journalists–What happened to valuing the truth? What happened to the healthy skepticism that has always been our profession's core characteristic? What happened to attempts at balance? What happened to multiple sourcing of contentious issues?

Numbers do matter—they matter to those of us who have been marching for 30 years as well as to critics of marchers. If you tell the world that one third of a city's adult population was at a march, you're implying that the population of this city very probably speaks with a single voice on this particular issue.

But if the real story is that fewer than one in ten of our people marched, well, the implications are very different.

The Western media likes to present Hong Kong people as a monolithic mass of China haters. This is not the case. As I mentioned before, active pan-dem supporters, the group that dislikes China, appears to number about 1.6 million, fewer than one in four of Hong Kong's 7.5 million people.

That's a lot of individuals. But it's not "the people of Hong Kong".

International media, your hostile agendas are showing. Raise your game.

Organizers of protest marches, stop working against the scientists and start working with them.

Hong Kong people, we need to remind the two groups above, the media and the organizers, that we value truth. We're not stupid.

And we're good at math!

* * *

I log onto the Internet at the Block X coffee shop at Polytechnic University and a colleague shows me a Facebook page called Hong Kong Moms.

This group seemed dominated by Westerners or Westernized people, and seemed to have little or no overlap with the Hong Kong mothers who wrote to me.

It was shocking. It apparently normally discusses toys and child-friendly meals.

But someone has posted a picture showing the face of a Hong Kong police officer and described him as a man "willing to shoot and even kill people who are pleading for a brighter future".

The apoplectic post was one of a large spate of name-and-shame Internet attacks on police officers assigned to duty at protest sites. Doxxing of police officers is spreading at high speed.

Horrified police chiefs this weekend set up internal hotlines so that defamatory posts can be reported as hate crimes. All the phone lines were quickly engaged.

Showered with flying objects for doing your job, and then coming home to find yourself unfairly libeled on Facebook—whatever your political view, a Hong Kong policeman's lot is not a happy one.

A well-known strategy of international protest is to dehumanize the police and ascribe all wrongdoing to them. They have to be present and must respond at every occasion, so it's relatively easy to make them the bad guys, simply by changing the order of events, and focusing on their every error, diverting attention from violent radicals who actually do throw bricks and light fires. This was precisely what was happening in Hong Kong.

Five Vignettes From June 24

1) No, we don't need to be airlifted out of our apartments. No, we have not been herded into communist re-education camps. No, tanks are not rolling into Prada in Causeway Bay.

Lovely, sweet people are writing to me (some from genuinely dangerous places) telling me they are praying for me and my family to survive the crushing of Hong Kong by the evil Chinese.

"Send food parcels," I reply to one. "Soy-poached guinea-fowl with caramelized onions, plus a bottle of Chateau Lynch-Bages 2008."

2) TV journalists from CNN stopped me and other people on the walkway outside Exchange Square asking questions as if they expected us to be packing our bags and fleeing.

I narrowly managed to stop myself saying what they clearly wanted to hear: "I'm running to the airport with only the Ascot Chang bespoke shirt on my back."

3) Most business people I've been chatting to are polite about the demonstrators—but it only takes one and a half drinks and a promise that their names will not be used for less supportive views to come out.

Tour industry people are horrified by mass cancellations. One top hotel saw its occupancy rate of 90 percent drop to a disastrous 55 percent, an employee of a hotel management group told me.

A senior executive at one of Asia's biggest property developers told me: "We're planning to cut apartment sales prices to move stock." (Hard to hide my smile at that one! Thank God! Carrie Lam, you've done it at last!)

4) Retailers in the malls around Admiralty (including Pacific Place, United Centre and Queensway) are furious because radicals and their supporters are sending out thousands of messages and emails warning people to avoid the area "for your own safety".

Shopkeepers pay at Pacific Place HK$1 million a month in rent or more.

None of the messages point out that the groups warning about the lack of safety are the exact same people who are gathering bricks and other objects to make the area unsafe.

5) One Westerner watching video clips of fighting at the doors of the Legislative Council Complex asks me why Hong Kong police don't use heavy weapons, machine guns and armored cars. "I mean, how come your guys mostly just use AEROSOL CANS?!" he says.

Yes, he was American.

CHAPTER 13

Unseen Hands Behind The Protests

In Which Obvious Anomalies Stick Out A Mile—Defend Whose Constitution?— We Besiege Police Headquarters— Hong Kong People Plead For Balanced Coverage

OH DEAR. Activists today, Wednesday, June 26, asked Donald Trump to free Hong Kong from China. The city needs to be "decolonized" from mainland China by the United States, they said.

Hong Kong people do not want this. These are unmistakable signs of interference by malicious groups manipulating these young people. But of course, I'm not going to write that. I need more evidence.

At this time, something else was worrying me more. Some of my own students joined others marching through the city wearing "Liberate Hong Kong" t-shirts and chanting "Free Hong Kong".

The phrases, of course, reflect the "Liberate Tibet" and "Free Tibet" campaigns that have been so successful for my generation. (Yes, I waved my little irony flag as I typed that sentence.)

The Tibet story, incidentally, has been a huge black eye in modern Western journalism. We wrote stories for years about the "Tibetan genocide" that turned out to have been planted by the US state department's media manipulation people.

Surveys and census results eventually revealed that Tibetans had the highest growth rate of any population in China, far higher than Han Chinese. Of course, Western journalists did not apologize for or correct their stories. They simply edited the narrative so that it evolved from "Tibetan genocide" to "Tibetan cultural genocide", much harder to disprove.

But regarding the Hong Kong youngsters, this author felt the mixed emotions all teachers suffer when they see their students interacting sharply with the real world: pride, nervousness, concern, hope, love, involuntary incontinence.

At the head of the parade, an organizer is confidently telling reporters there were 1,500 people in the march.

A hostile-looking local Hong Kong observer was skeptically shaking her head, so Your Humble Narrator decided to solve the problem by employing a little-used scientific crowd-analysis technique called Counting Them One By One With My Finger.

There were exactly 476 people with maybe 40 appearing to be journalists. The other person, a local former journalist who wanted only to be known as Emmy SY O, was also shocked at the gulf between what was happening in Hong Kong and what was being reported.

Like me, she felt that manipulation by hidden groups was obvious to anyone who glanced under the skin of the protests—and was horrified that the present generation of journalists was not interested in digging into that.

A little later, we scanned the news websites, some of whom were reporting live. Reporters were already confidently declaring to the world that 1,500 are present.

Emmy and I agreed that we didn't like the way local and international reporters carelessly rushed to allow themselves to be spoon-fed lies—and reporters from my newspaper, The Standard, were just as guilty as the notoriously biased ones, such as Apple Daily and the Hong Kong Free Press. But I was happy about the result for one selfish reason.

It neatly confirmed the old-school reporters' theory that if the crowd was small, the exaggeration factor was 300 percent. (The actual counting of the real number of people who turn up is "lost technology" for modern-day media.)

Anyway, it was interesting to listen to the chants and eavesdrop on the interviews. The marchers were saying that they were angry because "Hong Kong is not China" but China was treating Hong Kong "like a colony".

Ah. Right. I think we all agreed that Hong Kong was not a colony. It was part of the same country—that's closer than a colony. (But of course I don't say this.)

Arriving at the US Consulate General up the hill on Garden Road in Central, the group read out and handed in a letter to Donald Trump. The English translation said: "In desperation we seek your engagement and assistance to fight back against this authoritarian regime."

Dingalingalingaling! Alarm bells went off.

This was absolutely not a translation of a Chinese passage. The choice of words, the cadence, the rhythm, the tone—it was all wrong for a statement by a group of "grassroots" Hong Kongers.

Who wrote this?

Nobody would tell me.

Minutes later, Emmy and I compare the English version with the Chinese version. Logically, the English version should be a translation of the Chinese one. But the opposite appears to be true. What could that mean?

Of course we know the answer. There are undoubtedly English-speaking foreigners right at the heart of these protests. Nobody wants to mention the

CIA or Canvas or Amnesty International or the Oslo Freedom Forum or the more secretive groups and sound like conspiracy theorists, but there was definitely someone pulling strings.

This is a tricky issue to talk about, and you can't really even write about it. If you ever even hint in print that "foreign forces" are involved, you are instantly buried alive by pieces of hate-mail telling you that you are a paid Communist Party official pushing a "Beijing talking point", and "cancelled" as a credible source.

The trouble is that sometimes it's true that foreign forces are involved—and this was quite definitely one such case.

As if to confirm this, someone arrived with a big batch of posters saying "Free Hong Kong: Democracy Now" prominently printed *in English*, combining an independence message (which guarantees to annoy Beijing) with the magic word "democracy" (which guarantees sympathetic news coverage by Western media).

They were in full color and beautifully printed on glossy paper. Someone's got some serious money.

A few hours later, through gossip among journalists, I hear that activists have two or three bottomless funds backing them and have decided to send millions of dollars in the direction of the media covering the protests by buying entire newspaper pages. Woohoo! Good for us.

The cash will be used to buy ad space in which they tell the world about their "continuing" fight against the (dead) extradition bill—a story which everyone already knows and which we in the world's media are happily carrying free of charge on our front pages anyway. This makes no sense.

Er, thanks, guys! A few of the reporters present take a moment to discuss the fact that millions of dollars will soon be going to our employers.

As recently as 15 years ago, this would have triggered huge newsroom discussions about media ethics, money, balance, honesty, and morality.

But those days are gone. The modern media's level of interest in ethics has dropped to less than zero. I feel like such a dinosaur. Maybe I should just go back to my cave and gnaw on some bones.

Instead, I head out to talk to a group of Hong Kong families again.

You can find them at dining clubs, at churches, at schools, at anywhere ordinary people gather.

Many of the adults of Hong Kong are smart, calm, and completely reasonable—nothing like the apoplectic protest leaders that the media insists on interviewing, again and again, until we are all sick of them.

I find that this latest group of adults are all pro-democracy people, but they are also thoughtful, intelligent, and decidedly NOT anti-China. They have some serious reservations about much of what goes on in the world's most populous country, but they don't have the hate demonstrated by the radicals.

They strongly oppose the protests, but are equally strongly in favor of human rights—and thus don't exist in the way the media carves up Hong Kong society into "pro-democracy" and "pro-Beijing". Some of the children of this group are drawn to attend the protests out of curiosity, but even they are not fooled by the artificially polarized politics.

These multi-generational families are becoming my touchstone for the Real Hong Kong. Hong Kongers can deal with sophisticated political positions and know that it helps no one to go to one polarized extreme or the other—unless of course destabilization is your actual goal.

* * *

At the end of the day, I go back to Central to find a huge crowd has gathered at City Hall, including several of my students. I decide to tag along with the youngsters.

Emmy O is still there. She nudges me and points to a large group of young people holding signs which are almost entirely in English.

"Liberate Hong Kong", the signs all say. "Defend our constitution."

I gasp. My eyes widen into tennis balls. The initials "WTF?!" appear, hovering over my head, as my jaw hits the floor.

And then I slowly turn to catch her eye.

She gives me a knowing nod.

Woop-woop-woop-woop-woop!

Emergency alarm bells are ringing at full volume now, in both our heads.

These placards are extraordinary. They are an unmistakable sign of something dark and creepy going on.

It's the words "defend our constitution" that have set off the alarm bells.

You see, Hong Kong doesn't have a constitution. It's never had one.

The nearest thing it has is a book called the Basic Law, which is widely disliked by the radicals and by the pandem groups.

No Hong Konger on any side of any political debate would EVER print a kazillion signs in glorious color saying "Defend our constitution".

Nor would they gather in a large group to march with a phrase which is completely meaningless in a Hong Kong context.

These hundreds of placards are clear, physical proof that something bad is happening: They have undoubtedly been prepared by someone with little or no understanding of Hong Kong society.

Furthermore, a large group of young people have agreed to carry them for a reason that is unclear. They have either been told the signs mean something else, or they have been promised cash to make this protest, or both.

Anyway, for whatever reason, this particular group of radicalized young people are happy to carry this nonsensical phrase along the street in large numbers.

There are dozens of foreign reporters filming this procession who don't understand what's happening. None of them have noticed what we've noticed. They probably assume that Hong Kong has a constitution and that protesters want to defend it—not realizing that this is neatly and unmistakably reveals the presence of English-speaking forces hidden underneath this demonstration. (And singularly uninformed forces, too.)

Something seriously bad is going down in Hong Kong—and it's being at least partly orchestrated by outsiders. There is now not the slightest doubt about that.

But who are they? Loud, Western, anti-Chinese, ill-informed and dangerous: A friend of Emmy's decides to dub them "the Trumpettes".

* * *

As midnight approaches, things are turning dark again in more ways than one. A large group of us have marched from the City Hall waterfront to the Police Headquarters building in Wan Chai.

On the way, young people are stealing all the safety barriers from construction sites and road holes and using them to totally block both sides of Gloucester Road, the main thoroughfare through the busy part of Hong Kong Island.

Buses full of shift-workers trying to get home after a long day are stranded, and people are begging to be released from buses in the middle of the expressway. In cars, exhausted office workers rest their heads on their steering wheels. Misery descends.

I feel awful and I hope my students do too. But the public have to suffer for the cause, right?

I guess I should have asked how the young people knew that the Hong Kong public wanted their roads blocked as a call to Donald Trump to free Hong Kong from China (I couldn't imagine anything worse), but by that time we were in a gang of more than a thousand people besieging police headquarters.

Young people at the front of the crowd start to vandalize the building. They spray-paint obscene messages on the walls, destroy the logo, rename it "police dog headquarters", and hang a banner on it. At one stage, students try to grab a person in ordinary clothes heading to the building and he runs for safety.

I hear later that some people were taken ill inside the building, but ambulances were unable to get to them.

It's a horrible scene, balanced on the knife-edge of turning violent.

The police are standing on the steps and terrace of the station, almost Buddha-like in their calm. It's interesting: They are just standing there and taking the abuse. They are not dressed in riot gear, but in ordinary, light blue short-sleeved shirts.

(No one is photographing them. They show the police as what they are—human beings. Much of the media has decided to strictly limit itself to use of pictures of riot officers in full, dehumanizing riot gear, faceless stormtroopers from a Star Wars movie.)

Other officers, whom we passed on the road between City Hall and the police headquarters, were extremely polite and low profile, allowing radicals to create mild mayhem, and intervening only when serious problems loomed for the public. I'm impressed with their level of patience.

I think they must have been stunned by the irrational hostility of the media write-ups and in the past couple of weeks and have consciously decided to avoid doing anything that could be twisted to make it look like they were initiating the trouble.

So as I say, they are standing there and taking the abuse. Maybe they decided to use the ancient Chinese principle of *wu wei*, to respond by not responding, to act by not acting, to achieve without striving.

Or perhaps they just didn't know what to do.

Whatever their motivation, they showed an impressive adversity quotient. They reminded me of the guards outside Buckingham Palace.

As I stand there, I reflect on the fact that it's been an awful day for the police. This morning they revealed to the press that they had uncovered a protester-run website that had no other purpose than to list the full names of Hong Kong police officers and their home addresses so that their families and children can be "targeted", whatever that means.

What kind of people would do such a thing? A new and horrific slogan is being distributed on the opposition websites: "Wives and children of police should die too."

Whoever is working to drum up hate against the police are being extraordinarily successful.

In the end, the events of this evening all become oddly anti-climatic, thank goodness. The ultra-violent radicals of last Sunday night are apparently not present or have received instructions to tone it down.

In the early hours of the morning, people start to peel away and go home. I walk away along Jaffe Road towards the bar district. What I see amazes me.

Just one block away from this scene of screaming anger and sustained vandalism, happy drinkers are spilling out of every doorway. The party is just carrying on, oblivious to the almost-riot next door.

Happy crowds of revelers, mostly Western or Filipino, have spilled into the streets outside Typhoon and Delaney's and Neptune, drinking beer and watching sports on TV.

It's like two different planets.

Seven Vignettes From June 26

1) On my phone I find a video forwarded by my journalist colleague Ivan Tong, editor of The Standard.

It showed former Justice secretary Elsie Leung Oi-sie being screamed at by angry masked protestors as she walked through Pacific Place.

As a columnist I was 100 percent critical of her, year after year, but I felt awful watching this tiny little white-haired lady being abused by scary men who seemed close to violence.

My heart went out to her.

"These folks acted like red guards in the Cultural Revolution," Ivan said. True.

2) During recent demonstrations in the Tamar area there were countless angry speeches about how the evil mainland Chinese were oppressing and killing innocent Hong Kong people.

"Nobody seemed to notice that the People's Liberation Army base in Hong Kong is also in the middle of Tamar–and in fact was the one spot which was a calm oasis of peace the whole time!" wrote one amused reader named K. Au Yeung, who is not a pro-Beijing person.

I bet the soldiers were watching over their wall: laughing, baffled, horrified?

3) The creative coverage prize for journalism yesterday had to go to the China Daily newspaper, which published a picture of a small cluster of people and

a headline about protests in Hong Kong: "HK Parents March Against US Meddling," it says. Of course, there have been many much larger marches in Hong Kong, but they are not mentioned!

The irony, of course, is that you need both sides to get the full story of what's going on in Hong Kong. Yes, it would be nice if the China Daily made more mention of the big marches, and not just one small one.

And yes, it would be nice if the rest of the media covered the facts that many Hong Kong parents (and surely the majority of adults in this city) ARE upset about what's happening, and DO resent the US meddling that is certainly taking place.

While the picture showed only a few people daring to criticize the protesters, there was a very large contingent of unheard Hong Kong residents seriously worried about what was happening.

4) The absurd campaign to blame the police for everything is going into overdrive.

A nasty international hackers group called Anonymous announced that it is going to join the doxxing exercise and expose the personal details of Hong Kong police officers on the Internet to cause trouble.

"Your use of firearms and biological weapons has clearly violated the Hague Convention and the Geneva Convention," said an Anonymous spokesman. "You have nowhere to hide because we are everywhere."

This is baffling. Hong Kong police have used no firearms or biological weapons. Up till now, no side has.

The problem is Twitter, filled with still pictures or heavily edited 10-second videos that makes it look as if our police officers spend all their time beating innocent people.

5) The G7's international financial watchdog this week praised Hong Kong as the only place in Asia Pacific to get a top grade in battling cross-border money crimes.

What they did NOT do is remind people that the G7 Financial Action Task Force has been hassling Hong Kong for years to hurry up and get an extradition law that included China. Hong Kong's civil service followed their advice... and the rest is history.

Thanks, guys.

6) News about the existence of the shadowy English-speaking forces behind the protests continue to grow.

A foreign correspondent was skeptical yesterday about the suggestion that Wednesday night's "Free Hong Kong" protest campaign was aimed at the Western media.

Until a local reporter showed him a picture of the protest outside City Hall.

"Jesus," he said. "Every single banner is in English." (As mentioned earlier, Hong Kong's population is 92 percent ethnic Chinese and the main language of this city is Cantonese.)

7) Readers from the West were much amused by my report that Hong Kong activists had delivered a letter to the US Consulate in this city asking Donald Trump to "liberate Hong Kong" from China.

Andrew Schmidt replied to it via my newspaper column: "Dear Hong Kong, or China, or Russia, or Lichtenstein, or ANYONE, please liberate us Americans from Donald Trump."

* * *

Hong Kong adults continue to have much richer, more diverse views than the shallow anti-China stances of LIHKG, or the equivalent forums of Western expats.

While many in the mainstream media continue to spread the lie that the police are starting the violence, local people in my network point out that the police actually do have lethal weapons and could quite easily suppress any rioting before it begins, with a show of force—but are choosing not to do so.

"The Police, with their training and lethal weapons, could have initiated the attack," says Onon Chan.

"They could have ended their responsive assault with a much higher level of force (as seen in numerous confrontations in other parts of the world). Instead, they stood fast and exercised a reasonable level of force only when they were attacked and their defense line breached. They stopped immediately upon achieving their purpose of holding the line and arresting those breaking the laws.

"They were better armed, but not invincible and bullet proof. Should they have stood still? Would the mob listen to their warning? Do not keep wandering in a perpetual pantomime!

"The government could have adopted a better PR strategy. We all hope that Hong Kong can be spared as a haven for spies and a base station to overturn the mainland government's rule of China by foreign operatives.

:These, however, are not the concern of the Police. All they do is to uphold the law and order."

* * *

I'm now getting hundreds of messages, sometimes 1,000 comments, emails and texts in a single day. They come from a wide range of Hong Kong people, and many give me very insightful comments about what's going on.

I scan the latest ones.

John Chan writes: "Pandems are focused on criticizing the police for using force but deliberately miss out the fact that it was this gang of rioters who started the violence in the afternoon on 12/6. Police merely responded."

Like many correspondents, he is dismayed that the politicians and journalists are not separating the peaceful protesters from the violent rioters, but instead are grouping them together as being completely innocent, while trying to portray the police as the root of the violence.

"It's sad that the pandems choose to tie themselves and the other 99.9 percent who are peaceful protesters with this gang of rioters," he says.

Some Westerners are grateful to read my accounts, which are more detailed and carry a wider range of local voices than other media. "Thanks, Nury, appreciate this perspective," writes Todd Finnegan.

"Don't always agree with things you say, Nury, much more often than not, in fact," writes Ken Davey. "But thank you for this neutral account when it is far easier for commentators to jump on the bandwagon."

The vast majority of notes, messages, letters and emails from local Hong Kong people in particular emphasize the crucial need for balanced reports—something in which the international media has shockingly little interest.

"I support you to continue the neutral report," says Monnie Yu.

"Really appreciate your well-express viewpoints," writes Audrey Winsome. Her friend Peggy Wong adds: "He reported very honestly."

"It's such a shame a few people are spoiling the peaceful protest," writes Gabrielle Lyne.

It's gratifying to see my reports are being shared on many thousands of social media pages and accounts, but too much of what is going on still puzzles me, and readers too.

"I agree that there isn't enough to explain the pro-extradition side," writes Yvonne Tung. "Why has it been so hard to publish a fair and clear analysis on this?"

* * *

The many parents among the people who write to me are concerned that so many young people are involved.

"I have seen many secondary students putting their lives in danger," writes Michael Moon. "Try to understand why your kids want to go to the protest and protect them. There are no more peaceful demonstrations in HK."

Raymond Ho is anxious that the real story of what is happening here is told: "We need people telling more facts to youngsters instead of one side story raised by the politicians of willful blindness."

One letter comes from a former policewoman. "I am an ex-police," writes Margaret Chow. "So I know how difficult their job is, because part of their salary has always been compensation for taking the shit from unreasonable citizens."

But she is against the extradition bill and feels that many of the people in favor of it are rich people who can "flee the country when the extradition law passes".

Yet the protests are violent, she agrees. "That said, rallies can easily turn into riots when there are thugs amongst the people who are rallying peacefully, so on that point I do agree with you; because ultimately the general public just want to have a good and fair and uncorrupt government and live a peaceful life."

"Thank you for telling the truth," writes Matthew Y. Lam. "Unfortunately, most protestors are not willing to listen to different opinions at all. They don't accept any rational discussions or peaceful talks.

"I really hope the young protestors try to understand the whole story and think in different angles, not only follow the views of the media or politicians. God bless Hong Kong."

A particularly harsh message comes from Ilaria Maria Zucchina, a foreign correspondent who has been writing strongly one-sided articles, and is a columnist for the Hong Kong Free Press, alongside a local man, also very anti-police, named Kong Tsung-gan.

"Nury, this is beneath you," she writes. "This is an embarrassment of lies and opinions presented as facts. It serves no purpose to write something so dishonest. The protesters violence did not occur in a vacuum. The police has been overreacting for a long time: now they are armed to the teeth. The evidence is there and condemned by many who obviously have no ulterior motives. We cannot heal the rift in our society through lies."

But her view is in sharp contrast to the views of local Hong Kong people, who are grateful for my attempts at telling a more rounded story, and particularly value my habit of including details and numbers, and putting events into a wider context.

"Thank you," writes Ricky Wong Wai-hung. "We need facts, not lies. We support peaceful protest, but not violent deeds."

"Thanks for telling us the truth based on facts," says Michael Kung.

Many complain that there is no journal printing a balanced view. "Thank you for being impartial and truthful," writes Hoi Yat-tsoi. "Hong Kong's local media either go too far to the right or too far to the left. Most people don't understand that the truth is somewhere near the middle."

One correspondent, Bosco Tung, says he is watching from Canada. "While I'm not physically in Hong Kong, and I DO understand the fears of people and that they're not really marching against specifics (cuz no protest ever is, since mobilization will always be a tricky thing), these posts have been helpful in reflecting on more sides and wondering about things. Moderation is tricky, because we hear what we hear, and when we realize someone isn't fully 'on our side' we by default think they're against us."

A growing number of local people warn me that there are negative forces behind the protests. Michael Tam laments the difficulty of finding trustworthy facts "in this world drowned in fake news". He writes: "Obviously there are very powerful, dark and anti-China forces at work."

Many correspondents express sadness about the video in which Elsie Leung, the former justice minister, is abused and threatened by a large gang as she walks through a shopping mall.

"I really wanted to cry when I watched," said Winnie Lo. "I met this lady before a few times, she shouldn't deserve this. Or should say, nobody should deserve this, even if you disagree with them."

I replied: "Yes, that's how I felt. I have written many negative words about Elsie Leung Oi-sie but even so, I felt so sad watching this video. Nobody deserves that."

Mark Steven Yong added: "Unfortunately, those who support the young folk refuse to see that there are many scumbags among them."

CHAPTER 14

Breaking Into The Legislative Council Chamber

In Which More Love Is Declared For Trump—
Chemical Warfare—Radicals Break Into Hong Kong's Parliament—
An Old Observer's Wise Words

THIS IS WHAT happens in Hong Kong on July 1 every year. It's a public holiday, so the vast majority of Hong Kong people have a pleasant day off. Many take the time to relax or go for a walk in the forests and mountains.

But a minority join me on the annual march. Sometimes there are tens of thousands of us, and other times there are several hundred thousand of us.

The academics and police monitors use scientific methods to calculate how many people march, and come up with a number—on peaceful years, there may be just 60,000 of us, and on politically lively years, between three and six times that figure.

The organizers will often make an outlandish claim of a million or more, and the branches of the media which are more interested in their agenda than the facts will highlight that number.

It's almost always swelteringly hot. We're sweating, yet the atmosphere is upbeat. One year I remember police officers arriving with boxes of bottles of water, paid for by the government.

They handed them out to us with a smile as we reached Admiralty.

The march starts after lunch. We usually get to the beginning point at about 2 pm, and we're pretty much finished by 5 pm. The old route, which went to Central, is slightly longer than the revised route, but the distance is tiny, about three kilometers.

And this year?

Exactly the same thing happened.

Or so it seemed from the point of view of people like my neighbors, who obediently turned up after lunch, made the trek peacefully to Admiralty, and then returned home for a nice dinner after a pleasant walk.

They reported what they perceived as happening, and (except for the claim that there was a million people there) spoke the truth.

But those of us watching the story behind the story ended up with a very different memory of that day.

* * *

The violent radicals decided to steal a march on things scheduled to happen on Monday, July 1 by making their attack in the dark, in the early hours of the morning—long before the official march, for which people start to gather from about midday.

Nine hours earlier, at 3 am, a night shift of radical protesters was already on the move, gathering in quiet corners in Central, Admiralty and Wan Chai, and by 4 am, before the dawn, they made their move.

They raced onto the main roads around the Legislative Council Complex and blocked them with anything they could steal from nearby building sites or by taking the police force's own metal road blocks, the mills barriers.

The protesters piled up police cones, barriers and other objects on Lung Wo Road, Tim Mei Avenue and Harcourt Road, the streets around the government headquarters—the aim being to paralyze the area.

Iron poles, bricks and guard rails were gathered in heaps to use as weapons.

Other protesters formed a human chain to pluck bricks from building sites and transfer them, hand to hand, to places where they would be more useful.

The night shift of police, of course, were at hand, but were holding back.

It was so ironic. If you read the press, the major problem in Hong Kong is a brutal police force terrorizing the public. But if you are actually there on the spot, the problem appears to be the exact opposite—protesters are causing huge amounts of disruption and the main complaint you want to direct at the police is that they are far too restrained. You want to scream at them: Look what they're doing! They are clearly preparing for violence. Why don't you stop them? Do something!

And this is not a pro-government complaint. Opposition people are as upset at the massive amounts of thieving from building sites as Apols or China-friendly people.

But a glance at Twitter perhaps shows the logic of the police's "maximum restraint" policy. All police physical responses are presented, in text and pictures, as police attacking peaceful demonstrators. So they have evidently chosen to respond as little as possible, and delay responses of any kind for as long as they can.

Instead of making pro-active moves to stop them, some police try to quietly dismantle the barriers, but the biggest group of officers simply gathers in a cordon around the Legislative Council's main buildings. Anyway, there are simply not enough police staff to deal with the number of protesters coming at them from all directions.

After dawn has risen, a large group of protesters suddenly rushes the cordon, unleashing a huge shower of objects. This is at about 7.30 am. The attacks continue on and off, and at about 9.30 am, one group of protesters approaches and showers an unknown liquid over a group of officers.

The splashed officers retreat, trying to wipe the stuff off themselves. They experience difficulty in breathing and quickly find their arms and faces becoming swollen and itchy.

Officers pull back. Thirteen are sent to hospital for treatment. The case is referred to the Organised Crime and Triad Bureau. This is clearly some sort of chemical attack. The tension that moment creates lasts through the morning, with the police taking a more defensive attitude.

At about 1 pm, radical protesters again storm the Legislative Council Complex. Among senior police officers at this time, there is genuine worry about the level of violence, especially with the addition of a chemical weapon, and the police release a statement to news outlets: "Police absolutely respect people's freedom of assembly, procession and expression of opinion in a peaceful and orderly manner," it says.

"However, Police's risk assessment indicates that there is a serious safety threat in Admiralty and Wan Chai and thus advise members of the public to carefully consider whether to join the public procession on Hong Kong Island this afternoon.

"Police remind those who opt to take part, especially who will bring along young and elderly family members, to take extreme care."

On the Internet, this urgent safety warning is interpreted as an outrageous attempt by Beijing to remove people's rights. Sigh.

Over a short period of time,the message changed dramatically: It became all about Donald Trump, called for the US to decolonize Hong Kong from China, requested an invasion by US troops, and demanded that people "Defend Our Constitution" even though Hong Kong does not have one

* * *

And me? By mid-afternoon, I am on a raised footbridge, watching the main body of the march, and smiling rather mirthlessly.

A source earlier tipped me off that the mysterious "black hands" behind the protests have been preparing something special and eye-catching for the media on this particular occasion. Their local agents will get a lot of attention.

Eventually it hoves into sight, and I see what they mean.

They were right. Sections of the march, no surprise, are showing an extraordinary amount of love for Donald Trump, a point of view supported by expensive, full-color banners.

I still find myself resisting the temptation to print any allegations that there is secret funding from foreign sources, even though all the serious local sources now confirm that this is a significant factor. I am already getting way too much hate mail for departing from the standard media narrative.

But just take a look at what we can all see today.

The American group behind the Defend Our Constitution placards are plainly back in action. Big, illustrated banners printed with illustrations in full color on this Monday afternoon focus on Trump's catchphrases.

"Carrie Lam, you're fired" one says in English, taking a line from a US TV series called The Apprentice.

This series has NOT been dubbed into Cantonese for airing on Hong Kong's TV channels, so why is it here? It is very unlikely to have been generated locally.

"Make Hong Kong Great Again", says another, also in English.

The design and text of the banners, with its American-style wit and correctly spelled English lettering, come across as unmistakably Western.

But I don't say this to the tourist standing next to me, watching from a raised walkway. He is pleasantly surprised to see that so many of the banners are in English.

He asks why they are calling for Donald Trump to "liberate Hong Kong" from China.

"Maybe he's the only leader crazy enough to take it seriously," I suggest.

* * *

Later that afternoon, the Hong Kong government sends out an announcement that the "Children's Corner" and other normal Legislative Council Complex amenities were "suspended". This is not surprising.

Of course they couldn't have known it at the time, but the main activity inside the building on the evening of that day would turn out to be young people scrawling rude words on the walls of the Legislative Council Chamber—so some might say "Children's Corner" would soon actually be back on.

But I'm getting ahead of myself.

During the afternoon, I stayed with the main body of the march, away from the front end. Thank God for technology—I can be at the scene while monitoring the media and government announcements.

I look down at my phone again to find that the Hong Kong Fire Services Department has just sent out a press announcement. It is entitled "FSD Ready For The Storm".

Doesn't sound like the usual sort of press release. I click the link and the accompanying text turns out to be about long-term typhoon preparations; relatively dull stuff.

But as the hours pass, the title turns out to be prophetic—things turn nasty in the mid-afternoon, with protesters releasing a cloud of toxic powder as a weapon over police in front of the Legislative Council Complex. The

Fire Services Department receives an urgent call at 3.37 pm and is assigned the job of dealing with the problem.

Actually, that was a genuinely terrifying moment. The Fire Services Department sent five engines and three ambulances to the scene. Two policemen were sent to Queen Mary Hospital for treatment.

A team of fire officers in hazardous materials outfits examined the white power and concluded that it was p-phenylenediamine, which is a poisonous substance listed in Hong Kong as "dangerous goods category 4". While not deadly, it causes itchy eyes, skin redness and swelling, plus shortness of breath. If sufficient amounts are inhaled, it can cause serious respiratory tract burns.

The two chemical attacks on a single day are leaving officers worried. The danger level has risen considerably.

By this time, huge crowds are gathered outside the Legislative Council Building, and one can easily see that the ones in front are bent on attacking both people and property.

Inside, worried staff get a message on their screens.

The notice is a Red Alert.

What that means can be summed up in three words: Get out now.

* * *

Darkness has fallen. A relatively small company of police, trying to protect the Legislative Council Complex, is facing a huge angry crowd.

There's no way that they can win any sort of fight.

The police make a plan. They give themselves a clear goal: First, attempt to keep the peace as well as is humanly possible, but further than that, prioritize human safety over property damage. The days' chemical attacks have shaken them up.

The initial key task is to get all office staff working in the tower to safety. After that, the goal will be to keep both demonstrators and officers safe.

For the thousands of angry, shouting protesters outside, the main goal was more amorphous: Several of them have drawn up lists of demands, some clashing. There were Nine Demands and Eleven Demands and so on.

But there were no leaders in the building to deliver them to—so the structure itself, solid and unyielding, became a symbol of what they saw as the Hong Kong establishment's perfidy in daring to have truck with Beijing officials.

We've now gotten used to the normal evening scene. The main body of peaceful demonstrators has gone home. Some tens of thousands of young ones have stayed as a back up to support the much smaller number (a few hundred or perhaps a thousand) very violent ones in front. But emotions run through large groups like storm winds, and the anger of the radicals at the front is clearly infecting the larger crowd behind.

By 9.00 pm, police officers at the doors are told that the last staff member has been quietly spirited out of the premises.

But they remain worried. Their defense plan had been based on having layers of officers in the grounds outside the building. If protesters get inside, they'd need a whole different set of strategies.

Inside the building, senior officers discuss strategy rapidly. A fight with a huge angry mob using chemical weapons in corridors has to be avoided, for everyone's sake.

Then the lights go out.

Protesters seem to have reached the fuse boxes. Some parts of the building are completely dark.

While officers are thinking it can't get any worse, it does. Some can smell toxic smoke—the stench of sulphur and bad eggs.

This could be a repeat of the gas cloud problem that had hospitalized their colleagues earlier.

There's a huge crashing noise, following seconds after by another. Young men in black are crashing trollies into the glass doors, trying to smash through them.

Some pandem politicians, horrified by the violence they have unleashed, rush to the front to try to stop the violence on the building, but they are rudely thrown aside. One is physically grabbed and hauled away as if he was a child.

There can be no clearer demonstration of the fact that the violent radicals have literally and metaphorically taken control of the protests from the peaceful demonstrators.

Inside, senior officers decide that pitched battles inside a darkened building at midnight with the threat of poison gas would almost inevitably lead to serious injuries or worse.

HQ informs them that a back-up crew is being put together as fast as possible and will be sent to the building shortly. That gives them their plan.

Chemical warfare in a tightly enclosed, darkened space is not an option. They step back. There are no staff in the building, so no one to get hurt—only property.

Seconds later, protesters pour in through the smashed entrance and (not without difficulty) penetrate the steel shutters leading to the Legislative Council chamber.

They spray "FUCK" and "The Government Made Us Revolt" on the walls, vandalize the portraits, and raise a British colonial flag.

The violent radicals are followed by a group of more peaceful protesters, including a cluster of several Christian students. A handful of these genuinely try to limit the vandalization and bad behavior, paying for drinks they take from the canteen, but theirs is a token effort. There's massive needless vandalization.

But there is no fighting within the dark corridors—because there is no one to fight. The result is that no one is hurt. Whoever has the chemical weapons which have been used twice today already has no reason to use them a third time.

Some students (and many observers on the Internet) are expressing the view that this is clearly some sort of trap, a way to corner the intruders and arrest them—and some of the young people inside are so convinced of this that they pledge to stay in place in the chamber and let themselves be arrested.

"We stay together, or we leave together," one of the students shouts.

Thousands are watching on the Internet, and many of them are telling the vandals to stop and get out—it is definitely a trap, and will shortly be sprung. Messages are flying, unintentionally echoing the red alert warning that workers inside the building received earlier: GET OUT NOW.

But this was no trap.

The police priority was to avoid chemical-laced warfare in the corridors, and keep everyone safe until back up arrived.

After spraying graffiti onto the walls, the crowd inside starts to thin, and police officers re-emerge with a low-key dispersion plan to try to clear the building by simply ushering the intruders out of the building. Some officers hand out bottles of water.

The vandals are suspicious and surprised that police appear to be allowing them to walk free—including the ones who had most clearly committed acts of vandalism, and had allowed themselves to be filmed doing so.

It must be a trap. Maybe they'll be snatched when they get out into the forecourt?

But that doesn't happen.

As the majority leave the building, the other company of police officers arrives and the bulk of the crowd is dispersed with comparatively little tension and no injuries.

From the point of view of the violent radicals, the recent hours have been a triumph. They had taken their message and their flag to the heart of the Legislative Council Chamber. They've defaced Hong Kong and China emblems.

They'd taken reporters into the building with them to film their conquest for the world, and the international media was already broadcasting it.

From the police point of view, it has also been a success: A day which had been going badly, with two attacks of chemical warfare and many officers rushed to hospital, had ended with no further injuries on either side.

And what about arrests for vandalism and destruction of public property, which would surely amount to millions of dollars? The protesters had encouraged people to film them—if the public prosecution services decide to press ahead with charges in due time, the evidence is all there, conveniently provided by the perpetrators themselves.

The ending of that day, with few people hurt, was something to be happy about. Still, all in all, it was not a good day for Hong Kong. When the biggest political message of the evening is a young vandal writing FUCK on the wall of the parliamentary chamber, something has gone badly wrong,

Late that night, I reflect that the really curious thing is that people at both extremes—the violent radicals and the China-friendly people—are intensely irritated with pandem legislators. Tonight, they've been punished with bruises, and not just to their egos.

* * *

The next morning, TV reporters stop an older white male outside the damaged Legislative Council Complex, probably expecting him to be a tourist.

But I recognize him immediately: It's Peter Bentley, a much-respected Hong Kong businessman who has been operating in this city and the mainland for almost 40 years.

A clever, witty individual, he has been a contributor to my columns for decades. But there is no amusement in his voice today. His response to questions was so passionate that the clip immediately goes viral, soon to be seen by millions of people.

He tells the interviewer that when he saw how the Legislative Council building had been treated "I just cried. I love Hong Kong and I love China. But I know these things have set back the progress of peaceful evolution of democracy in Hong Kong by at least two or three generations."

He's right. The international press is portraying the radicals as "the people of Hong Kong" fighting for "the democracy they were promised" but Hong Kong people of all backgrounds know that the situation is far more complex than this. Violent anti-Chinese-immigrant radicals and independence campaigners, some financed by overseas sources, are going against the wishes of the people of Hong Kong, yet have found themselves being portrayed as heroes by the world's biggest media.

This is a dangerous mistake and the people best-positioned to correct it are the pandem politicians—but their silence is deafening. They are smart enough to know that the error will ultimately be in their favor.

There is a huge amount of manipulation going on, but little interest in exposing it. It's an argument I put in print and on social media to the dismay of Western critics of China, but to a stream of thank you messages from local Hong Kong people.

The network is soon buzzing.

"Thx Nury for your unbiased message again," says Billy Leung. "I think that's very important to really help HK, a city I live in and love. We HKers should calm down instead of keeping on provoking any side to harm HK again."

Ben Lim is melancholic: "The irony, of course, is that in their attempts at a 'better future for Hong Kong', they have single handedly ruined it. For one of the reasons why businesses put their money in HK is political stability. Increasingly, the money is now flowing into their biggest business competitor Singapore."

Many are surprised at how one-sided the media is. "You are the only media on Facebook that tells the truth of both sides in Hong Kong," writes Colwin Tham. "All of the hong kong online media use their emotion to think and state something that benefit their side only. None of them are neutral enough to broadcast the whole story."

Basil Hwang, a well-respected senior Hong Kong lawyer, writes: "It's courageous being a voice of reason when folks are hell-bent on promoting a particular fairytale narrative. You tend to get shouted down. Keep up the good work. And on the comment by your friend regarding similarities with the Cultural Revolution, while I was not there, I have aunts and uncles who were both red guards and their victims, and what I saw (I live and work in Admiralty) brought to life for me their dinnertime stories about it."

Teacher Jim Lewis writes: "I appreciate the effort you make in pointing out both sides of the arguments, Nury. It is unfair to be labelled as a stooge when clearly you are still presumably more in sympathy with the protests than the government, but any attempt to sit on the fence in such a situation is liable to wind people up. (I have the same problem when I try to debate Brexit with my Brit friends)."

He goes on to say, “In reference to the aggression shown by a minority of protesters, has there been evidence of agent provocateurs involved - i.e. undercover elements from the CCP masquerading as students? There was certainly rumour of this on the first day of the mass protests-i.e., unidentified types lifting up paving slabs, charging into police, and then mysteriously melting away.”

Indeed, there is a sharp difference between the peaceful protesters and the violent troublemakers—but it’s becoming clear that they are not mainland agents, but the opposite: People from the anti-mainlander groups in Hong Kong and the West. It appears that somebody has ordered the Chinese communists to keep their distance.

As the arguments fly, dozens of angry Westerners defriend me on social media for daring to depart from the ordained narrative, but local Hong Kong people have been joining my friends and followers lists in their thousands.

“Came across your posts when this all started, out of a mere frustration with both the local and international media (news agencies and social media alike)”, writes Jasmine Chan. “Thank you for speaking out the truth and giving us all a proper and balanced view to the issue.”

“It’s super-hard to find unbiased journalists out there,” says Sinead Lee.

But the most generous note today is one I read from Lillian Tsoi: “Thank you for being a journalist with a soul.”

Clearly I deserve none of this praise. I spend most of my time either writing what I see, or simply talking to Hong Kong people and passing on their wisdom to the world. If there was any justice, my job title would simply say: “Typist”.

CHAPTER 15

The Secret War

In Which A Meeting Is Eye-Opening—Why The Death Of 1C2S Is Being Pushed

OKAY, NOW HERE'S the thing. It's mid-July now, and several things are becoming clear.

First, we know for sure that people outside Hong Kong are actively involved in promoting the protests, with cash and practical help.

The "Defend our constitution" placards have been distributed and displayed again. No one has bothered to correct the people printing them. Or perhaps nobody among them cares about the facts.

Furthermore, media are now receiving images of demonstrators posed with images of Donald Trump that pretend to be pictures from the protests but are clearly the result of "photo ops", with everything neatly arranged and in focus. The message of the manufactured images is to emphasize the link between Hong Kong and its putative savior, the US President. The manipulators are overplaying the "love Donald" line like mad—only an astonishingly lazy or wilfully blind journalist could fail to realize what this means.

The cash from the West is not just paying for visual aids, but warm bodies too, with paid attendence now an option. These rumors have been circulating for a couple of weeks, but on this topic I am listening *only* to direct reports from people I know personally.

Adults, youths, school children, and even domestic helpers have told me that they have been offered cash in significant amounts—sometimes thousands of Hong Kong dollars—to join the protests.

Teachers tell me children from their schools, kids who were clearly under 18, were offered HK$300 each (that's about US$40) to bulk up the numbers at protests. They just needed to turn up in black and do some shouting, throw a few bricks and that sort of thing.

They were told they would be informed of a spot nearby at which the paymaster will stand. Payments would be in cash. Marshals would be present to keep them safe.

Adults get more. Domestic helpers are being offered up to HK$3,000 to get to the front of protests and take active roles in the violence.

In the poorer parts of town, a community leader for South Asians tells me he has been called by members who have been offered significant sums of money, several thousand Hong Kong dollars, to participate in violence.

To be sure, there are certainly a very great many honest people at the protests, motivated by nothing more than a genuine and worthy desire to fight for the retention of Hong Kong's identity.

But there are also many figures in the background with a clear aim of de-stabilizing the city—and they have the money and connections to make it happen.

Reading the editorials of newspapers in Hong Kong and around the world, we see constant repeated allegations that China has killed "one country, two systems", or 1C2S, the concept that keeps Hong Kong a capitalist place with a free press.

This is a puzzle.

1C2S has been far, far more successful than anyone expected. Its success is visible every day, every hour, every minute. You get up and hear anti-government news on RTHK radio. You read news critical of the government in the newspaper as you go to work. On one side of your bus are courts which are operating on a British common-law style system. On the other side of your bus are offices in which businesses are operating in the same Western capitalistic system they have always used. Your savings are rising in the stock market because it is being run in classic London-New York fashion.

At the office water cooler, conversations can be about anything you like, and jokes poking fun at Western and Eastern leaders are all over the Internet, many by this author. You log on to Hong Kong-based 9Gag or Reddit's Hong Kong section and find them filled with often rather crude anti-China jokes, and endless images of Xi Jinping dressed up as Winnie the Pooh.

No honest person can say that 1C2S is dead. On the contrary: Our economic and legal systems remain British, and our level of free press is pretty much unbeatable.

So why is there such a concerted effort to mislead the world? The vast majority of Hong Kong people know it has worked spectacularly well and surely want to keep it.

I go to the place where I know I will most likely find answers—the coffee shop at the Stock Exchange, where I gather some good sources together.

The Chatham House rules are declared (information disclosed during a meeting may be reported but sources may not be explicitly or implicitly identified), and the discussion starts.

Here's a summary of what I was told.

Yes, the Hong Kong people know that 1C2S works and desperately want to keep it. We like our freedoms. However, the community has been caught up in a complex secret war involving many other forces with very different aims—and they desperately want to either destroy 1C2S or convince the world that it is already gone.

1) The pandems are trying to portray 1C2S as a total failure, because its obvious success makes China look good, and they are now motivated mainly by an active dislike of the mainland, supported by large amounts of cash, encouragement and practical advice in the form of grants from the United States. Many activist groups have quite literally been on the US payroll since the 1990s. Some of these sums are on the record and can be checked.

2) A secretive group of American operatives want to kill 1C2S because it shines a positive light on the superpower that will inevitably usurp the United States as the largest global superpower very soon. By creating hate against China, the rest of the world's countries will gravitate towards America. Further, the Americans need to convince Taiwan that 1C2S is a failure, so that the island can continue to be used as a military and intelligence base for the US.

3) The Taiwanese anti-China campaigners and their supporters in Hong Kong want to kill 1C2S because its success has empowered their political rivals, damaging their hopes of re-electing the America-friendly but highly unpopular President Tsai Ing-wen in the upcoming election, set for January.

4) Violent radicals in Hong Kong want to kill 1C2S because they, unlike the majority of Hong Kong people, want to fight for independence/self-

determination/full autonomy from the mainland. The success of 1C2S gives the lie to their attempts to convince the world that the mainland has crushed Hong Kong. They need people to believe 1C2S has been crushed, or they need to goad Beijing into actual destroying it by sending in the People's Liberation Army or replacing Hong Kong's legal system.

(The radicals, it should be noted, pay lip-service to democracy for Hong Kong but are actually against it. Anything like a democratic vote or referendum on the matter would certainly see Hong Kong people vote against separation from mainland China. So the people the Western media most energetically portrays as pro-democracy "poster boys" in truth actively oppose democracy, which is why their slogans emphasize "freeing" Hong Kong rather than introducing suffrage.)

5) Some of the mainland Chinese want to kill 1C2S because if it dies, China can take over Hong Kong and run it.

Groups 1, 2 and 4 (the pandems, the Americans, and the radicals) are working closely together. The pandems have huge numbers of supporters, the Americans have the money and the backstage agents to stir up anger, while the radicals have the youth, energy and willingness to do violent acts of disruption that grab global media attention.

Groups 2 and 3 (the Americans, and the Taiwanese independence campaigners) are working together, too. The Americans need Taiwan to be run by a group hostile to China, but polls earlier this year showed that the Taiwanese people would almost certainly use their democratic vote to choose a pro-engagement party instead. The Americans and the Taiwanese separatists feel that the general public of Taiwan is making a mistake which needs to be "corrected". They know that fomenting maximum unrest in Hong

Kong is their opportunity to reverse the situation in Taiwan.

At the beginning of this year, that seemed like a tall order. The polls showed that the Taiwanese equivalent of the pandems was badly lagging in popularity, and US-supported Taiwan leader Tsai Ing-wen was almost certain to lose the election coming up in January of 2020.

But in March and April, as angry debate was ignited about China's "imposition of an instant mass deportation law" in Hong Kong, the polls started to show a change. In June and July, with the media showing chaos in Hong Kong, the US-favored Tsai Ing-wen had shot up in popularity, and was now leading the polls. Job done. Now all they had to do was maintain the story until January.

Groups 1, 2, 3, and 4 all see that working together and encouraging each other benefits them. To this end, the more chaotic and ungovernable Hong Kong becomes, the better.

Ideally, an invasion by the People's Liberation Army using tanks, preferably with significant numbers of deaths (or claims of deaths) would kill 1C2S completely and give all these groups the long-term triumph they want. If that's not possible, the chaos should continue until China clamps down in other ways, such as suspending 1C2S or taking over the judiciary or replacing Hong Kong law with Chinese law.

Group 5, the "hawkish" elements among the mainland Chinese, is in some ways the most dangerous cluster of all. China is huge, Hong Kong is tiny, and the chaos is giving them a logical reason to invoke already-existing laws which allow them to come in and take over.

And on top of all this we have the global media, who like to simplify the battle into an absurd morality tale: Teen Heroes Battle Evil Empire, with the deeply bigoted anti-mainland-immigrant vandals portrayed as noble heroes and the soft-handed, largely blameless Hong Kong civil service portrayed as vile agents of communism.

All the elements of the perfect storm were in place and working in overdrive.

And who was trying to stop this storm? Ordinary Hong Kong people, many of whom are mothers who feel voiceless, who feel abandoned by the media, and who have no idea what to do. The mainland media was useless and the Western media uninterested.

Yes, it was pretty scary.

But the thing that stuck in my mind from that discussion was something else. The most important fight at the moment was one that was never seen, never discussed, and no one knows was happening, the financiers tell me.

It's a behind-closed-doors fight in which senior people in Hong Kong desperately try to persuade the hawkish elements in mainland China to stay out of the battle, to allow the city to maintain its "high degree of autonomy" and keep the 1C2S policy going. In every other battle like this around the world, troops have been called in. But these Hong Kong individuals are trying to persuade China that the PLA should continue to stand on the sidelines.

No one knows that particular debate is going on, so those Hong Kongers have no one rooting for them—on the contrary, all the political groups, and all the international and local media, are attacking them.

If you think your position is hard, just think about theirs.

Interestingly, I also learn that the Hong Kong Police have a "secret" aim, too: And this is to prevent the mayhem from rising to a level that makes Army intervention necessary. And to do this without killing a single protester. Not going to be easy.

* * *

Several hours have passed. I'm now meeting people at my main office, the coffee shop at Block X of the Polytechnic University, when I get an interesting piece of news about the black hand group behind the protests. It comes from a financial source, a father of one, who has come to see me in my home territory.

The US segment of the secret committee organizing the protest have asked protesters to replace the British Hong Kong flags they are carrying with US flags, he says. They want the stars and stripes flying over the rallies.

I find that hard to believe. I tell him: "But why? That makes no sense at all. It would be like California separatists carrying Chinese flags. It's totally illogical. It's meaningless." I point out that the British Hong Kong flag carries a message of nostalgia for the colonialists. But the Stars and Stripes would carry none at all.

He replies by rubbing his thumb across his middle and index fingers in the classic sign for money. The protesters WILL carry the US flag. There are at least three fat bank accounts supporting them.

I nod politely but I am skeptical. The colonial British flag has been carried by extreme pro-colonialist elements of the pandems for literally 20 years. No way is a bit of cash going to persuade the protesters to make an entirely nonsensical switch to the stars and stripes.

As usual, I was wrong. At the next protests, at least six protesters, right at the front of recent protests, turned up with giant US flags.

One lovely old lady, known to everyone as Granny Wong, was still wedded to her British "Union Jack" flag, but she was now outnumbered by far.

Yet the problem I highlighted earlier—that this did not make sense—did get people talking. Pro-Beijing types, Apoliticals and China critics all complained about it.

"I want to scream at the students to stop involving Westerners, because it's our affair, not theirs," an older protester says to me in a direct message. "But I'm scared I'll sound like a Beijing official."

That's a remarkable thought—and surely a first. Peaceful protesters and Beijing officials are saying THE EXACT SAME THING. Western elements are way too deeply embedded in this battle.

But it takes an awareness of nuance to see these things—and too much of the international media has no time for that.

CHAPTER 16

A Wager Is Laid

In Which The Narrator Debates A Media Man—
Peaceful Protesters Complain—A Wager Is Laid—
The Heavyweight Candidate—A Disinformation Campaign

"DON'T GO," MY WIFE PLEADS.

"Don't worry; it'll be fine," I say and slip out of the apartment as dusk descends.

But actually I'm nervous. This columnist is heading to Central to take part in a live debate with Evan Fowler, co-founder of the Hong Kong Free Press, who is now living in the UK.

That web publication favors the overwhelmingly dominant Western media narrative, a cartoon about selfless hero protesters versus dastardly villainous officials from a Nazi-like vision of China.

In contrast, my attempts to use my columns to return just a bit of nuance to the situation has led to my being labeled "CCP puppet" by that website's followers, from whom I am now getting enormous amounts of hate mail.

Knowing the debate organizer, an admirable young man named Simon Lau, I realize that there's a chance of balance. But I also realized that many audience members will be Westernized Asians or Westerners, and Hong Kong Free Press readers—so I am expecting hostility.

Forty minutes later, I'm at the venue in Central, and Simon, in the role of moderator, declares the debate open.

In his opening speech, Evan Fowler expresses deep pessimism about Hong Kong's future, and highlights the extradition bill as part of the problem.

Nevertheless, he is far more reasonable and balanced than his former colleagues at the Hong Kong Free Press, I am happy to find. Still, he is very negative about the mainland, and says that China disregards laws anyway.

Most worryingly, he tells the audience that innocent Hong Kong citizens are already being snatched off the street and secretly being taken across the border in significant numbers at this moment.

His allegations are seriously scary stuff. He doesn't give any evidence for this dramatic story of high volume body-snatching—but I assume his connections at the Hong Kong Free Press will do so shortly.

Then it's my turn.

I have a much simpler opening message. I tell the audience that the present debate in Hong Kong is not about the ditched extradition bill at all. It's an expression of fears about the inevitable loss of Hong Kong identity as a larger community and a smaller one became more integrated. It's about people's fear or dislike of mainland China. The violence we see can be tracked back to the localists associated with a particular incident in Mong Kok—radicalized youths, favoring physical attacks and arson.

Some members of the young, mixed audience have been nodding grimly at Mr. Fowler's vision of China As Active Kidnapper of Innocent Hong Kongers, but others seem to gel with this author's assertion that the real story is not the one we read in the media, and Hong Kong will survive and thrive.

In the end, the questions asked by the attendees show that many have taken in what I have said. The group of mostly young people turns out to be far more open-minded and sophisticated than I'd expected. By the end of it, I feel quite cheered. There's hope.

* * *

Back at the Block X coffee shop office the next morning, I am amused to see business-friendly newspapers like The Times of London idolizing Hong Kong's Joshua Wong.

Their writers probably don't know that young Mr. Wong's party is dedicated to releasing society "from capitalist hegemony".

Someone should tell them.

Meanwhile, I am fascinated by the widening gap between the artificial narrative that has now gone global and the complexity of the real situation.

"We have misgivings about China, and with good reason," says a message from Mel Ng, a mother of one. "But we're not stupid."

People assume that the folk who are rallying behind me are "pro-Beijing" (or "from the blue camp" in the local shorthand) but the truth is that most of them are apolitical or are fans of peaceful protests, and some are decidedly critical of China (or "from the yellow camp").

But there are two areas of full agreement. First, people on all sides of the debate have been dismayed by the way the local protest movement has adopted the deeply bigoted stance of the Hong Kong localists.

The second is the way the movement is increasingly identifying itself with Western politicians, Western media, English slogans, and even Western flags.

Indeed, I would say that my largest group of contributors, the disillusioned peaceful protesters, hate this even development more than the readers who actually do lean towards a pro-Beijing position.

There's a lot of criticism, but the US flags, the mention of Trump's name, and even pictures of him, are proliferating.

* * *

Mr F.R., a frequent contributor to my column, challenges me to a bet.

"Led by the pandems, the Hong Kong people will rise up and overthrow this communist Hong Kong government within 100 days," he says. "And Beijing will send in the tanks to retake Hong Kong. We are on the verge of revolution."

I scold him for his unoriginal thinking. That scenario has been circulating for weeks. The Twittersphere has announced the arrival of the tanks umpteen times, but all have been false.

"It's rubbish," I say. "The vast majority of the Hong Kong people aren't pandem members, and the vast majority of the pandems are not violent radicals."

I make a counter-prediction that the numbers of protesters will fall steadily as the peaceful ones continue to flee, until the violent radicals are pretty much back to their original low numbers, a few hundred people who dress in black and carry Hong Kong independence banners.

"You're crazy," he says. "There were two million people at the march in June. Are you saying that 99 percent of the marchers will back off?"

"No," I say, doing some quick mathematics in my head. "Not 99 percent. I'm saying that 99.9 percent of your so-called 'two million marchers' will soon stop marching."

"You're an idiot," he says.

"Whatever."

"So how many people is that?"

I grab a paper napkin. I show him how one percent of two million is 20,000. I show him that one tenth of one percent is 2,000.

By December, there will still be violent radicals in Hong Kong, but it will be mostly be the original numbers of a few hundred, certainly less than 2,000. "And 1C2S will still hold fast," I add, although I have my doubts about that.

We shake hands.

The bet is on.

@#$%!

I might lose this.

* * *

A week has passed. It's Monday, July 8, and I am talking to people at the Yacht Club in Causeway Bay. Former senior government staffer Mike Rowse is present.

Mike tells me he was intrigued to hear people talking about the lack of a suitably experienced, heavyweight successor to leader Carrie Lam.

A common response to civil unrest is for the people in charge to shuffle officials. But everyone says the same thing: who would want that job?

Mike has the answer.

"They could have me," he says.

I laugh.

But then I realize that they could, in theory. You see, there's no requirement for the leader of Hong Kong to have been born here, or even to be of Chinese ethnicity. That's how extraordinarily international Hong Kong's laws are.

The law only requires that our leader must have a Hong Kong passport and no other.

Mike is one of relatively few *gwai lo* ("foreign devil") to qualify. He famously gave up his British passport for a Hong Kong one some years ago—I think I may even have broken the news in my newspaper column.

Passing by at that moment is Peter Bentley, who has overheard this conversation.

He points to Mike's generous midriff and says with a laugh: "You'd definitely be a heavyweight candidate."

* * *

These are tough times. Hong Kong is beset by disinformation campaigns run by the various secretive anti-government groups at the moment. Many come from LIHKG or Apple Daily. Here are four out of more than a dozen that are filling social media channels in the past couple of days:

1) "If you have a recently issued Hong Kong ID card, Xi Jinping can track all your movements."

2) "Lampposts in Hong Kong have Chinese facial recognition programs and are watching you, sending your face to Beijing."

3) "Mainland China's social credit system will begin in Hong Kong very soon, within days."

4) "A curfew preventing anyone from leaving their homes at night will be implemented later this week."

None are remotely true—but all are widely circulated.

I tell my protester friends that there's a very good reason why they should stop spreading these things: "You'll give Xi Jinping ideas."

They laugh.

Later that day, I am talking to a police officer when one more conspiracy theory pops up on the Internet: "A large number of Hong Kong police officers are actually PLA soldiers in disguise. They have been secretly replaced."

The officer likes that one.

"We could do with a break," he says.

I seem to have found a job for myself—making both sides smile.

* * *

In the evening, I get a tale from a journalistic colleague. A protester was boasting to a foreign reporter that the students were entirely spontaneous "with no leader and no organization".

Unfortunately for him, that was the exact moment that a photo popped up on social media showing the contents of arrested protesters' backpacks: hundreds of Octopus cards and food vouchers, all carefully organized, worth tens of thousands of dollars.

Not only are the protests organized, but they are very well organized indeed. Who is behind them on the Hong Kong side? Certain names keep popping up as possibly having the connections, money and smarts to be a major player in what is happening in Hong Kong.

These include Apple Daily founder Jimmy Lai, a newspaper proprietor with strong connections to the US government, and Simon Shen, an academic who runs a think tank, and various law professors at universities in the city, who continually take issue with whatever the government says, coming across as unbalanced voices pushing undisguised anti-China arguments.

Later that evening, a source claims that the protesters have a foreign bank account and at least two proper local bank accounts, each of which contains millions of dollars—"And that's millions of US dollars, not Hong Kong dollars."

Agents from the West are openly financing a destabilization program in Hong Kong but most people don't want to know—and so miss the evidence that people are carrying around right in front of the world's TV cameras.

Defend Our Constitution.

CHAPTER 17

Police Brutality Allegations

In Which We Discuss The Truth About Housing In Hong Kong—Where Girls Can Jog At Midnight—Waiting For The PLA—Reflections On The Rule of Law—Police Brutality Allegations Reviewed

NOW EVERY COMMUNITY loves its young people, so the commentators are starting to look for reasons why mayhem is breaking out.

Youthful thugs and criminals exist in every city, there's no doubt about that. But Hong Kong young people are seen as good, decent, hardworking citizens, famous for doing tons of homework. Why are some of them signing up to join the violent radicals?

The most common reason given is the price of property.

I read a few of these op-eds and then sigh and toss them aside.

A lot of rubbish is talked about Hong Kong property by people who have never bought a flat here, so it may be worth taking a few pages to put the record straight.

The general theme of these editorials goes like this: Hong Kong has the world's most expensive real estate, so it stands to reason that no one can afford to buy the stuff except the mega-rich.

This has caused most people, especially young ones, to despair that they can ever own property.

Thus they feel justified in throwing bricks.

This argument is ill-informed and misleading. It implies that the mega-rich own all the property and the rest of us are locked out of the system.

I automatically dislike the mega-rich as much as anyone—it's almost a requirement for anyone who wants to get into the journalistic profession.

But Hong Kong is not really like that at all. Where does the error come from? Probably from the fact that Western journalists living here almost always rent their homes. They naturally resent paying large rents and assume that everyone else in Hong Kong is in the same position.

That's not the case. Here's the real story.

About 50 percent of Hong Kong people live in self-owned property. That means we live in flats that we own, often outright with no mortgage, and their average value has risen to a degree that makes them worth more than equivalent (or larger) homes in virtually ANY OTHER CITY in the world—yes, and I am including London, Tokyo and New York.

So, for half of the population, news that Hong Kong property is the most expensive in the world is not something to despair about. The exact opposite is true. It has made us comparatively wealthy. To be frank, there is something rather nice to know that you could sell your single smallish apartment in Hong Kong and buy a whole house in New York or a whole street in most other places around the world.

A vast number of Hong Kong people have had the same experience over the years. We have bought tiny flats and have surprisingly quickly seen them take our net worth above a million US dollars, above a million euros, even above a million British pounds.

And the other 50 percent of Hong Kong people? Are they struggling to pay rents for expat-standard apartments in Mid-Levels, like foreign correspondents writing those editorials?

Again, no. The majority of non-owners (roughly 30 percent of Hong Kong people) live in public-sponsored housing, which means that they pay only token rents. Now without getting all Daily Mail about "scroungers", we can still say that it's a well known truism among Hong Kong people that the government is rather slack about things such as means-testing. The majority of public housing tenants are good, deserving people, but they regularly report that some of their neighbors wear Prada and own the latest Tesla.

Officials do occasionally swoop on estates to crack down on the people gaming the system, but they can't get anywhere close to wiping out the abuse. Hong Kong has very strong privacy laws.

Between the roughly 50 percent who are capital-rich owners and the roughly 30 percent who are public housing dwellers, there's about 18 percent who are neither. These are sometimes called the "sandwich class". There are a large number of schemes designed especially for them—and most of which aim to get them into the category of the 50 percent who own apartments. The schemes are extremely popular and widely used.

So that's the majority of local people—the 50 percent, the 30 percent and the 18 percent.

But a small number of people fail to join any of these groups and simply try to rent property at market prices—and yes, many of the Western journalists are among them.

The result is that they end up paying eye-wateringly high rents to Hong Kong people who own or sub-let the apartments.

And they are the ones who write editorials about how no one in Hong Kong can afford a flat.

This is not to say that there are not problems in Hong Kong. Of course there's a challenge for any people trying to make their way through life in the world's most expensive city. I have young people in my own family, so I know the truth of that.

All I am saying is that the expat journalists' experience of struggling to pay outrageous amounts of rent for comfortable Mid-Levels apartments, is not, by any means, the full story or even a typical story.

* * *

Hallelujah! By now, the end of July, it's finally becoming obvious to even the slow-witted foreign correspondents that the on-going protest is not about the dead extradition bill.

Some have started writing that it has "morphed into a pro-democracy protest" which is also not really true. The reality is that these are pro-independence, anti-China protests, pushed by destabilization agents from the United States and Europe—as shown by the growing number of participants using Edward Leung's line: "Free Hong Kong: revolution now".

Meanwhile, Twitter is still regularly awash with clips of PLA vehicles "invading" Hong Kong. In every case they turn out to be simply delivery trips to the PLA base here, but people are using them to work each other into a fury.

"You watch," says Mr F. R. "Within days, the PLA will have taken over."

Yeah yeah yeah.

Friday, 13 July

People keep writing to me from overseas to ask if Hong Kong is safe to visit.

Let's talk about that.

My teenage daughter used to go jogging at midnight by herself. She was 16 at the time, a beautiful, petite, delicate child. Did I watch her from a distance, worried about her safety?

No. I went to bed.

I knew she'd return fine and well. That's how safe Hong Kong has been until this year. (And yes, I know I am writing this on Friday the 13th.)

Until now, Hong Kong has been arguably the safest big city in the world. Here are some numbers.

In the first four months of this year, London had 12,500 robberies. Hong Kong had 29.

In London, about 2,500 rapes were reported. In Hong Kong, it was 20.

Hong Kong is not perfect, but it is an astonishingly well-behaved community with an excellent policing system.

Anyone who has lived in any other country knows that it's really worth working hard on all sides to keep the positive citizen-police relationship that we have in our city.

Oh, wait, I forget. We have exceptionally brutal police, right? I keep reading that fact in the (pause to roll eyes) media from the United States.

* * *

The next morning, a reader sends me some notes from an international crime convention. They make interesting reading.

The foundation of the rule of law in international crime co-operation is the return of fugitives, it says.

Since 2006, Hong Kong has asked China for the return of several hundred fugitives, and the mainland has returned 248 to this city. Mainland China wants 300 fugitives returned from Hong Kong, and we have returned... none.

So which side is following the rule of law?

This is a hugely embarrassing thing for a dedicated long-term China critic such as myself to have to write.

* * *

Tee-hee! Okay, now I'm laughing. The US agents involved behind the scenes at the protests are getting an increasing amount of stick from all sides. This week, an even wider range of people are decrying the over-use of "Western friends" and the carrying of United States flags—the complaints are from peaceful protesters, apoliticals, friends of China, and expats from Asian and Western nations.

"Trump's face is everywhere. It's ludicrous and shows that what is being reported is not what is happening," says A. Luen.

"We in Hong Kong have told Xi Jinping to keep his hands away so that we can solve this problem by ourselves," writes Melinda Mo. "He has kept his mitts out, so far. And then we ran to place it in the hands of Donald Trump!"

My upstairs neighbor, a US passport holder and mother of two named Terri Appel, who has been an active peaceful participant in the marches, explains it well.

"It's as if a group of Texas separatists demands self-determination for their state. And then refuses to talk to the US government but starts carrying Chinese flags and sending Texas representatives to Beijing to get verbal support. It makes no sense at all."

* * *

Meanwhile, this reporter, like many others, had been shocked by some of the images of police brutality that came out of protest coverage.

In particular, there was one video that stayed with me. A police officer had his boot on the back of a man's head. The man was clearly injured, his face in a pool of blood, his teeth damaged, and he was begging to be released, to no avail.

A few Hong Kong dads decided to get together to look seriously into these incidents.

Fortunately, our job was made easier by the fact that many people shared "evidence of police brutality" files, so it was easy to find image collections on the Internet.

But we quickly came up with a problem. The vast number of pieces of evidence were "partials"—they covered only a tiny part of an incident.

Not only that, but more than 90 percent of the material consisted of still images. In analysis of hand-to-hand combat incidents, still images are more or less useless. Depending on the moment the picture was taken, they can show brutality on one side or the other or neither or both. Indeed, the very same arm movement photographed from different angles can have the full range of implications.

It took less than an hour to find that the vast majority of examples of "evidence of police brutality" widely shared on Twitter or other websites consisted of still images clearly chosen for the purpose of making officers look excessively heavy-handed. They were almost entirely useless, doing nothing but feed people's confirmation bias.

So we set the stills aside and looked for video clips.

Again, we found a problem. The vast majority of videos were tightly edited scenes showing police officers at the moment just after a young man had been arrested and restrained. They didn't show the previous seconds in which protesters resisted arrest, nor did they show the incident that precipitated the interaction.

All three of the dads in this review exercise had been at the protests and had seen the standard order of events. A group of young men shower the police with spears or bricks, and then run for it. Typically, most will escape but one may be caught. He (it is almost always a male) will usually struggle fiercely, causing several officers to join forces to subdue him. Eventually he stops resisting.

And that's the moment, when several police officers are positioned over a still individual, that gets caught on camera and broadcast to the world.

In a few cases, we found individual incidents which were simultaneously captured as stills, as short edits, and as longer pieces of video. In those cases, the stills and short edits appeared to show the incident as one of police brutality, but the longer videos gave a different story: for example, the capture of an arsonist and his attempts to resist arrest, or a gang surrounding an officer, who then fights back.

This is not to say that there were no incidents of actual police brutality. The protests frequently descended into what looked like war zones—and it would be ridiculous to argue that police had faultlessly followed procedure in every interaction with protesters. When men are screaming at each other, and there is definitely a chance of injury or loss of life, both sides will do what they feel needs to be done to preserve their own safety and subdue the other party.

So, in short, we were quite sure that incidents of police brutality would certainly have happened, and we did find longer videos in which we could see officers behaving very roughly, pushing people, intimidating them, and screaming at them, and even hurting them. Indeed, all three of us had been intimidated by police officers ourselves.

Yet did this mean that Hong Kong police were guilty of generalized or widespread brutality? From the evidence we saw—and we looked at hundreds of still images and videos—we found surprisingly little evidence of this. And comparing them with clips of police forces in other places, our local officers seemed similar to most, and indeed came across as far less violent than many.

What really seemed to be happening was that the ordained narrative from whoever was organizing the protests required Hong Kong police to be painted as excessively brutal thugs from mainland China, so that's how they were painted.

By distribution of huge numbers of carefully chosen still images, they had certainly created a general feeling that the police had somehow changed into a very badly behaved group of thugs. We dubbed this process "transmogrification theory"–the belief that Hong Kong police had instantly and miraculously been transformed overnight from one of the best-loved police forces in the world to the most brutal police force in the world.

We also looked back at statistics. The most recent Police Service Satisfaction Survey at the time was the one taken just last year, in 2018, in which 84 percent of respondents were either "quite satisfied" or "very satisfied" with the overall service performance of the police. Furthermore, 79 percent of respondents were either "quite confident" or "very confident" in the police. These were record high scores. No doubt the figures will plummet in future, given the success of the people pushing transmogrification theory.

Interestingly, several of us noted that the "revolution industry" that existed around groups such Serbia's Canvas group and the Oslo Freedom Foundations (which, despite its name, is headquartered not in Norway but in the United States) had various strategies for destabilizing a country: and a key one was to dehumanize and delegitimize the police force.

Strategy: When bad things happen, remove the protesters entirely from the reports, and make police misbehavior the key element. This was definitely happening in Hong Kong.

We also discussed the related conspiracy theory allegations that Hong Kong police had been replaced by or augmented with police officers from the mysterious land to the north. They were "PLA men" in disguise, according to literally hundreds of allegations on LIHKG, Twitter and other media.

All such claims could be quickly dismissed for one simple reason. The "informed" people spreading the stories didn't once even get the initials correct! The Chinese police are the PAP (People's Armed Police), or the Chenguan, who are civil administrators with some police-like authority.

PLA stands for People's Liberation Army, and refers to the Chinese military. Get it right!

* * *

My inbox was now getting far more messages than I could hope to read. But I scanned as many notes as I could and tried to reflect what people were saying. My part in what was happening in Hong Kong was tiny, but I felt privileged to do it.

I was getting letters from blue camp people, and yellow camp people, but mostly from people who did not fit into either stereotype, the apolitical individuals who formed Hong Kong's majority.

What could be done to return this city to peace?

As for the yellows and blues, ultimately, the big step would be for people in general to recognize the reconciliation principle: When two sincere groups of people disagree about something, both are right.

Hong Kong peaceful protesters wanted to express their nervousness about China and had the right to do so.

People who were not nervous about China were right when they said that the protests themselves, and the way they were covered, showed the situation was being manipulated in an attempt to force Beijing's hand to clamp down on Hong Kong.

Unlike most foreign correspondents, the residents of Hong Kong were realizing that things weren't what they seemed to be. I was already seeing dramatic drops in the number of people at the protests. If all went well, the demonstrations would become steadily smaller and calmer—violence would disappear, peace would come, and I would win my bet early.

But as usual, I got it wrong.

I had figured without another complicating factor entering into the equation: Hong Kong's infamous triads.

Gangsters had pricked up their ears and noticed what was going down.

This was going to get rough. Seriously.

CHAPTER 18

What Really Happened On July 21?

In Which We Review The Start Of A Violent Day—March Ends but Radicals Take Over Central—Altercation Five Days Earlier

THERE ARE TWO STORIES told about a gangster-related event which took place during one humid week in July in Hong Kong.

One is the popular media version, which you will find in the press, on websites, on posters and so on.

Let's start with that, since it is short and easy to take in.

A mob of white-shirted gangsters attacked innocent passengers at Yuen Long MTR station on the evening of Sunday, July 21. As the fighting began, police deliberately ran away from the scene to allow the violence to take place. They ignored 999 calls and returned only when it was over. The incident proved that the Hong Kong police force is in cahoots with the triads, or, more likely, is an active unit of the triads. Afterwards, police refused to arrest any of the gangsters, confirming this beyond doubt.

That's it—the whole story.

It is endlessly repeated in the media, any chance they get. And it's also the basis of the Wikipedia version of the account of what happened on July 21 in Hong Kong. Notice something? It doesn't involve the protesters at all. They are totally missing as characters in the story. Curious, that, right?

And the second version of the story?

Well, that one cannot be reduced to a single paragraph—and it concerns events that happened over a week, from Sunday, July 21 to Saturday, July 27.

Here's that second version. It's longer and much more detailed.

And guess what, protesters actually *were* much involved in the events of that period. Read the full story, then make up your mind.

* * *

The morning of July 21 was blisteringly hot and humid.

Hundreds of police officers worked during the day to make arrangements for public safety during two events.

There was to be a relatively brief rally due to start at 3 pm in the football pitches of Victoria Park, followed by a march to Wan Chai.

Even though this would be a short march, there were more than 100 road closures, traffic diversions, bus-reroutings and public safety barriers to set up.

But police were finished in good time, thankfully, as people were streaming into the park soon after lunch.

After various rousing speeches, by 4:00 pm, the rally part was coming to an end and the procession was underway. People were pouring out of Victoria Park and into the shopping streets.

The first thing that stuck out to observers was the small size of the crowd: numbers had dropped dramatically.

Those who stopped for a while and counted the people moving from the park into the streets where the march would take place noticed this. A count using standard scientific crowd-flow methods showed about 60,000 people moving through Causeway Bay at that time, plus about the same number in the park waiting to join. Assuming that a few thousand would join *en route*, observers realized that the total would likely be in the region of 125,000, or perhaps 140,000 at the most.

(But of course, the organizers would likely follow their normal procedure and claim a much larger number, which the media would obediently present as the truth. Three hundred thousand? Four hundred thousand?)

It was all pretty calm at this stage, but that wasn't unusual.

The marches themselves are rarely a problem. The difficulties start when groups of the more radicalized individuals either stop moving and cluster at a specific area targeted for vandalism, or bypass the procession's end point and surge onto other roads and start blocking them. On this occasion, the march route ran from Victoria Park to Wan Chai, not even two kilometers away.

But by 4.30 pm, many black-clad youths, mostly male, were spilling past the Wan Chai end point.

The agreement had been for the march to end at a point between Johnston Road and Luard Road in Wan Chai, and then disperse through Queen's Road East or Wan Chai Road. In theory, the police had a right to stop them if they departed from the agreed arrangements.

But, as usual, officers had been told to exercise maximum restraint. They asked demonstrators to stay within the agreed area, but were ignored.

Police took no action at this stage, instead moving their own officers back towards Admiralty.

Within 30 minutes, the protesters' pledge to remain in an agreed area had been completely abandoned. The crowds swiftly surged past police barriers into roads which had been set aside for the public and for emergency vehicles. Police were busy, rapidly rerouting vehicles to keep the traveling public and the protesters safe.

Government staff and police officers arranged for extra ferries to be run from the Wan Chai Ferry Pier so that anyone who wanted to leave the area could easily do so.

By 5.20 pm, a large group of young people in black had fanned out onto Harcourt Road, a major highway between Admiralty and Central, blocking it completely.

Discussions started between clusters of marchers. What to do next?

One group wanted to stay were they were, because the police headquarters building was nearby, ripe for abusing, as was the much-battered Legislative Council Complex.

A second group was bored with all that—been there, done that, right?

They wanted to try something fresh, and suggested moving to the Court of Final Appeal in Central—after all, judges and Hong Kong's entire legal system were seen as "the enemy" too.

A third group then pointed out that the original plan called for a show of strength in Yuen Long that night.

A message confirming that fact had already been distributed.

Some of the "brothers" would go there and expect backing from the rest of them.

But that could be done later in the evening. What to do now?

Others suggested marching to the Liaison Office, which is mainland China's de facto "consulate" in Hong Kong. (The full name is the Liaison Office of the Central People's Government, and is abbreviated to LOCPG.)

They wanted to actually try to break into the building, the same way that they smashed their way into the Legislative Council Chamber at the beginning of this month.

Once inside, the aim would be to do much the same thing—they could deface the emblems, tear down the portraits and perhaps graffiti the word FUCK or other noble messages on the inside, as before.

Eventually one of the groups started moving towards the center of town, shouting "Go to Central! Go to Central!", and several hundred individuals started to follow, while a smaller group headed to the police headquarters.

By 6 pm, a large group, several hundred strong, had taken control of the main thoroughfares in Central including Connaught Road and the feeder roads around it.

And the police? Instead of stopping the flow of protesters, officers focused on enabling public access in a difficult and unpredictable situation.

The protesters soon occupied all three lanes of Connaught Road heading West, and part of the eastbound carriage way too—but police worked to keep a sliver of road open for ambulances and trapped buses.

Enjoying their dominance of the situation, protesters surged southwards to block Des Voeux Road, another main thoroughfare, too.

Police watched from a distance and helped angry trapped motorists find ways around the unscheduled blockages.

But inevitably, many cars were soon trapped and tempers flared.

Reporters spotted Denise Ho, a singer, among the protesters.

"Police have not properly guided us to where we should disband, so I am just finding my way home," she told them. Ms. Ho has had a long association with the Oslo Freedom Foundation.

Her version of the story was that police were to blame for the chaos the protesters' instant roadblocks were creating.

Meanwhile, a separate group of hundreds of black-clad individuals, the ones who stayed behind in the area between Wan Chai and Admiralty, had risen to their feet and were now clustering outside the police headquarters there, shouting foul language.

A group focused laser pointers at the eyes of officers standing at the gates. Laser pointers tend to deliver between one and five milliwatts of laser light—and at the top end of that range, serious eye damage can occur.

Then, a Christian band arrived and set up a keyboard to accompany them as they sang hymns.

As had become common, they told reporters that they were here to urge people on all sides to behave well—but as usual, they turned a blind eye to the vandalism and abuse from the protesters' side, reserving their criticism and warnings purely for the police, who were doing nothing at all.

Back in Central, part of the large group there decided to move further to the west, marching to the offices of the Chinese government in Sheung Wan.

The splintering of the groups was causing huge challenges to police. Riot squads on standby were spread out. Protesters were in multiple areas by now, and each needed a block of officers to divert traffic and keep everyone safe. Police had never been so stretched.

The light was starting to fade. It was now about 6.45 pm and there were still a large number of stragglers from the march scattered between Victoria Park in Causeway Bay and Wan Chai. A company of police was enabling the safe procession of the remaining people on the roads in that area.

There was also a big crowd of people blocking the main road in Admiralty, plus the earlier mentioned groups, one outside the police headquarters in Admiralty, and another more dissipated cluster blocking all the major roads in Central.

The police companies on duty, spread thinly over the whole area, found it difficult to predict which way the groups were heading. They noted that a breakaway mob from Central seemed to be heading towards Sheung Wan.

Throughout this whole period, the police had been telling marchers that the agreed, legal event was now over and they should now go home, as they had pledged to do when the demonstration achieved public approval.

Both sides know that extreme vandalism, violence and worse were likely to ensue if they protesters don't go home at this point. People would be hurt.

But no one was listening.

And now another problematic element came to the attention of reporters. One segment of the protest organizers had earlier that week promised that there would be a march in Yuen Long, a town in the north West of the New Territories, that evening. This would be the latest in a series of protests in the new towns and far-flung suburbs of the city. Posters and notices had been distributed about it.

But at that time in Central, communications devices sprang to life with news that people in Yuen Long were ready for them—in surprisingly large numbers.

The images distributed on phone screens showed clusters of men in white shirts holding sticks. They looked dangerous.

* * *

What was going on? The key to understanding this event is to realize that five days earlier, on July 16, a group of protesters had travelled to Yuen Long and set up a display to screen protest films in the central area of the New Territories rural town. The messages were extremely hostile about the governance of Hong Kong and mainland China, as usual.

The local triad society had not welcomed the visitors at all, and rather contemptuously encouraged them to leave, even physically shoving at least one participant. The young men, angry at the treatment they received, promised to return at the weekend with a large group of supporters.

They then distributed a poster calling on protesters to go to Yuen Long five days later, on Sunday evening—on July 21. This was distributed through social media to all the followers who use their many channels.

On their part, triads in Yuen Long distributed a poster calling on their supporters to be ready for a performance of traditional Chinese disciplines such as "martial arts and stick-fighting".

They felt they had the moral high ground–they were simply defending their territory from people who were known troublemakers and lawbreakers. (Yes, there is more than a little irony there.)

In short, a factional war had been called between radical protesters and the triads of Yuen Long, and the showdown had been scheduled for July 21.

CHAPTER 19

White Shirts Wait For Trouble

In Which People In Yuen Long Are Ready To Rumble—
Trouble Breaks Out In Central Instead

THE PICTURES BEING shown on people's phones around the city that evening showed men spread over several streets in Yuen Long, so it was hard to get an exact number but it was at least 70, and quite possibly more than 100.

Yuen Long is a largely rural district in the part of Hong Kong closest to the mainland border. Its political identity is complex. It is sometimes described as a "gangster-led" area (as is Sai Kung, another rural district).

But the presence of triads doesn't mean that it is some kind of crime capital where everyone has guns. This isn't the movies.

Instead, these groups are more like local Chinese equivalents of the West's freemason lodges—male-dominated groups of insiders who sometimes provide advantages and help, if needed, to other members of their communities.

Some of these groups are quite definitely on the wrong side of the law, for sure. Others less so.

In fact, the whole image of Hong Kong triads as a slick gangster army is misleading. In reality, there are more than 40 separate triad groups in Hong Kong, and they range from nasty organized criminal groups to clusters of people more akin to old men's benevolent societies.

Only about seven are formally organized in anything like formal military style, and perhaps three are associated with regular, hard-nosed violence.

Hong Kong's police force has an active unit called the Organized Crime and Triad Bureau which keeps an enormous number of files on these groups and individuals, and conducts frequent raids.

Other triad societies waver between different styles of social group. Many are calm, "insider" style mutual aid organizations most of the time, but if they feel threatened they will suddenly snap to attention. The nastier ones can get hold of guns if need be, while the less be-weaponed ones depend on knives, or even just sticks.

Most of the groups, thankfully, stay low profile and stick rigidly to their own territory. Because that's what it's all about: Territory. The individuals have a shared history of living in a particular area, such as Yuen Long. The principle by which they abide is all to do with "home bases".

We won't bother you in your home base, but please don't come and cause trouble in our home base.

In other parts of Hong Kong, they have a shared historical "heung ha", or ancestral home—so a society on the North Point side of Causeway Bay district, where I live, traces its roots back to Fujian province in China.

These societies' position, as they see it, is highly ethical and even pro-justice. They seem themselves as neighborhood watch groups, as seen in communities in the Western world.

"We're a community defense force," they say. "We keep violent lawbreakers out of our communities."

They also keep the peace, deliver their own form of "village justice", and sometimes work as staff unions, or political lobby groups, protecting their interests. North Point, for example, is a thriving community where a variety of groups of people from different origins live together in a low-crime area.

In Yuen Long, the triads had a much tougher, scarier reputation. It was clear that they had taken a threat by protesters to visit on Sunday evening seriously. They had assembled in the streets from 6:46 pm, and they waited patiently.

They would wait a long time.

* * *

That was not because the protesters were scared—not necessarily, anyway. They were just busy. Consider the atmosphere in Central.

The protest leaders were swaggering around Central and Admiralty, shutting down major thoroughfares at will. They well and truly owned the city. The police were keeping their distance.

These young men had taken control of the business district of the world's most expensive city simply by marching into the streets and demanding that all vehicles stop. Besides, they were heroes; Time magazine said so, the New York Times said so, the BBC said so, CNN said so, Fox News said so. No one was going to shut them up.

But the reminder about paying a visit to Yuen Long was now being discussed by some of the leaders. To them, images of men patrolling the streets of a satellite town waiting for them was the red rag to the proverbial bull. The Yuen Long men wore white — and it looked very much like the color had been deliberately chosen to contrast with the black t-shirts of the protesters. Which of course was true.

Discussions began as to whether some of them should go to Yuen Long to face down the white shirts right now, as they had promised to do. This was just after 7 pm. Or should they do that later?

There was another "main attraction" still being discussed—and the Liaison Office of the Central People's Government was much nearer. They could just walk there in ten minutes. (Yuen Long was a good 40 minutes away.)

The enthusiasm for the idea of sending a large group north to Yuen Long dissipated among the larger crowd. They decided to go west instead. They could head to Yuen Long afterwards.

Dusk was falling, making the light hazy. By about 7.25 pm, a large group of protesters had reached Western District, where the China Liaison Office was, and moved aside the barriers that police had assembled there.

They set up their own road blockages, this time on the junction between Des Voeux Road West and Western Street.

The demonstrators then gathered outside Beijing's offices in Hong Kong. Men who were completely masked were lifted high to spray paint onto the CCTV security cameras.

Attention then turned to the radicals' famously well-trained engineering team, who tried to break into the building. They were unable to do so. The gates were locked firmly and it was hard to reach any windows.

So instead, they turned their attention to the large Chinese emblem and the nameplate, smearing them and defacing them.

Black paint was splashed onto the Chinese equivalent of a coat of arms. Next came a large shower of eggs. (Eggs are a good weapon for civil unrest in Hong Kong, because the high summer temperatures mean they soon stink.)

Another group aimed green lasers at the retinas of anyone who looked out of the windows. "Blind the commie bastards," they yelled in Cantonese.

Then followed a period of chanting and shouting, and the etching of foul language onto the walls of the building.

Again, it was not an edifying way for young people to spend their evening, but by this stage such behavior was no longer a surprise.

* * *

Police commanders were in a bigger quandary than usual. In recent weeks, they had been repeatedly accused of brutality—even if the reality was that the trouble came from a few bad apples, while the vast majority of officers spent their time enabling protests, authorized and unauthorized, by diverting traffic and re-routing buses, and occasionally make justified arrests of people committing criminal activity.

But evenings were dangerous. They feared that the hotheads among the protesters would soon start taking violent action—and of course any police response, however justifiable, would be written up by the media as cases of a rogue force attacking peaceful demonstrators. Stay back, stay calm, keep everyone safe—that was their guiding principle.

It was now almost eight, four hours since the protesters had broken away from their original agreed route and started causing disruption across the heart of the city. Police had at this time arrested nobody, had allowed vandalism to progress without any kind of interference, and had let the protesters block major roads at will.

The only thing officers had done was to consistently and politely ask protesters to go home—to no effect.

At this stage, it seemed inevitable that the officers' hand would soon be forced. But for the moment, they continued the maximum restraint policy.

At 8.10 pm, police bulletins went out on social media asking people to avoid going to Western district, and to clear the streets if they were already there.

There were simply too many bodies in that small space, achieving nothing except to make themselves angrier.

Riot police gathered nearby to respond to any outbreak of violence from the crowds near the Liaison Office.

But fighting unexpectedly broke out in Central instead.

The protesters had blocked a road tunnel, and the driver of a dark blue van complained. He demanded that they let his vehicle out of the underpass in which he and other drivers had been trapped.

After many abusive words were exchanged, he climbed out of his van. Big mistake.

A large group of black-clad men raced to surround him and immediately started raining punches down on him, They pummeled the driver with their fists and hit him with objects. Others soon joined in the increasingly horrifying attack, a huge crowd surrounding a single individual.

Others spray-painted his vehicle with the paint cans they had been using for anti-China graffiti.

They smashed the windows of the van and pulled the door open so widely that its hinges snapped. It dangled uselessly, like a broken wing.

A reporter heard the man call out to his attackers: “You can play and do whatever you want. But don’t do this to me.”

They ignored his pleas. Hugely outnumbered, the man was kicked in the head and body. He fell to the floor and they stamped on him. He was quickly turned into a bloodied mess on the road in one of the most horrifying acts of the protests so far.

The bloody attack was over in minutes and the assailants ran away before police and ambulance staff arrived.

* * *

By 8.30 pm, the protesters in Western District had grown tired of screaming obscenities about mainlanders at the Liaison Office. They had failed to penetrate the building and so abandoned that plan and headed back to Central.

There, the group joined members of the Civil Human Rights Front, who sent out their claim about the number of people at the march to the media.

It was 430,000 people, they said—almost exactly three times the actual number of people present according to any scientific method of counting. I immediately knew that the media would report to the world tomorrow, as a fact, that 430,000 people marched. Truly, Western media was leading the way into a post-truth period. Choose a card, any card. Make up a number, any number.

Minutes later, one of the protesters spotted a banner hanging on street-side railings belonging to a political party, the Democratic Alliance for the Betterment and Progress of Hong Kong. This party, known as the DAB, frequently gets more votes from the public in democratic elections than pan-dem politicians. The DAB people were actually well known for working hard for their local constituents—but none of that counted. They were not sufficiently hostile to China. End of. That made them the enemy.

So the banner was cut down from the railing and thrown away. It's hard to imagine clearer evidence that the radical protesters had not the slightest interest in democracy: They were there to denounce anyone who doesn't share their hatred of the people to the north.

* * *

In Yuen Long, an altercation broke out between one youth and a crowd of men in white shirts. He'd quickly been soundly beaten with sticks. Police heard about the dispute and went in search of the youth, eventually finding him and asked for details. He claimed to have done nothing to provoke the attack and blamed it on the fact that he was wearing a dark t-shirt. But this story was problematic—many people were wearing dark tops in Yuen Long that night, but had not been attacked.

Still, the men in white shirts were puzzled. Where were the rest of the protesters?

* * *

The answer was that they were still on Hong Kong Island. By 9 pm, a large group of protesters had gathered around the main police station in Central, working hard at smashing its windows with bricks and writing obscenities on its walls. Its cameras were spray-painted first, to prevent identification of the vandals.

Around the corner the original main group was standing around rather aimlessly—and nobody wanted to go home.

Many of them just sat on the ground at one of the main junctions of central, where Des Voeux Road met Pedder Street. Others clustered on nearby Connaught Road West.

Then came a moment that was chilling for some observers—for anyone who remembered the ultra-violent night of February 8, 2016, during which 124 people were injured.

A group of radicalized localists arrived from the direction of the Liaison Office chanting a slogan: "Free Hong Kong: revolution now!"

The whole crowd took up the cry and started chanting it. It was a visual illustration of the fact that the stance of the violent anti-Chinese-immigrant radicals was spreading through the remainder of the more general protest movement.

Observers could not help but recall that in 2016, the violent radicals were a group just a few hundred strong, yet they caused immense harm with their endless appetite for violence and arson.

If their number swelled to thousands, problems would escalate to a level which did not bear thinking about.

In any other city suffering vandalism on this scale, troops would be called in. If the same thing happened in Hong Kong, it would be politically disastrous.

Our ill-experienced police force would just have to do the best it could —or the PLA would finally have to be called in.

* * *

And reporters? A number of my sources and colleagues were at the scene.

They said that another reason police were treading very carefully on this date was because of certain events over the previous two days.

A member of the Hong Kong National Front had been arrested in a raid on Friday night.

Police had searched a factory unit connected to him in Tsuen Wan. Over the past 48 hours, details had emerged about what had been found.

As well as petrol bombs and pro-independence campaign material, officers had found about 2 kilos of triacetone triperoxide, a powerful explosive used in the London bombings of 2005. This material was associated with the most deadly forms of terrorism on the planet. It had also been used by Islamic terrorists and Sri Lankan militants.

By rights, this discovery should have been the biggest news story of this weekend, and should have been internationally reported. But it would soon be overtaken by other events.

CHAPTER 20

Fighting In Yuen Long MTR

In Which Molotov Cocktails Appear—Trouble Escalates

IT WAS NOW about 9.45 pm and the protesters on Hong Kong Island were still not going home. Finally, one group headed to the Central MTR station to take the train to Yuen Long to teach the white shirts a lesson, while the rest headed to reinforce the numbers of people on Connaught Road.

Police chiefs decided that the time had finally come for officers to take stronger action and brings the chaos to an end. A company of riot police and a group of special tactics officers moved towards Connaught Road West.

And there it was! Tear gas exploded.

Suddenly people were choking. Some youths leapt to their feet to move away.

There was puzzlement. It seemed that this time police had given no one any warning, as they claimed they always did. They simply fired a canister straight at the protesters.

Or had they? As the smoke cleared, with some individuals spraying water on it, it became evident that things were not as they seemed.

It was not the police, but a group of protesters who had set off the smoke bomb—the police were still some distance away at that time.

It became clear that the protesters had fired some sort of home-made tear gas bomb or petrol-based explosive towards the police, who were on Connaught Road West, outside the Shun Tak Center. But it had fallen short and much of the smoke had blown back towards the protesters.

Police officers then approached and asked the protesters to stop the road blockage and disperse. There was no response except abuse and the throwing of bricks—and, to the horror of some bystanders, a number of protesters were seen putting together and throwing Molotov cocktails. These burning petrol bombs would be a hugely unwelcome addition to the protests.

Officers then followed their usual procedure of raising their warning flag—telling protesters to leave the scene as "tear smoke" (technically the material used by the officers was smoke, although it was referred to as tear gas informally) would soon be fired.

At this point, the two groups were facing each other outside the Shun Tak Center, home of the Macau Ferry Terminal, standing 25 to 30 meters apart.

After the requisite 10-minute warning period, the tear gas was duly fired. Some ran away, but others were wearing gas masks and were largely unaffected.

They started throwing glass bottles at officers, but many had shields and manage to deflect them.

At about 10.35 pm, a second volley of tear gas was fired—and this time protesters grabbed metal barriers and charged towards the police, using the same tactic that they used in the first violent protest, on June 9.

* * *

Meanwhile in Yuen Long, trouble had broken out.

At 10.40 pm, a significant group of about 100 radical protesters, some in black, some in ordinary clothing, had arrived at Yuen Long MTR station.

More than 30 people from the faction dressed in white rushed into the station to face them down.

Both groups expressed hostility to a third group of people—the police, of whom there were just three present at the time, two together and one standing separately. But mostly, the two factions just strutted around in front of each other, shouting abuse.

No one watching the videos of that evening would say these were innocent passers-by trying to get home. These were two angry gangs confronting each other.

Some passengers did enter the station but turned round and left immediately. The fury in the air was palpable.

Station staff phoned the main MTR control center at 10.45 pm saying that there was a serious problem there. Remaining members of the public who had been on the train fled, and train staff watched nervously through monitors.

There was a minor skirmish between the two factions, but it ended quickly and the confrontation settled into a shouting match, at which point a pair of police officers was seen (and filmed) leaving—and were assumed to be running back to the police station.

But they weren't. In fact, they'd been told to go to their patrol car where they'd be joined by reinforcements. It would be insane to step between these two large groups of furious people, mostly men. A second patrol car, containing three more uniformed officers, was dispatched at this time, which was 10.45 pm, from the police station towards the railway station.

* * *

Meanwhile on Hong Kong Island, in Western district, the stand-off continued.

A politician named Ted Hui Chi-fung, a pandem lawmaker often found at the scene of the angriest protests, strode into the space between the two groups.

He blamed the police for the stand-off, and demanded that officers stop moving towards the protesters.

As a response to this, an officer holding a loudspeaker patiently explained that the protesters had been attacking the police, adding: "Why should we retreat? It wasn't us who wanted to use tear gas. They threw bricks at us."

Hui had no answer to this.

Protesters again flatly ignored requests to disperse, and officers fired a third round of tear gas at 11 pm. More officers were dispatched to the scene. It was going to be another long night.

* * *

Meanwhile, some members of the public in Yuen Long had physically walked to the police station to tell officers about the trouble at the MTR, since there was no way to phone police—an organized protester attack on the phone system, with hundreds of calls made one after the other, had disabled the police phone exchange.

Back at the train station, the fury started to escalate on the MTR concourse area by about 10.45 pm, with increasing shouting and threats. One protester grabbed a fire hose and sprayed the men in white.

Three minutes later, at 10.48 pm, another group of scary-looking white-dressed men arrived, holding flags, sticks and umbrellas.

The three extra police officers arrived at 10.52 pm.

Why such a small response from the police?

It's a reasonable question. Commanders could argue that two factions screaming at each other is unpleasant, but it was relatively mild compared to what was going on 30 kilometers away on Hong Kong Island. In terms of concentration of manpower, the riot police were where they needed to be.

Still, there is a case that police have to answer. They could have sent more regular officers. Why did they send so few?

Perhaps they really had been paid off by the triads, and were deliberately stalling. Perhaps they were just angry and felt that the protesters needed to be taught a lesson by someone. Perhaps they were just scared—no small, under-equipped group of people would want to march into two large groups of angry men hitting each other with sticks.

Or maybe they were just being sensible, waiting for back up—a large company of trained and properly equipped riot police might be able to bring the situation under control, but a small group of country officers with no experience of riots would have precisely zero chance of getting this situation under control.

But whatever the reason or reasons, the initial police response was low key. Yet the police delay was literally only a matter of minutes, with an upgraded response soon to follow.

At 10.55 pm, protesters apparently blocked the doors of the train on the platform, preventing the driver from continuing his journey to Tuen Mun. This caused a number of members of the public to be trapped at this location.

Yuen Long police chiefs seemed to have a premonition that more manpower would very soon be needed. At 10.57 pm, they ordered the deployment of a Quick Response Team and a group of Tier III officers. While these officers were being briefed and putting on their equipment at the police station, the anger between the two factions at the MTR station boiled over.

At 11:02 pm, the faction dressed in white jumped over the ticket gates into the paid area where the faction dressed in black were standing.

People in black, on the upper level, dropped heavy objects onto the heads of the people in white on the lower level. By 11.05 pm, the verbal confrontation had turned into a massive brawl.

The men in white quickly gained the upper hand, and the people in black retreated up the stairs. The triads followed at 11.06 pm.

While this was happening, the larger group of better equipped police officers left the police station at 11.07 pm to head to the train station.

The violence in and around the MTR train itself took place between 11.08 pm and 11.13 pm. Men in white got into the train and lashed out with their sticks at anyone they could reach. While it was clear that they were aiming for the protesters, there were some members of the public there, who were returning to their homes on the Tuen Mun-bound train. These innocent passengers were caught up in the battle.

At one point, a man in a white shirt appeared and blocked the doorway of the train, trying to stop his fellow white shirts re-boarding the train. There were several similar incidents at other points during the fighting. (I was fascinated by this: it was a phenomenon I had seen among the protesters: many attack, but one "nicer one" tries to stop the others. I didn't expect to see this among triad members.)

The police raced into the railway station at 11:14 pm, just as that brief period of fighting came to an end.

But that wasn't the end of the story, but just a single episode in a much longer story. The officers would soon find themselves busier than ever.

Radical protesters from Central quickly headed to Yuen Long to continue the fighting. Battles between the two factions would go on for many hours, at the station and at other locations, between there and the next MTR station, Long Ping, almost exactly one kilometer away.

* * *

Back on Hong Kong Island, another statement flashed up on phones from the Hong Kong government.

It said that the government members were "concerned that a small number of radicals incited the masses in an organised manner" and such "acts threaten the law and order in the SAR and 'one country, two systems'."

The biggest concentration of Hong Kong's riot police was still very busy on Hong Kong Island.

At about 11.15 pm, they watched as a Civic Party lawmaker named Alvin Yeung stepped forward into the impasse outside the Macau Ferry Terminal.

By this stage, police had been asking protesters to go home for close to five hours.

Yeung told police officers that they must "give protesters' time" to leave the scene, a remarkably ill-judged suggestion, given the situation, and the fact that they had done little else since the afternoon but keep people safe and tell them to go home.

An officer wryly responded to Yeung that the officers had given them an inordinate amount of time already.

"Just ask them to leave," he added. "It's that simple."

The protesters also defied Yeung, by hurling a shower of objects at police, some of which hit their targets.

At 11.23 pm, a police commander calmly told the crowd that if they continued with the violence, officers would have no choice but to move towards the use of rubber bullets.

This piece of news finally had some effect on the crowd. A few started to leave the scene, and the group visibly thinned. Within ten minutes, almost the whole crowd was walking back towards Central.

It was over for the evening.

Or was it?

* * *

By this time, a little after 11.30 pm, news was flashing up on many people's phones about the brief but violent skirmish in which black shirts battled white shirts at Yuen Long—and word that a revenge attack was needed on behalf of the protesters.

Black-clad brothers needed help to wreak vengeance on our enemies!

Protesters leaving Central descended into the Central MTR.

Below ground, black-shirt wearers were told to change garments to other colors if they were going to Yuen Long. They needed to look like members of the public.

The "moneybags" were present, too.

They had used their bottomless secret funds to purchase large numbers of one-way MTR tickets so that protesters could speedily move from place to place.

They stood by the turnstiles, handing out free tickets. By 11.45 pm, many were using them.

There was also a pile of spare baggy t-shirts placed at the MTR turnstiles to help people disguise themselves.

Some male protesters ignored the cash men handing out the tickets—preferring to jump over the turnstiles. But others took the tickets and the spare t-shirts, realizing that there were all sorts of potential benefits if they presented themselves as innocent members of the public.

Above ground, as midnight passed, protest marshals in Central warned people using a megaphone that there was trouble in Yuen Long and going to the spot wearing "civilian" clothing may not protect you. "They'll hit you, even if you change," one voice warned. He made it sound like there was a war in Yuen Long.

But the angriest, bravest individuals were not put off, and more people poured down the MTR stairs to head to the trains.

* * *

In Yuen Long, the situation had changed after midnight. Most people had fled, but a small number remained, including individuals from both sides.

Then, at about 12.30 am, came an incident straight from the script of a comedy-crime movie.

Police and MTR staff working together had managed to lock the white shirts out of the station. The Yuen Long men were behind a floor-to-ceiling shutter. It was a slatted metal roller shutter, so that people inside the station could see the angry white-shirt men—but the triad members could not enter.

Their opponents, the black shirts, taunted them from inside, where they had free reign. Both groups had sticks and were screaming abuse at each other.

One young man on the black shirt side ran up to the shutters and poked his stick through the narrow openings, sneering as if he was tormenting animals at the zoo. A white shirted man tried to grab the stick but he was too slow.

The taunting continued for some minutes.

All of a sudden the white shirts managed to snap the locks holding the roller shutter down—and it started to roll upwards.

The black shirts immediately stopped sneering and turned to run away, as the white shirts give chase.

It's hard not to think of scenes in cartoons where a character is taunting a chained bulldog—and the chain snaps.

At about 12.50 am, after another skirmish, things had calmed down again. A few members of the press arrived and a man told them that he thought the police deliberately opened the gate to let white shirt attackers in. Several journalists reported this. (However, this allegation was untrue — the video clearly showed the white-shirt men tearing open the gate by themselves.)

* * *

It was now 1.06 am and the Hong Kong government released a second statement. This condemned the gratuitous violence in the Sheung Wan/ Western district area. "These outrageous, violent acts included hurling petrol bombs, setting fires and throwing bricks. Thoroughfares were also blocked," it said.

The statement went on to condemn the violence and intimidation in Yuen Long.

"It led to confrontations and injuries ... This is absolutely unacceptable to Hong Kong as a society that observes the rule of law. The SAR government strongly condemns any violence and will seriously take enforcement actions."

* * *

Yuen Long police were kept very busy indeed over the next few hours, with the fighting between the two factions moving to Nam Pin Wai village, close to the station.

Officers had been continuously requesting help from riot police from Hong Kong Island, and they finally arrived. Over these hours, there were several different groups of police involved in attempts to keep the peace, and this resulted in some confusion.

Around 4.00 am, there was another burst of activity: A Crime Investigation Department team arrived at Nam Pin Wai village, just behind Yuen Long MTR station, and marched in for an inspection. By this time, the triads had stashed their sticks and were empty-handed.

After the inspection, a spokesman for the team said in front of the media that they had not seen any weapons. This was an accurate statement, and referred to the inspection that had just been completed.

Unfortunately, the way the media reported the story, it sounded as if he was referring to the earlier battles—the men in white were clearly holding sticks during the skirmishes at 10.40 pm, at 11.02 pm, at 00.23 am, and several others between 1.00 am and 4.00 am.

Then, one officer, trying to keep the peace, put his hand on the shoulder of a man in a white t-shirt and encouraged him to go home. The police then patted a man in a black t-shirt on the shoulder with the exact same message.

The media edited the clip to show *only* the first "pat" and it was quickly all over Twitter as proof of the police's close relationship to the gangsters.

* * *

As dawn started to rise on July 22, the last of the protesters headed away from Yuen Long. But they were already planning a return visit—they set the date for the evening of Saturday, July 27.

With a few thousand friends. Or maybe a few hundred thousand friends. Maybe a million friends! This was not over.

* * *

A lot of shocking things happened on July 21, and into the early hours of the next morning, from the way protesters blocked kilometers of roads on Hong Kong Island, to the way they beat the van driver in Central, to the attack on the Liaison Office, to the protesters' first major use of petrol bombs, to the hours-long series of four or more battles between white shirts and black shirts in Yuen Long.

But people behind the scenes absurdly recast the story so that the protesters were entirely removed from the tale. The tale was revised so that the only characters were the police, the white shirts, and innocent members of the travelling public.

That tiny two-second clip of two police officers leaving the train station was played again and again on every protester-supporting media channel available—it was "proof" that the Hong Kong police were a unit of the gangsters. On walls all over Hong Kong, we started to see a line being written in English and Chinese: "Police Is Triads".

And the international media? Although the vast majority of crimes committed on that day had been by black-clad people, they failed to see any of it, blaming all of the day's trouble on police. The media painted the protesters as victims only.

CNN's news report was ludicrously biased, opening with these words: "Hong Kong descended into scenes of chaos Sunday night, after riot police fired tear gas and rubber bullets at protesters, and a mob armed with batons attacked people in a metro station."

CNN was operating as the mirror image of the People's Daily, uninterested in the truth, and simply pushing a manufactured storyline in which the most energetic lawbreakers were re-cast as innocent victims.

CHAPTER 21

Reclaiming Yuen Long

In Which A Return Visit Is Made—Fearfulness—
Police Are Preferred Target

A WEEK HAD PASSED. It was July 27, and another march was taking place.

Press reports were presenting this rally as the latest in a series of public protests. But this was misleading: it was absolutely not the same thing at all. Most of the earlier marches, at least in their initial stages, attempted to be peaceful, legal processions in which the public exercised their civil rights.

This was something entirely different.

Today's march was illegal and unlicensed from the start. More than that, the principle that was driving it was in direct contravention of the rule of law—the attendees were not hiding the fact that they are there to beat the crap out of perceived enemies.

Some reporters, watching the gathering, mentioned that they could perhaps praise the marchers for displaying courage in facing up to "dangerous gangsters".

That could be true—if there wasn't such a big focus on building up numbers. The intention was to hugely outnumber the enemy, and then beat the crap out of them.

In view of falling numbers, all other protest events planned for this weekend had been put on hold so that everyone could be summoned to this spot.

Even among the reporters who were sympathetic to the radicals (and that meant all of them), observers could sense some discomfort at the way that so many young men were arriving hungry for violence.

The central theme of the event was to "Reclaim Yuen Long" in revenge for a despicable "police-enabled" triad attack on innocent train passengers a week earlier.

But for many people in Yuen Long and around Hong Kong, the theme didn't make sense. Residents of the area, in particular, were reacting angrily, asking a simple question: How can these young people "reclaim" a place that most of them have never visited in their lives? And what does it mean when outsiders are saying they are there to reclaim a town from the people who have lived there generation after generation? You can't "reclaim" someone else's home.

Few of the young people seemed to understand that villagers had a long, complex, historical relationship with the traditional societies in their midst.

This should have been a moment for pandem leaders to stand up and call for peace. An event focused on violence was clearly anathema to everything they claimed they stood for.

But that didn't happen. Only a few were present, and they were happy to join in the "let's teach them a lesson" vibe.

Police were dreading the event, too. Intimidation and violence had been close under the surface of earlier marches and erupted towards the end of them—but never before had it been the openly discussed, intended and desired outcome for an entire large group of protesters.

In any moral sense, the Reclaim Yuen Long event was far worse than the previous weekend's fight at the train station.

Furthermore, police had made a series of arrests of Yuen Long triad members after last week's events, so the gangsters and their supporters were furious with them too.

Both sides were inclined to blame the police for the sins of their enemies.

In the event, the day's events shifted in an unexpected way.

As people spilled out of the MTR train and gathered outside Yuen Long Police Station at about 1 pm, there was a feeling of fear.

But as the size of the crowd grew, it diminished. The "reclaimers" felt they had the power of numbers on their side. They were the ants facing down the locusts. They were the good guys. Their aim was noble.

A million people would gather and teach the few hundred triads a lesson!

One group of young men donned masks and identified themselves with red ribbons. They strutted around like superheroes.

Another masked group called themselves The Vigilantes. They compared weapons, and discussed battle strategy and how to outwit the police to hit their enemies hard, hurting them badly—and unconsciously replicating the worst examples of the gangs they wanted to confront.

By 3.20 pm, large numbers of angry masked protesters were pouring out of the train station. Instead of reclaiming Yuen Long, most marched directly towards Nam Pin Wai, the village said to be main home of the triad gang which fought with protesters a week earlier.

Half an hour later, hundreds of marchers were massed right outside the village's main entry point.

Barriers had been erected and police were present. Masked protesters shouted into the village: "Gang members! Come out and fight!"

They forcibly removed the protective barricades placed at the village entrance. Movement could be seen within the village, but the individuals inside chose not to react. The doors of the village ancestral hall remained shut.

Should the huge mob rush in? Would the triads come out? There was high tension at this point.

But neither out of the two outcomes took place. The assembled group of protesters, large as it was, seemed strangely unwilling to pour into the village and do what they had come to do.

After 20 minutes of inaction, the frustrated protesters turned to an easier target: The police there to protect everyone's safety.

At 4.23 pm, two police vans arrived with extra officers and demonstrators turned to rush at them, shouting: "Triads! Triads!"

As the focus of tension outside Nam Pin Wai changed, by 4.41 pm another group of demonstrators was marching through the main part of Yuen Long holding a British colonial flag.

A third group of protesters had gathered in the village of Sai Pin Wai, a hamlet on the West side. Rumors said that white-shirted men in safety helmets had been seen there—and photographs were circulated showing "the enemy" apparently ready for action, with sticks and gas masks.

In some places, villagers had put up "no entry" signs and drawn red lines on the street, telling the protesters to keep away.

But again, the awaited showdown between the protesters and the villagers or gangsters failed to materialize—and by 5.10 pm, that crowd had also re-channeled its anger, again in the direction of police officers.

Why? Police officers tended to take whatever you inflicted on them, and then they jumped on some of you and arrested a few. They may treat you roughly, but they don't actually break your bones or kill you.

Protesters at Sai Pin Wai spun on their heels to face the police and quickly took action. A masked group of men wearing black surged in front of a police van to stop it moving.

They then attacked the vehicle with weapons. They smashed the windows, destroyed the headlights, and spray-painted the names of triad groups on the van.

There were four officers trapped inside. The protesters shouted at them: "Why do you protect the triads?"

This was ironic. On Sunday, the previous week, the list of offenses by black-shirts was far, far longer than the list of offenses by white-shirts. Yet far more men in white had been arrested.

At this stage, police in other parts of the town noticed that protesters were now openly wielding metal rods, bricks and sticks. Normally, this happened late at night, at the end of protests—it was unusual for it to be happening so early. At 5.17 pm, officers released a statement as a news release: *"Given that some protesters were holding iron poles, self-made shields and even removing fences from roads, police are concerned about possible deterioration of the situation."*

Through loudspeakers, police told protesters that they had clearly made their point and should now leave the villages. Officers knew this was when the trouble tended to escalate: the more peaceable protesters would back off, but hardcore ones took "dispersal requests" as their cue to attack.

Sure enough, by 5.21 pm, objects were flying through the air at the police.

Officers gave notice that they would use tear gas, and some minutes later, canisters were fired.

A pandem politician complained to police that they should not be using tear gas, as an old folks' home was nearby. But staff at the home told media that the windows were shut and residents were not affected: "They just continued to watch television."

By now the word was out among the protesters about the revised strategy: Attack the police, not the gangsters. One group of protesters headed back towards the Yuen Long Police Station and by 5.49 pm it was besieged.

In another part of the town, shortly after 6 pm, two huge groups of protesters then discovered that one smaller group of police officers was trapped between them.

They brutally attacked the officers, hitting them with umbrellas, their fists and any other hard objects they could find. The police attempted to defend themselves with aerosol pepper sprays and tear gas but were heavily outnumbered.

They were badly beaten and bruised.

By 7.10 pm, darkness was falling and the majority of protesters started to leave the scene.

As was now standard practice, they blamed police for the violence, claiming to have the legal right to be "peacefully demonstrating" and decrying the "excessive" use of tear gas and pepper spray. (They seemed to have forgotten that this was an illegal gathering with the express purpose of conducting a violent revenge attack as a payback for the previous weekend's factional fighting.)

Just after eight o'clock in the evening, excitement again mounted after a protester looked through the window of a parked car, a luxury black Lexus—and saw a cluster of sticks. He called to his friends.

The sticks resembled gangster batons. The protesters decided this must be the triad leader's vehicle. At last, a chance to hit the gangsters!

They trashed the car, smashed the windows and kicked in the side panels.

The hardcore protesters continued to fight the police in the darkness until after 9.30 pm, but the numbers were falling steadily.

Police asked MTR staff to run extra trains and open all barriers, so that people could leave easily and conveniently without paying.

By 10.03 pm, the last protester groups left the villages and headed to Yuen Long train station. One group shot laser pointers into the eyes of police officers working to maintain order at the station. But police managed to get most people onto the trains by about 10.40 pm.

At 10.49 pm, police officers outside the villages of Nam Pin Wai and Sai Pin Wai were given orders to stand down, and climbed into police vans to finally go off duty. It seemed that the drama was finished. In the so-called villages of the gangsters, the streets were dark and quiet.

CHAPTER 22

Peaceful Protesters Withdraw Support

In Which Our Narrator Is Grabbed On The Street—Holding Court In PolyU—Reflections

TODAY I WAS GRABBED by a group of black-clad protesters in Causeway Bay. It was a Sunday, the day after the big "teach the gangsters a lesson" session that had flopped badly the previous night. No triads had been hurt, but plenty of police officers were injured, and any right the protesters had to the moral high ground had been jettisoned.

Protests started relatively late today, and people didn't surge into Causeway Bay until mid-afternoon today, Sunday, July 28.

Once more, the protesters had abandoned their British Hong Kong flags and were carrying US flags instead. The exception was Granny Wong, who had her usual British Union Jack.

Quite a few reporters were present, filming the protest. We stood on the side of the road with cameras as they marched into the heart of the world's priciest shopping district. Near the front was a young woman nicknamed English Placard Girl, who was getting lots of attention from everyone, as usual, for her rather charming English-language hand-written denunciation of the "commies".

There was the aforementioned Granny Wong, with her politically incorrect Union Flag of Great Britain. (She made us stop filming so she could comb her hair before posing for us.)

Then the leaders of the march had a discussion in a tight cluster and some decisions were made.

The problem seemed to be that the atmosphere was too nice. Even though the march was illegal, police had diverted the buses, and created new routes for other vehicular traffic.

There was no real "trouble" as such. The organizers were looking rather annoyed about this.

So the leaders of the group decided to go into lawlessness mode, ripping up the safety railings, building metal blockades in the middle of the road, graffiti-ing slogans everywhere they could, and generally ramping up the bad behavior. "We need to burn stuff," one of the youths said. They seemed to *need* trouble.

To begin the process, someone raised the umbrella signal.

We ought to talk about this. Until recently, umbrellas had been seen as a very positive thing among Hong Kong protesters—they became a somewhat noble symbol of defiance during the Umbrella Movement in 2014, and provided a charming, colorful contrast to the dark-clothed riot officers with their shields and tear gas guns.

But by August of 2019, radical protesters were always followed by a group carrying dark umbrellas—and they had a very specific job.

A hand-signal was given (two fisted hands sliding apart vertically, as if opening an umbrella) and the censorship cohort instantly snapped into action. They had a very specific job—to prevent the media or the public taking pictures of them indulging in illegal acts.

This thoroughly annoyed me. First, they had taken something rather beautiful and positive from the peaceful protesters of the Umbrella Movement and turned it into something harsh and negative for use by law-breaking vandals.

Second, there was a basic dishonesty about the way they would instantly switch from a "film me, film me" attitude when they were marching peacefully to the "you film me, you DIE" attitude when they wanted to commit any sort of crime.

I guess I should have been even more irritated that so many members of the media obeyed their orders instantly and without question, but nothing could shock me any more. At the protesters' orders, most people lowered their cameras or camera-phones.

Not me.

When the vandalism started, I continued to film with my phone. I tried to find angles that would get past the umbrellas they were using as censorship shields.

I filmed them getting out a secret set of tools that enabled them to remove safety railings within minutes.

I filmed them painting slogans onto the zebra crossing so that everyone who used them would see their anti-democratic demand for Hong Kong to be freed from China.

I filmed them building barricades in the road.

My camera phone kept rolling as they vandalized public property, kicked over garbage bins, trashed construction sites and stole items from them to be repurposed as weapons.

And then I was spotted.

"He's filming. That guy," someone shouted in Cantonese. A group of men ran over to me.

I was quickly surrounded by large, frightening masked youths in black clothes and hoods—they really looked like they had stepped out of a Middle Eastern desert execution video.

"Delete your photos," the largest one shouted in Chinese.

His friend repeated the command in English. As usual, there was one nice one, who was marginally more polite than the others. "Friend," he said in English, with a classic passive-aggressive smile. "We need you to delete the photos you just took. Understand?"

I did as I was told.

After carefully satisfying themselves that the material had all been wiped, they released me.

I counted to ten, to let them get a little distance away, and then I turned and strolled away.

I then turned my phone back on.

I pressed "Album", then "Recently Deleted" and then "Recover All".

The footage came right back.

As I went through the recovered clips later, I felt smug. Ha! I had totally outsmarted them.

But the truth was that I was incredibly stupid. Because I promptly wrote up what I had done as a funny anecdote and put it on the Internet.

The following morning, I started receiving a large number of poorly written and abusive comments in both English and Chinese. Some of them were very unpleasant and threatening. The trickle turned into a torrent.

I had to abandon all forms of social media for a few days.

"The VRs [violent radicals] read your story," one of my sources explained. "They found a picture of your face and put it on a couple of the black shirts' forum. You are dead meat, my friend."

But I wasn't. Not immediately. Nobody killed me that day or the next, and eventually the hate mail from "the VR people" disappeared, to be replaced by my normal hate mail, mostly from Western expats. Whatever.

* * *

Another day, another dollar. I love being interviewed by reporters from the West. You can basically say anything you like and they will write it down: "In China, it's considered bad luck to be eaten by bears on your birthday."

It's Friday, August 2 and Coffee Court is in session at the Block X café in PolyU. The international correspondent interviewing me has just left after writing down my words of wisdom about being eaten by a bear and I am sitting with some students in a companionable silence, as we each get on with our work. They are writing essays, I am writing columns and features for newspapers and magazines.

The new university term won't start for another month, so the people in the coffee shop today are mostly teachers and people doing summer courses, which means students from the mainland or from Europe.

But there had been a cluster of local students in here earlier in the week.

It was funny. On Monday, the representatives of this city's 11 universities jointly announced that Hong Kong was now a "police state"—and then went off to drink Frappuccinos, organize illegal rallies and write openly on websites about how the evil Hong Kong authorities had removed all freedom of speech.

Clearly we have a new definition of "police state".

* * *

I noted that the biggest news story in Hong Kong at the moment was being missed by every media outlet: the mass exodus of peaceful protesters from the regular demonstrations.

But reporters can't be blamed for this — they are trained to report on the things they see in front of them, not on things that are missing.

So they are continuing to tell the world about the thousands of protesters who are on the streets and what they're up to. But they are not telling them about the much, much larger numbers who are throwing up their hands in horror and staying at home. In June, there were huge numbers of people on the streets, maybe half a million. The biggest number in the past week was about 10,000, at most.

It is vital to remember that these are not just numbers. These are people. These are people with names, and some of them are people I know personally.

Ah-Kin, Ah-Lum, Tak, Man, Ah-Sin, Sally L, Sally S., Lung, Terry, Man, Esther, Li-yi and literally hundreds of thousands of others have voted with their feet against the radicals. I wish I could just take the whole newspaper to record all their names.

Most of this latest batch of escapees are in their 20s (a large percentage of older people left earlier).

The remaining protesters are the harder hardliners who are increasingly loud but whose support is narrowing.

The big grey area of peaceful protesters who are in no way "pro-Beijing" but are very uncomfortable with the violence-filled protests is growing big and fat: I think of them as my people.

We are strongly pro-democracy, we are in favor of peaceful protests, we are in favor of free press, we are not scared of shooting off our mouths at China OR America OR anyone else.

But we don't like violence and we definitely don't want to destroy Hong Kong at all. (Unbelievably, the "destruction of the Hong Kong economy" has become a specific goal of the protests.). The Cantonese phrase, pronounced "laam tsow" literally means "we'll fry together". It's translated as "mutual destruction" by some English outlets.

The radicals had stolen the tagline from The Hunger Games movie series: "If we burn, you burn with us." We were starting to see it in posters around the city.

So they had openly said they wanted to destroy the economy—and yet the foreign correspondents STILL pretend that this was the voice of the Hong Kong people, a community known for peacefulness and financial acumen. Journalists' ability to delude themselves was staggering.

Many people were hoping that the first day of the 2019-2020 university term, September 2, exactly one month ahead of us at that point, would calm things down—but I didn't know. I had just heard from the young people in the coffee shop that student union leaders had called on all students to boycott all lectures. They were calling for them to take the whole semester off.

Seriously? I couldn't see that happening. They were over-estimating their level of support.

As a back-up plan for people who refused to do that, there was the "easy option" which *was* declared compulsory—there would be at the very least a total strike of all students for the entire first two weeks of the semester. The universities would be dead for that period, and Hong Kong's thousands of students will join the protest.

"That sounds bad," I said.

But the students shook their heads. "I don't think it will happen," one of them said. "Most people don't really support the student union leaders. We like to study." (Only in Hong Kong would a student say that without a hint of irony.) His stance sounded like the students I knew, the ones I had been teaching for years.

But had he correctly inferred the feelings of students in general? Or was he really talking about himself and his mates? They were at the university working during the summer break, so it may be that he was a super-swot assuming that everyone was like him.

But then I thought of the classes I had taught. We never discussed politics, as such, even though it inevitably came up in general discourse. Many seemed to be apolitical and some were gentle, religious people. Many of them were very homework oriented.

My university, PolyU, was the largest in the city, but was pretty low down the ladder in terms of status—in fifth or sixth place on the city's university league tables. And yet many students were ambitious.

* * *

In the local and international newspapers, media bigmouths were speculating on what Chinese premier Xi Jinping would do about the violent unrest in Hong Kong.

They were missing the bigger story. Xi Jinping's focus was surely on what the activism might do on the mainland—and measures were already being rolled out, I could tell from talking to teachers.

Example: Students from a Hong Kong international school who just went to a youth conference in Beijing were given electronic security tags to wear—and were sternly warned not to lose them. If they did, they'd be sent straight to the airport to leave China.

As repercussions escalate, China could become like one of those dreadful, scary countries where there is no privacy for travellers.

Such as the United States, where last year alone (that is, in 2018) border guards forced 33,295 travellers to reveal passwords for laptops and phones (not joking!).

Now tell me again about the wonderful civil liberties in America?

* * *

As we scan the papers, we note that people among the international media are belatedly starting to realize that the protests are not about the extradition bill and ALSO not pro-democracy either. Some are starting to describe them as "anti-government" protests. Slowly, slowly, the truth will out.

The secretive committee behind the protests are pushing for independence—not because they really want it or think they can achieve it, but because they are anti-China and pro-US. Their aim is to destabilize China, and they can use these young people to achieve that.

On their part, many of the radical protesters really do want Hong Kong to be "liberated" from China, and recolonized by the United States, or given full independence or self-determination, and they have been persuaded that escalating violence is the way to achieve it.

Out of the thousands of posters large and small on the Lennon Walls, very few mention democracy at all. Instead, the vast majority express great hostility towards China, and towards the Hong Kong government and the police force, portrayed as agents of China.

The chants of the radicals are demands for the liberation of Hong Kong from China in a revolution, not calls for democracy.

The graffiti sprayed all over the city doesn't call for democracy but for revolution. It's all painfully obvious to anyone who attends the protests, but I guess people see what they want to see.

There's also a deeper question here: Many of the violent radicals are thuggish young men, nothing like the (now vanished) peaceful protesters, many of whom are quite sophisticated and educated. So how come the radicals are so well organized and well financed?

That's a question we need to answer before moving on.

CHAPTER 23

Uncovering Foreign Funding And Training

In Which We Pool Knowledge—Cash From Across the Water—Revolutionary Training Specialists—Removing The Police Pillar

MY NETWORK WAS no longer mainly Hong Kong mothers and fathers. So many young people and non-Chinese people had become friends or followers or readers or contributors that I had a much wider range of sources.

Among these were quite a few well-connected, highly educated individuals, including business people with a knowledge of geopolitical intelligence.

One afternoon, we sat down and shared information about the foreign backers of the protests.

This had to be done offline, since it would otherwise attract the conspiracy theorists had we made it public—and it was a topic that needed to stay factual and evidence-based.

The conversations were long and fascinating, as were the people involved and the accounts of the detective work done.

But there was so much material uncovered, that we need to just summarize it in this chapter.

* * *

The increasingly violent insurgency in Hong Kong is being engineered and amplified by hidden geopolitical groups working to destabilize the region.

Western agents are working behind the scenes and have financed the unrest, and trained and radicalized protesters against China. They are even paying for the development of hi-tech tools to enable them to evade detection.

Millions of dollars are coming from the United States, while training, strategy and media skills came from a mixture of European and American "professional revolution consultants".

This year alone, the US has budgeted US$643,000 (HK$5 million) for pro-US anti-China activists in Hong Kong through the National Endowment for Democracy (NED), the CIA's regime-change arm—but other large sums are being sent through other groups.

These include the Open Technology Fund, which presents itself on its website as a non-profit independent organization, but is a US government-led operation to boost protester organizations' communications capabilities.

Funds are also coming from the US Agency for Global Media, which runs disinformation units such as Radio Free Asia, founded by the CIA and listed in the original US government documents as a "Propaganda Asset".

Separately, Hong Kong activists have received practical training in street-protest strategy and media control through meetings and exchanges with "revolution consultants" from at least January 2013 onwards. In that year, they met top people from the Oslo Freedom Foundation, the Albert Einstein Institute, and the Serbian group known as Canvas.

All three specialize in creating and sharing strategies for over-turning governments using street protests.

Some sort of Ukraine-Hong Kong "friendship group" has been set up—but it sounds decidedly politicized. Its Facebook page is called the Free Hong Kong Center and discussions are virulently anti-China. A Ukrainian group called Gonor, which specializes in providing masterclasses for street protests, are said to be interested in Hong Kong, although we could not find any evidence of interaction yet.

On the local front in Hong Kong, key players include right wing billionaire publisher Jimmy Lai Chee-ying, and union federation leader Lee Cheuk-yan, whose organization received regular large sums from the United States from at least 1996 onwards.

Why is this happening? The CIA's aim is clearly to provoke Beijing into damaging or removing the "one country, two systems" policy. Doing this would empower pro-US, anti-China elements on China's coast, and thus ensure that Hong Kong could remain a US intelligence base, and Taiwan an intelligence and military base.

While it has long been known to some people that foreign forces have been participating in the Hong Kong unrest, it is always denied and never written about. Few people realize how successful the project has been, nor how long it has been going on.

For example, many Hong Kong people knew that the 2003 protest which prevented the introduction of Article 23, an anti-subversion law, was organized by two Hong Kong activist groups—but few know that both groups were partly bankrolled by the United States, as listed in NED files. Nor do people realize that the law would have impeded the CIA's ability to operate in Hong Kong.

Similarly, many Hong Kong people know that the Umbrella Movement started making headlines in in September, 2014—but few know that 18 months earlier, the Oslo Freedom Forum and other groups provided detailed training and materials for 1,000 Hong Kong activists to prepare for it.

By any measure of geopolitical maneuvering, the extent of US activity and involvement in Hong Kong politics is extraordinary.

Had Chinese or Russian sources equipped, trained or financed anti-government elements to this level in the United States, it would be considered an international outrage.

And let's remember, the 2019 protests are simply another stage in a process which has been going on, literally, for decades.

To take one example, the city's main workers' group has always been the Hong Kong Federation of Trade Unions, founded in 1948. But in 1990, an alternative group called the Hong Kong Confederation of Trade Unions was set up which largely duplicated the work of the existing organization. The new group promptly labelled the original group "pro-Beijing", but in fact it was the newcomer organisation which was political, taking a strongly pro-US, anti-China position.

This second group, since the 1990s, has regularly received significant sums of money from the United States, some of which are recorded in US government files. A typical entry is the one for 2003, the year of the Article 23 protest, which says US$260,434 was sent to Hong Kong for the use of *"Hong Kong Confederation of Trade Unions and other Hong Kong-based labor rights NGOs trade unions"*. Although the sum was listed as a gift from the American Center for International Labor Solidarity, it appears in US government files as a donation from CIA-founded NED.

The trade union group has been a key organizer of protests and demonstrations expressing strongly negative views about mainland China, with leader Lee Cheuk-yan becoming a household name.

Another example: A group called the Hong Kong Human Rights Monitor was *"established in 1995 in anticipation of Hong Kong's 1997 transfer of sovereignty"*, NED officials said in a report. NED's financing of the activist group meant it was *"poised to expand its capacity to lead a coordinated campaign for democracy in Hong Kong through the mobilization of activists and the general public"*.

And that's the key. The natural nervousness of some elements of the Hong Kong public about mainland China could be "weaponized" in street protests — and that word came from people at the Oslo Freedom Foundation meetings, not from its critics.

Expert skills in media presentation would ensure that major news organizations, including Fox, CNN, BBC, Reuters, The New York Times, The Guardian, The Washington Post, Agence France-Press, and Associated Press, would present the news slanted to the pro-US, anti-China side.

So, for example, reporters were inspired to go to great lengths to avoid showing Jimmy Lai as many Hong Kong people see him: a billionaire pro-Trump tycoon running a coarse, right wing, racially insensitive, anti-immigrant newspaper, while being involved in supporting a CIA-backed insurgency.

Instead, the international press portrays him as the beleaguered noble fighter for press freedom—despite the fact that at no time has Apple Daily or any other Hong Kong newspaper been shut down or prevented from publishing editorials critical of the government.

Similarly, the international media are downplaying or omitting coverage of Hong Kong radicals' burning of numerous shops and restaurants set up by mainland China immigrants, trashing the offices of democratically elected politicians perceived as friendly to China, or attacking people in the street for having the "wrong" accent.

Again, this is not to say that there aren't many honest, sincere, pro-democracy protesters involved in the unrest, expressing genuine fears about the future. They were present in huge numbers in June, but many have been scared away by the violence and twisted politics.

If you are in Hong Kong, and interacting with people who know what's going on, it's not difficult to detect the layers of anti-China forces at work in Hong Kong, through the many signs of foreign involvement, including the placards and banners in American English.

Ironically, the group which is the biggest loser from the US interference in Hong Kong are the good, honest ordinary people of the city, whose nuanced, complex relationship with mainland China has been polarized and subverted, leaving the populace angry and divided.

* * *

We should also talk about the involvement of the "professional revolution industry".

Between January of 2013 and September of 2014, numerous Hong Kong activists met with and received materials from revolution specialists. They jointly created a plan to block roads in an "occupy Wall Street" type event calling for 10,000 participants.

Briefings and detailed material were given to Hong Kong team leaders and passed down to train a large number of "marshals" for the forthcoming protests in the city—Oslo sources originally said there were about 1,000 Hong Kong individuals involved.

Write-ups about the Umbrella Movement, which started in September of 2014, presented it as a textbook case of a non-violent protest, without realizing that the phrase was literally accurate: It was organized according to a textbook—or various handbooks of protest strategies.

But of course it eventually splintered, with the original organizers and the students falling out—and then the radical localists turned the Hong Kong protest movement sour in February of 2016 with their violence and arson.

And well before that date, the behind-the-scenes coalition had fallen apart and Europeans criticized the radicals' leadership.

In 2015, Srda Popovic, founder of Serbian protest advisory group Canvas, complained about the wrong direction the activists had taken in an interview with the UK's Guardian newspaper: *"In Hong Kong, they simply occupied the same space every day, and mainland China knew all it had to do was wait. You see, what you want in a campaign are what we call low-risk, inclusive tactics of dispersal. Occupy is a high-risk, divisive tactic of concentration: getting everyone in one place, fighting with the police, and pissing off the people–like shopkeepers–you need to win over."*

But returning to 2014, in October of that year, Oslo Freedom Forum leaders spoke openly and proudly about their involvement with Hong Kong anti-China activists to multiple people.

The relationship stopped being a secret at that time, and many journalists who had written positively about the Umbrella Movement as a spontaneous outburst of civil disobedience, including this author, then writing for the New York Times, were shocked.

BBC journalist Laura Kuenssberg even filmed a news report from the gathering in Oslo, saying: *"To topple a government for good you have to be organized and plan meticulously. And activists here have been helping to organize the current protests in Hong Kong. Their plan to put thousands of people on the streets was hatched nearly two years ago."*

The BBC video report went on to describe the way that pro-democracy marchers could be used as "a weapon of mass destruction". It also featured

Jamila Raqib, executive director of the Albert Einstein Institute, explaining its involvement. (The Institute was founded by Gene Sharp, a US academic specializing in civil disobedience tactics.)

Ms. Raqib said: *"Protesters were taught how to behave during a protest: so, how to keep ranks, how to speak to police, how to manage their own movements, how to use marshals with their movements — these are people who are specially trained.... how to manage a water cannon being used against you and other types of police violence."*

In a BBC written report that repeated much of the same information, Kuenssberg also reported the presence at the Oslo meeting of Popovic, co-founder of Canvas, and his involvement in multiple regime changes.

The BBC reports, video and text, were published on October 21, 2014. They created immediate fireworks in both Hong Kong and the United States.

The problem was not that Ms. Kuenssberg had got the facts wrong. The problem was that she had got them right, and put them on a high profile platform, contrary to recommended strategies.

The Hong Kong Umbrella Movement protests had been one of the greatest *undercover* triumphs of a long-term process which some people were calling "the Anglo-American destabilization of China". The protests had been seen as entirely spontaneous and homegrown — even to the vast majority of participants. That's because, to some extent, they were natural and organic. Journalists too, including me, had initially been taken in.

The protests were superbly well organized, with enormous attention to detail, a huge budget, and were not just impressive, but came across as impressively good-natured, at least in the opening days. A constant flow of positive stories about the event were provided to journalists.

But the truth is that really successful "spontaneous" operations of that scale needed to be carefully planned and delicately steered. And making revolutions seem "homegrown" is a core, bedrock technique of the systems pushed by the Oslo Freedom Forum, the Albert Einstein Institute, Canvas, and other groups in that space.

Yet it couldn't last. The Hong Kong event was designed as a relatively short "occupy Wall Street" type protest, and the original organizers soon lost control of it.

But the organizers, all the different layers of them, preferred to keep the details out of the public eye—especially the involvement of people from the West.

Ms. Kuenssberg had done her job too well.

In October of 2014, unhappy messages were passed between Hong Kong, the United States, and the BBC newsroom. The basic theme of the complaint was straightforward: The preferred story was that the Hong Kong protests were entirely homegrown, and NOT foreign influenced at all.

Furthermore, the BBC report could be said to be wrong in one sense: while leading localists campaigning for the unpopular cause for independence WERE present in Oslo, the "official" leaders of the 2014 protest at the time it started were university professor Benny Tai and his team in a group called Occupy Central With Love and Peace, who had not been present.

Nine days later, on October 30, the BBC report re-appeared with amendments. The new text was followed by a statement: *"This article has been amended after an earlier version may have given the impression that the Hong Kong pro-democracy protests were planned by foreign activists. The amended version makes clear that the planning for the Hong Kong demonstrations was carried out in Hong Kong, with support from abroad. It includes a statement from Occupy Central with Love and Peace (OCLP), saying that none of its members had attended the Oslo Freedom Forum or received 'any specific training' from the organisations men-*

tioned in this report. The amended article also makes clear that Mr Popovic has not had any involvement with the Hong Kong protests."

From that moment on, foreign involvement in Hong Kong protests would be kept under deep cover. Every detail had to be perfect. The word that was repeated continuously was "meticulous".

They hadn't planned on US agents flying to Hong Kong handing out large numbers of placards saying "Defend Our Constitution" when the city doesn't have one.

* * *

Some of the Hong Kong parents had been focusing on the money trail, so let's review that in more detail. The non-secret regular cash payment to Hong Kong activists from NED had grown to about US$640,000 (or HK$5 million) a year. For 2019, that budget was US$642,900.

The secret funds were much larger amounts, with some sources reporting sums in excess of US$2 million (HK$15.6 million).

Could it be argued that these were charitable donations, sent with good intentions?

One could try. But the trouble is this: The most regular complaint is that NED always claimed to support democracy, but actually ended up financing whichever minority groups were perceived to be more friendly to the US and hostile to its enemies—so its actual actions were often the precise opposite of democracy. It's real aim was to bolster the influence of America, which was of course a foreign power, at the expense of relationships with other countries. Sometimes NED cash was switched from one recipient to a rival one, as US agents tried to work out who was most likely to be friendly to America.

Where exactly had the cash sent to Hong Kong gone? NED officials always claimed to have detailed records, but when you traced the cash, it tended to filter down to vaguely named NGOs with titles such as Solidarity Center or to general phrases about NGOs which "advance the cause of democracy".

One source said that HK$82 million had been sent to Hong Kong for funding activists during the past six years in total from NED-related groups. That appeared confirmable: NED's own records showed that it had sent US$22 million (or HK$170 million) to China and or Hong Kong since 2014 to "advance the cause of democracy", that is, to make sure pro-US people were in the ascendancy.

And in truth, 2019 in Hong Kong was a special occasion, so a host of other cash pots had become available in the city, with almost all the traceable ones coming from the United States.

Many seemed to have been steered through the US Agency for Global Media, a very powerful but rather low profile office. This is a wealthy agency which funds Voice of America, Radio Free Asia and other units, which are conspicuous for their repeated reporting on subjects such as the so-called Uyghur "concentration camps" containing three million (or ten million or 12 million) people that has caused so much hatred of China.

Also listed under the control of the same US agency, and involved in the Hong Kong protests, was the Open Technology Fund (OTF). While the OTF presents itself on its website as a non-profit independent organization, its own funding and organizational charts show that it is US government led. We didn't know at the time how much cash was coming from that unit. But OTF cash earmarked for Hong Kong anti-government activists during this period was in the range of several million US dollars, Time magazine would later report. But we did already know at that time that millions of US dollars was spent on protester technology to give anyone who used it power over the police.

The protesters used Signal, developed with OTF cash, plus Telegram, plus other cutting edge apps such as a live map which showed in real time where in Hong Kong police vehicles or police officers were. This app in particular was a lawbreaker's dream.

Separately, a rather more untraceable pot of cash, sometimes known as the "rapid response fund", meant that the hidden committee behind the protests could quickly and easily obtain instant money for any spontaneous civil disobedience event or related need.

No major media outlet from the international press investigated any of these sums, or mentioned them, or acknowledged their existence. On the contrary, they actively pushed the idea that they didn't exist and anyone who said they did was pushing a tired lie. The New York Times said the notion that foreign forces were involved in the protests was "a shopworn canard" originated by the Chinese Communist Party.

One person present at our meeting quoted John Stockwell, a former CIA staffer who wrote about covert international projects in a bestselling book titled In Search of Enemies. In a speech at the time, Stockwell said: "It is the function, I suggest, of the CIA, with its 50 de-stabilization programs going around the world today, to keep the world unstable."

This year, as several parts of planet earth burst into flames, one had to admit: They're good at what they do.

* * *

Moving on: By now, it was well established that a large amount of cash and advice and technological help for the Hong Kong opposition came from the United States government. Who else was involved? What about the Europeans?

Another name that kept coming up was the aforementioned Centre for Applied Nonviolent Action and Strategies, better known as Canvas. It was set up in 2004 by two Serbians, Srda Popovic and Slobodan Dinovic, who had helped to overthrow their country's government, led by Slobodan Milosevic.

Officially, this innocuous sounding organization was non-profit, non-violent and purely educational. Its website makes it sound like an entirely harmless group with a Gandhian hatred of violence and a good sense of humor.

But, just like NED, a look at what they actually did gives a different impression.

Canvas has been linked to numerous government-toppling movements that had been far from peaceful. Staff admit to involvement in more than 50 different countries and territories, and talk about having taken part in the successful overthrow of at least half a dozen governments.

For example, the staff of Canvas admit to playing an important role in Egypt's revolution and a similar coup in Syria. But Egypt ended up with a pair of highly unstable authoritarian governments, and Syria descended into civil war. These were not happy endings for the suffering peoples of those countries.

Canvas has long claimed to be entirely free of involvement with government security forces — but that was shown to be untrue in 2011. That year, the underground hacker group known as Anonymous broke into the computer network of Stratfor, a US geopolitical intelligence platform, and released data it found there to Wikileaks.

Wikileaks revealed email discussions between Canvas leader Srda Popovic and senior Stratfor staff. They clearly had a close relationship. (Stratfor staff attended his wedding.)

Canvas was also widely accused of involvement in the breakdown of society in Venezuela. In 2013, journalists revealed that Canvas received funding from a US ambassador. Ex-US military people were also involved.

Some of the group's critics were blunt about the group's negative role. For example, Saudi Arabia listed it as a terrorist organization.

The Canvas website, interestingly, was later found to include a section promoting the writings and books of a self-claimed Hong Kong local who was widely quoted in the international media.

This man, who gave his name as Kong Tsung-gan, wrote mainly for the anti-government website known as the Hong Kong Free Press, run by a British man named Tom Grundy. It claimed to be funded mostly by donators, but could not release names because of "privacy concerns".

Kong, who claimed to have been born in Hong Kong and educated in a band one (top academic level) school, relentlessly criticized China and constantly pushed Western liberal democracy with a religious fervor. His rather bland articles contained words such as "freedom struggle" multiple times.

Another name that kept coming up was Amnesty International. This group continually misrepresented what was happening in Hong Kong, and it was hard to fathom just how they managed to get the story so twisted — until you realized that it seemed intentional. They were among the sources pushing hardest on the "police brutality" angle.

It was difficult to learn about all the aspects of their involvement, since Amnesty's policy was to use non-local staff to examine issues. Thus their report on Hong Kong was written by staff from the UK.

But there was clear local involvement, too.

To take one example, researcher Laura Ruggeri, a Hong Kong writer and academic, would later reveal that students from the University of Hong Kong were given an all-expenses-paid trip to the UK in 2018. They spent time with an Amnesty International division called the Digital Verification Corps, or DVC.

The students focused on media evidence on two topics: Police brutality and gassed civilians, she said. This turned out to be a fortunate coincidence, because two themes which flooded media coverage of the protests in Hong Kong the following year were, yes, police brutality and gassed civilians.

This is not to say that reporters and foreign correspondents were corrupt or paid to push a certain line. The activists were extremely well trained by the revolution consultants to choose which stories to push that fed into reporters' own prejudices and assumptions.

So the Hong Kong police needed to be painted as a group of ultra-violent Beijing agents despite the fact that they were locals, most of whom had never been anywhere near Beijing, and who had killed fewer protesters (none) than their counterparts in a large number of other protests around the world at the time. And the media was happy to print the oft-reported claims that tear gas caused serious, permanent harm, although the allegation would later prove unfounded.

* * *

While there is no space in this book to do a detailed review of the lessons that pro-revolutionary groups gave to Hong Kong activists, there are several aspects that are worth mentioning.

1) Pro-revolution groups emphasize the need to recognize the police as a key pillar of the government's support—and to do whatever could be done to delegitimize this pillar, removing it entirely if possible by calling for the cutting of police funding or the abolition of the force. Thus the police

needed to be portrayed as faceless agents of evil. Press photographers prefer to limit their coverage of police individuals to helmeted black-clad riot officers, anyway, so they tended to do this without prompting.

2) A key strategy was to get police to admit to sometimes using plainclothes officers (a sign of a good force), and then telling the public that the police had just admitted to having disguised instigators (a sign of a corrupt force) –this was built on the assumption that many members of the public would not know the difference.

3) Radicalized revolutionaries tended to be in their late teens or 20s. But their media agents were advised to create and pass to the press images of any participants who were school children or white-haired older people. This would create the impression that the revolution-hungry minority was actually the full spread of people of all ages. This was easy in Hong Kong in the opening days of the protests but became problematic when the older and younger people left and the ones remained were limited to a small age range, comprising teenagers and people in their 20s.

4) The dispute was presented as "the Hong Kong people against China", instead of the reality, which was that the dispute was between a minority of people who favored independence, against the majority of the Hong Kong people, who wanted a positive relationship with China. (In Hong Kong, the people who wanted independence varied from about 5 percent to 17 percent, fewer than one in five in all surveys, fewer than one in 20 in others.)

5) The pro-revolution groups also recommended a focus on the lethality of the weapons used by the army, with their tanks and machine guns, in

contrast to the innocent protesters' empty hands.

In Hong Kong, this was again a major problem since the army was never called out. The police were left to do the job the army did in other countries. More than 99.999 percent of police activity involved items from the non-lethal armoury: Sponge rounds, tear smoke, bean-bag projectiles and so on.

Bullets were almost never used, and the police had not killed anyone. Instead, the protesters had to find ways to blame the police for deaths by other causes.

Another difficulty was that the most active section of the protesters, the angry anti-immigrant groups, were using weapons that were dangerous and potentially lethal—Molotov cocktails, sharpened metal rods, hammers, slingshots, bricks. It was inevitable that they would kill or seriously injure someone, either on the other side, or on their own side.

Thus the media arm of the revolutionaries in Hong Kong had a tough job ahead of them. They would have to plant and push stories that a police force using tear gas was somehow far worse than army troops using live ammunition, and somehow deserved ten times as many negative headlines.

This was an uphill task, but they managed it. There were easily 20 times as many stories published about police using tear gas in Hong Kong as there were about protests elsewhere in which troops used live guns and multiple protesters died.

Many media outlets picked up the tear gas story and presented a report suggesting that the massive use of tear gas would cause permanent damage to "the people". CNN went to town on the story, discussing deformed babies and generations of harmed people.

The evidence that the allegation was untrue was right on the spot in Hong Kong itself, as mentioned before. One of the biggest uses of tear gas in a small urban area in the world took place in Hong Kong during the 1966-1967 pro-China riots under British rule. Scientists found that there was no lasting damage.

6) As well as recommending that the police should be made the protagonists of each story, advice from some revolution consultants told protesters to remove themselves from all headlines and opening paragraphs if possible. Indeed, they should be completely excised from the entire story.

We'd already seen this process used with great success. In the most commonly printed short versions of what happened on July 21 in Yuen Long, the protesters do not appear at all. The real story, that there was an hours-long fight between black shirt and white shirt factions prepared days in advance, disappeared. The distributed version of the story said simply that police fled from Yuen Long MTR station to allow triads to attack train passengers.

We would see this particular process used again and again in the following weeks.

CHAPTER 24

Violence Comes To North Point

In Which The Narrator Has A Date Night—A Torrid Day—Trapped In A Car—The Difference Between Hong Kong, London and New York

SO MY WIFE AND I decided to have a Date Night. I needed a calm, quiet break after spending a day, Monday, August 5, monitoring the most violent day yet in Hong Kong's insane summer.

Where to go? How about home?

We decided to nip out in the car just to drop our offspring in town to feed and entertain themselves, and then rush home to enjoy peace and quiet and a home-cooked meal, followed by a crossword or a TV detective show. (One of the most important discoveries of adulthood is that the little things in life are actually the big things in life.)

So we jumped in the car, dropped the kids off at various places, and turned around to head home to the quiet suburb of North Point where we live. We decided to stop briefly at shops on Electric Road and then go home via Java Road. Big mistake. We were very soon trapped at a place where bad things were about to happen.

But before sharing that story, I should mention what transpired earlier that day.

Today started with the media reporting that "industrial action" in the shape of a "general strike" was taking place.

This was not true. Stopping work for political reasons doesn't count as a general strike, legally or in any normal definition of the term.

Furthermore, the media were being careful to omit the fact that the people who have stopped work were a small minority—but ruined the plans of the majority.

The people of Hong Kong had not stopped work. What had really happened was that a radical minority had attacked the city's transport system, trying to foul up the MTR, the Light Rail, and the bus system. Their aim was to stop the ordinary citizens going to their offices, schools and factories.

Throughout the morning, arguments broke out on the mass transit railway as radical protesters jammed doors to prevent the trains moving, while people who needed to get places begged them to stop.

"We respect your right to protest; please respect our right to disagree," one passenger pleaded to deaf ears. His plea was surely repeated a hundred times on a hundred different trains.

The miserable commuters who eventually abandoned the blocked trains to search for buses were soon trapped AGAIN—as protesters blocked major roads, roundabouts and tunnels.

Most desperate were the people trying to catch flights: Protesters blocked the sole airport train at one stage. Families trying to reunite, business people trying to close deals, people going on holiday—all were left frustrated, and many were tearful. Many had non-refundable air tickets.

Those who eventually managed to get to the airport, fraught with anxiety and late for their flights, found anger and disruption even inside the main terminal. The misery was both in the departure area and the arrivals section.

People who had just landed at the airport were met with trouble even before they headed unhappily to our crippled transport system.

Radical protesters assembled in the arrivals hall and "welcomed" tourists with cries of "Go home! It's not safe here!"

The protesters forgot to mention that their actions were the reason why Hong Kong was no longer safe.

One observer told me she saw two or three tourists, taken in by the international media presentation of Hong Kong's story as one of hero teens fighting Nazi-like monsters, gave a thumbs-up to the protesters, getting a cheer in return.

But these were few and far between. The majority of tourists kept their heads down and tried to get through as fast as they could.

Children hid behind their mothers' legs, and some tourists emerged from the airside area only to turn around and walk straight back to the customs area.

* * *

It was a ghastly day for Hong Kong—and the peaceful protesters suffered the most, our reputations torn to shreds by our radical brethren as violence spread.

As evening fell, things got worse.

One gang of hardline protesters surrounded the family homes of police in Tuen Mun, shouting abuse and shining laser beams through apartment windows in the hope of harming residents' eyes.

In Central, at about 7.30 pm, protesters ripped down China's flag and threw it in the sea, raising a black flag saying "Independent Hong Kong".

* * *

It was a grim day for reporters covering the mayhem, so for this journalist, an evening thinking about something else was much needed.

Just five minutes' drive from home, the traffic stopped moving. We were trapped in our car.

A block or two ahead of us, radical protesters surrounded an entire block in North Point. Beyond that, they were showering police with glass bottles.

Angry high-rise residents leaned out of their windows to complain (and occasionally drop water).

Protesters responded by trying to shine laser beams up into the eyes of residents looking down from their flats.

At that moment, I was not sure if all these protesters were aware that North Point was also a popular residential area for triad members, people who are never happy about OTHER people behaving badly on their turf.

"Hey! That's OUR job," is their normal reaction to such events.

As we waited and watched (not having a choice), a few of these somewhat scary residents eventually came downstairs and moved onto the streets to "comment" on proceedings.

The result was very unpleasant indeed. The two groups started hitting each other with sticks and other objects. This time, the white shirts were in small enough numbers for the black-clad protesters to face them down and even have the upper hand.

After a brawl, one group of North Point residents ran into a building and up the stairs into a flat.

The black-shirt protesters assembled outside, throwing projectiles through the windows, showering glass onto themselves.

What was happening to my neighborhood?

After our cars were stuck for more than an hour, tempers started to fray. A short distance ahead, one driver right at the front lost his temper completely and tried to steer his car through the barricade the radical protesters had set up.

He was instantly surrounded by a black-dressed crowd who punched him and smashed his windscreen. I waited and prayed for the fabled nice one to appear, and he did—a young man in black approached his comrades beating the driver and intervened, bringing the violence to an end.

As for us, a slight loosening of the gridlock after 80 minutes gave us the opportunity we needed. We manage to get away when my wife, who had the wheel, turned the car 180 degrees and sped off, driving the wrong way down a one-way three-lane road in classic Hollywood style.

I should add: she is normally an EXCESSIVELY law-abiding driver, obeying all known laws and making up extra ones, but these days one sometimes has to do this sort of thing.

Finally reaching home, I logged on to the Internet (date night abandoned) to talk to people on my network, mothers and fathers scattered around Hong Kong, augmented now by literally thousands of ex-protesters.

I learned that hundreds of radical protesters had gathered outside the family quarters of disciplined services staff in Wong Tai Sin. They had been throwing bricks into the homes, smashing the windows, and terrifying children and other people inside.

Protesters then set fire to a tree which bordered the building.

In front of the building, they wrote "Wives and children of police must die".

From my inbox, I can see that the withdrawal of support is turning into an exodus.

The pandem leaders and pro-independence leaders are not condemning what is going on at all—and honest, peaceful protesters of Hong Kong see this and are dismayed. Western reporters omit these elements from their stories, keeping their readers' sympathies with the violent radicals, and focusing their readers' anger on the victims.

My screen is filled with notes from people who are passionately pro-democracy but are horrified by what is happening. This is surely by far the biggest group of political people in Hong Kong by now, but most international correspondents won't even acknowledge their existence.

Even some of the most passionate pro-democracy individuals writing to me are calling for firmer action by the police—or even the PLA.

"Let's not go that far," I write to one of them.

Late that night, mentally reviewing the events of the day, I realized that something else needed to be said.

The ordinary working Hong Kong people were hit by astonishing amounts of undeserved provocation all day today (or yesterday, as I am writing this past midnight), from the moment they tried to get to school or work in the morning, to the moment they got home at night.

Yet I saw very few violent responses, even from the many who disagreed entirely with the protesters' politics—and that means the ex-protesters, the so-called blue camp, and Hong Kong's majority group, the apoliticals.

The vast majority of Hong Kong people just put up with the trouble without fisticuffs. They sighed, they glared, they shook their heads disapprovingly—but they didn't hit out. In most cases, they quietly left their blocked buses and patiently went to look for other ways to get to where they were going. Their restraint should be recognized.

It was actually really impressive. If protesters built random barricades across roads in New York or London, I'm telling you, there would be NO POLICE NECESSARY. (I have brothers in both cities.)

Residents of those cities would just roll up their sleeves, remove the barricades, and give everyone nearby a solid kicking for good measure. You lookin' at me, punk?

* * *

Days later, it seemed as if we were in some sort of time loop when it came to confrontations between white shirt factions and black shirt factions.

It was time for history to repeat itself—but this time on my home patch. The next day, the radicals announced that they were going to "Reclaim North Point" from "the gangsters". And again, it was going to be on a Sunday night. The black-clad protesters had tangled with the white shirts on Monday, August 5, and now are going to use their strength of numbers to get "revenge" on Sunday, August 11. So far, so similar.

But there were marked differences between the two events.

While the radical protesters beloved by Western media were pushing the message that wives and children of police officers must die, the joint Fujianese clans of Hong Kong put out a message of peace.

Ng Woon-him, head of the Hong Kong Federation of Fujian Associations, called a meeting of all clans (there are more than 240 of them) on Saturday, August 10 to agree on their response plan for the arrival of radical protesters in their territory.

The plan was literally "to stay home and have a cup of tea". The theme of the mass social gathering on that day was: "Stopping violence, opposing independence and protecting our home".

Confrontation, violence, vandalism and arson were not characteristic of Hong Kong, they said, and were not what the Hong Kong people wanted.

The Fujianese clans would hold their ground in their home territory but refuse to initiate any violence of any kind. They wanted to make it clear that they would not be the cause of trouble in Hong Kong.

This was greeted by immense skepticism in the hostile sections of the local press, of course. It was unthinkable that immigrants should have any kind of moral superiority over the "indigenous" Hong Kong people.

But before that could happen, another incident from this city grabbed the world's attention.

CHAPTER 25

How Not To Reclaim North Point

In Which A Woman Doesn't Lose An Eye—
A Showdown Is Planned—Last Minute Change Of Plan

THIS WAS ONE OF the nastiest injuries yet. On Sunday, August 11, shocking news went out around the world about a protester whose eye was "shot out by police".

The write-ups said she was standing among protesters on Nathan Road near the Tsim Sha Tsui police station when a police projectile destroyed her right eye.

The "lost eye woman" (who did not give her name to the media) quickly became "a symbol of the protests" in numerous write-ups, since her shocking case appeared to represent goodness and innocence against brutality.

"Hong Kong protests get figurehead in woman injured by police," said the UK's Guardian.

The story seemed to be featured in every major media outlet on the planet. To make her even more sympathetic, it was reported that she was not a protester at all, but a "volunteer medic".

TV news reporters in the US covered one eye with a hand in "solidarity" after reporting the story. Numerous images of Hong Kong protesters with a single eye covered to support her appeared everywhere.

But later in the month, the case started to unravel.

First, there were indications from doctors and nurses that she hadn't lost her eye at all, but had quickly recovered.

The report was pointedly NOT denied by either the woman or her lawyers although one would have expected them to do so immediately.

Nor was there any clear evidence that she had been a medic, but may well have been simply besieging and attacking the police station with her fellows.

Most damningly, it also became increasingly clear that the harm may not have come from a police bean bag at all, but from a protester's pellet. The revised story said that she was really a radical protester on the attack when she was accidentally shot by someone on her own side.

The photos from the scene were carefully re-examined. They showed a pair of bloodstained safety goggles with a police beanbag round embedded in it, but it was odd; the beanbag was strangely free of blood, as if it had been inserted later. Furthermore, it was caught by the safety goggles, held away from the eyeball.

All sides called for a full investigation—because they knew the doctors would undoubtedly be able to give the real story.

But the doctors were silent and the woman disappeared. When a press conference was held, there was some puzzlement – some said the woman who appeared (but let others do most of the talking) wasn't the victim but an unknown person.

The entire community, peaceful protesters at the forefront, continued to demand an investigation but the woman worked really hard to prevent this from occurring, which seemed illogical. Surely she should be demanding an investigation, not preventing one?

What really happened? It became obvious that whoever was organizing the protests saw the stories being distributed about the woman as hugely advantageous to their cause and pulled out all the stops to make sure no other version of the story (such as what really happened) leaked out.

Police eventually used a warrant to get the medical reports.

The story became more bizarre. High-powered lawyers quickly appeared, who filed briefs preventing officers from looking at them! Why were they doing this? And who was paying for this?

The police could easily have leaked them to the media, of course, but chose not to.

Of course, the media version that had gone out worldwide was the tale that evil police blinded an innocent young woman, and the press showed no interest in the follow-up stories that debunked the entire story.

The secretive committee managing the story of the Hong Kong protests had pulled off another brilliant coup.

(Sadly, in a clash the following month, a woman really would lose one eye to a rubber bullet fired by a police officer. Indonesian journalist Veby Mega Indah, 39, the associate editor of Suara Hong Kong News, was hit on the forehead by a bullet on September 29, the force of which ruptured an eyeball beyond repair. Ironically, this genuine case got a fraction of the coverage of the earlier, discredited story. The foreign correspondent's tale did not fit the required media narrative of police brutalizing an innocent Hong Kong protester.)

* * *

But we've got ahead of ourselves. We need to go back to Sunday, August 11.

Ding! A Hong Kong government press release arrived on my phone that day, about unsafe waves: *"Red Flags Hoisted at Several Beaches."*

By coincidence I read the note while driving through King's Road in North Point—and men were hoisting red flags there, too. (But those had little yellow stars.)

If you highlight the words "red flag" on your phone, the built-in dictionary helpfully explains: "A sign of danger."

It was all rather prophetic about what was going to happen later that day, it turned out.

* * *

It's Sunday evening—time for the final showdown between the white shirts and the black shirts. I'm using technology to discuss details with members of my network, in preparation for the Reclaim North Point confrontation tonight.

As far as we can tell, the North Point triad society is nothing like the Yuen Long equivalent, and certainly very unlike the famous triad groups, such as the Sun Yee On and the 14k.

For a start, our local secret society is not very secret at all. Everyone knows about it. This group is mostly a middle aged or elderly cluster of people united by having roots in Fujian province. They are not known for violence (quite the opposite), but are largely a social group, with particular restaurants where they have regular meetings.

But, like other triad groups, they do have an "emergency response" mode.

Again, to understand them, you have to realize that it's all about territory. If their turf is invaded by troublemakers of any kind, they will send out messages to the males in the group, who will gather at the Foo Lam Restaurant on King's Road, North Point. They don't have guns or knives, but some of them are large, tough, dangerous men.

Yet one has to be honest, most are rather short and past their prime. And the leaders of the Fujianese community yesterday firmly called for zero initiation of any trouble—they were determined to be "the source of peace, not the source of trouble". It sounded very noble, but I still remained worried. There were more than a few hard-looking men who could definitely do some harm.

The media has dubbed them "white shirts", but actually their official color was red, and most of them wear standard civilian clothes most of the time.

* * *

Night has fallen. My wife used her car to drop me close to the center of the action on King's Road, in my usual fade-into-the-background gear: black t-shirt, dark trousers, camera, and my fastest running shoes.

I quietly walk to the center of the area as she drives away.

And then I notice people are giving me the evil eye. Why should this be?

A thought strikes me. What an idiot I am. At that moment I realize that I had chosen the WORST OUTFIT POSSIBLE. I looked like black-clad radical protester.

Once I had worked out the geography of the battle area, I realized that I was in the middle of a large police cordon in North Point, designed specifically to keep black shirts out.

And I was the ONLY person inside the cordon dressed all in black—so I was quickly attracting hostile looks.

Backing away, I scanned the high street to look for a clothes shop—but they had all been shuttered in anticipation of the biggest black-shirts versus white-shirts battle ever. One man suspiciously pointed me out to his friends, and I was soon rapidly moving away. As soon as I could, I broke into a trot.

But where to go? Behind me were the white shirts, and ahead of me was a cordon of riot police.

Quick geography lesson: The black-clad radicals, that is, people dressed like me, were in Causeway Bay and Quarry Bay. Between those two areas were Tin Hau, Fortress Hill, and North Point. That's where the white-clads were. (Plus me.)

I needed to urgently find a non-black outfit — preferably white or red. But where to go? All the shops had closed early (who could blame them?). I even stooped to picking through alleyway garbage bins (a smelly and unpleasant job) in the hope of finding discarded garments, but there were none.

I stopped running when I eventually found an open supermarket. It was a small branch of Wellcome Supermarket. "Any clothes?" I asked.

Staff, trying to help, pointed me to the only garments they had: A rack of "disposable ladies' panties". Aiyeeah!

In the end, I remembered that the t-shirt I was wearing had some sort of logo on the back. So I slipped off my top and put it on back to front so there was a random picture on my chest. Then I bought some shopping in a supermarket bag.

Now I looked like some ditzy old brown guy who'd gone shopping and had accidentally wandered into a war zone. (The cap did kind of fit.)

Conspiracy theorists and the Apple Daily newspaper had warned that the fight could be horrendous: Large squads of trained "red shirt" gangsters had been secretly sent from mainland China to protect residents and fight protesters, the reports said.

What a load of bollards. In truth, the residents on the street consisted of a motley crew of a few hundred middle-aged people.

There were a few dressed in traditional Fujianese red shirts, and a few beefy males in the white shirts that some triads had adopted recently—but the vast majority were normal people in ordinary clothes (high fashion in North Point is to wear a knock-off Polo shirt rolled up to the manboobs to allow breezes to cool the beer belly). Quite a few were women and old people.

This writer has lived in different parts of this area for many years, so sees these residents regularly. I would say that a few are borderline scary, but in general, they are not the Sopranos.

By 7.28 pm, everyone in North Point was ready and waiting for the Great Black Shirt Versus White Shirt Showdown to begin.

But where were the radical protesters?

Residents, police and reporters were plugged in via digital information streams to follow what was happening elsewhere in Hong Kong, so we had plenty of sources to check.

First surprise: We learned that numbers of the black clad radicals seemed to have collapsed again. Reports were soon coming through that the biggest groups roaming tonight were only about 800 to 900, and the smaller ones were about 200, with some just clusters of 50 or fewer.

When black shirts confronted triads in Yuen Long, they claimed to be a group of almost a quarter of a million people. How had 99 percent of their supporters disappeared? Part of the answer is that none of the numbers you read in the press were ever true. But still, the number of black-clads was unusually small.

Second surprise: At about 8.41 pm, we heard that an argument blew up between the remaining protesters at Causeway Bay station. They no longer outnumbered police by a big enough margin to feel confident.

The heated debate lasted several minutes and eventually caused them to worsen their problems by splitting into different groups.

One group, we heard, was heading directly to North Point. To us! Finally, Monochrome T-shirt Armageddon was about to start. It was now about 9.20 pm. The serious photographers changed their camera batteries.

The senior police officers at the scene received information on a headset and decided to shift the residents another block away from the North Point MTR station for safety's sake. By this time, residents and police were getting on surprisingly well—after all, they both felt unjustly maligned by both protesters and the media, who they believed, pretty accurately, were all firmly on the side of the people causing the trouble.

Police didn't use loudhailers but just called out instructions: "Move further down. Walk to your left."

Residents immediately started shuffling along, calling out to each other: "They want us to move, let's move, people."

The police commander looked stunned—after nine weeks when calls for movement or dispersal led to flying bricks or petrol bombs, the instant obedience was a surprise—especially from a group assumed to be on the criminal end of the spectrum.

Still, officers, mindful of the conspiracy theory that the police itself was a unit operated by triads, made an effort to remain brusque and hostile.

Policemen roughly discouraged residents from waving China flags, and had earlier detained two people who threatened reporters.

As North Point residents moved, they started chanting *"Ging chat ga yau! Ging chat ga yau!"* ("Power to the police!" "Power to the police!").

I had to laugh. This was NEVER going to be covered in the media, I said to myself: A large group of triads cheering police officers who had arrested two of their members. It was just all too complex for nuance-hating reporters.

A police cameraman arrived and painstakingly walked along the street, focusing on the crowd. His aim seemed to be to get pictures of every face, so that there would be records of all the North Point society members. This reporter's face was recorded among them.

Third surprise: The black shirts finally arrived. At 9.39 pm, their train pulled into North Point station. Anticipation ran high.

But nothing happened. Not one person in black came up the stairs from the station entrance.

Eventually, news from reporters travelling with them revealed what the problem was. After being told that police and North Point residents were waiting upstairs on King's Road, the group of about 50 decided to get back on the train.

We surmised that they were going to join a bigger group of protesters at the next stop, Quarry Bay station, and then double back to North Point.

But that didn't happen either.

After waiting even longer, we were told that protesters were arguing again, the digital info channels told us.

A South China Morning Post reporter put one protester's words on the Internet: "The police are everywhere and we are being chased here and there on the MTR. This is crazy. Police are spreading our manpower so thin. I say we just go up to the exit and fight them directly, once and for all."

By 10.05 pm, it was becoming clear that protesters did not want to fight North Point residents, preferring to fight the police instead.

The youths clad in black went back to the train platforms and went further east, and ended up engaging in small skirmishes with police in Taikoo Shing and Sai Wan Ho.

At 10.14 pm, police apparently received intelligence from plainclothes officers secreted among or near the protesters.

Nobody wanted to go to North Point to fight the gangsters.

Officers told the residents that they may as well go home now. The Monochrome Battle of North Point was not going to happen, thank God.

Residents started to disperse. *"Ging chat ga yau! Ging chat ga yau!"* the residents chorused again as they marched away, laughing.

Police officers, who had removed their helmets by this time, desperately struggled not to smile.

I walked back towards Causeway Bay, deep in thought. Nothing is ever what it seems here.

Behind me, police officers stared, shaking their heads in wonder.

* * *

Later, Tom Guendert, a New Yorker living in Wan Chai, shared a fascinating observation about the way young people in this part of the world were behaving in two different ways.

Mainland youths were dressing in Zara, eating at McDonald's, and setting up start-ups.

Hong Kong youths were marching in black "uniforms", denouncing anyone who isn't a loyalist, and following Joshua Wong, that self-proclaimed fighter against "capitalist hegemony".

Tom asked: "So which looks like free market capitalism and which looks like new communism?"

He made me laugh. But he was dead right—the increasingly small number of young people who were still protesting in my circles came across as organized radical socialists, while the mainland students in my classes were definitely capitalist entrepreneurs, with several of them literally running start-ups while still at university. The world changes quietly and few people notice.

* * *

Reader Joseph Chin arrived late for his latte one morning in mid-August. He told me that he had recently flown back to Hong Kong from a conference overseas. As he emerged into the arrivals hall at the Hong Kong International Airport, he was greeted by a group of radical protesters with big X-shapes taped over their mouths.

"What does that signify?" he asked them.

"It's because we have been silenced," came a reply from their (untaped) spokeswoman.

Joe said to me with a wry smile: "They're been on every newspaper, TV station and news website for two months. Interesting definition of 'silenced'."

It was the opposite of the truth to say that Hong Kong had silenced them. But of course, the secretive committee running the PR for the protests was genius at this kind of thing.

These mystery people were playing the biggest media in the world, using them as tools. They knew a young pretty face with an X over it makes for an irresistible photograph for the international media if it comes with an implicit criticism of China.

Two days later, I made a point of crossing the coffee shop to talk to a group of students who I know have been fiercely anti-government for years.

In the discussion, I quickly noticed that the most penetrating criticism of the continuing disruptive events didn't come from any "pro-Beijing" people but from disillusioned ex-protesters.

The violence felt alien to them.

I responded that I felt the same. I tried to spread some tolerance: "To revise a cliché, if you're 20 and you're NOT out on the street stirring things up to call for more democracy, there might be something wrong with your heart," I said. "But if you're STILL out on the street stirring things up when the conversation is being conducted with petrol bombs and bricks, there might be something wrong with your head."

One of the students, a girl called Jenny, nodded. She clearly knew many who fitted that description.

It was clear then that the young people of Hong Kong are NOT the problem, not at all. The radicalization of a very small minority by people behind the scenes was the problem.

In the afternoon, I received reports that backed up Tom Guendert's observation about curious parallels.

China border officials were picking Hong Kong people dressed in black out of immigration lines and forcibly checking photographs on their phones.

Hong Kong hardline protesters were picking people NOT dressed in black out of lines of observers and forcibly checking photographs on their phones.

At least it was balanced!

On a related issue: The present writer has an otaku son at home with an entirely black wardrobe, who now feels obliged to wear horribly bright, garish colors—such as dark grey, so as not to be mistaken for a violent radical.

He feels hard done by.

CHAPTER 26

Chopping Down A Lamppost

In Which The Family Goes On An Outing—Mourning Lampposts

EVEN IF YOU FEEL you are living in a war zone, you have to keep normal life going, right? Especially if you have children. So this author was taking his family on an outing to see the Studio Ghibli exhibition in Kowloon Bay. It was Saturday, August 24, a bright, sunny morning. Like so many young people today, my son is fascinated by Japanese entertainment, and so we were off to see a show featuring animation.

He was guiding us by looking at Google Maps on his phone.

Suddenly his expression changed to one of puzzlement. "What's this?" he asked. The road ahead was blocked, according to the map, with a floating "no entry" icon.

And so was the next one. As he watched, a whole series of red icons popped up on the screen. Yikes!

The area ahead was suddenly covered with tiny red No Entry signs—and showed numerous blocked streets. We'd never seen this before on Google Maps.

"Protesters?" he guessed.

We slowed the car and soon discovered that he was right.

On the pavement next to us, we saw running young men in black, their heads and faces covered.

It quickly became evident that radical protesters were in a riotous mood, lighting fires and throwing bricks and petrol bombs in Kowloon Bay.

We quickly made a plan: At the next opportunity, the car would pause long enough for me to jump out and continue in the direction of the trouble, while wife and children would turn off onto a side road, hoping to meet up later.

Thanks for the heads-up, Google Maps.

Five minutes later, I had travelled on foot to the heart of the trouble. I noted that protesters had a new target: They were killing the area's Smart Lampposts. One had been toppled as if it was a large tree. This was quite impressive, since they were tall, metal objects. Someone had sliced through steel. This must have taken a lot of planning, plus the obtaining of special equipment.

It fell rather suddenly, and narrowly missed killing one of the protesters.

With green, leaf-shaped metal tops, the lampposts were designed to turn Hong Kong into a "smart city" by giving out 5G signals and providing data to kill traffic jams and boost anti-pollution measures.

But this morning, 20 of them, worth millions of dollars, were being systematically destroyed, mostly by having their innards pulled out. (This was quicker than toppling them.)

I found myself standing over one. I knew it wasn't a real tree, but I still felt like waiting reverently by its corpse for a moment to mourn it.

Around the corner, groups of protesters were ripping out other smart lampposts' entrails, proudly announcing to the others that some of the stuff inside was "Made in China"!

Ah ha! That PROVED it was evil!

Guys, pretty much EVERYTHING is made in China these days. (I didn't say that out loud. I'm not completely crazy.)

As the spouse of a motorist, I shared the general hostility to the lampposts because of the way they over-policed drivers, but I had to admit that they were probably not the robotic communist spies that the radicals were saying they were. If the lampposts had a birthplace, it would be in the offices of Hong Kong people working at the universities and at Science Park in Tai Po.

I looked at my phone screen and saw that on the Internet, people were already blaming "police disguised as protesters" for the destruction of the lampposts.

But I was physically standing with police and reporters as I read that, and I knew it wasn't true.

It struck me that if your main information source was Twitter or LIHKG or if you followed biased propaganda outlets such as, well, CNN or the Wall Street Journal or pretty much all the media sources out there, you could genuinely accept Transmogrification Theory as true. At a wave of a magic wand, a respected Cantonese-speaking police forced had instantly turned into a group of Mandarin-speaking murderers.

But when you were actually there on the spot, the theory was laughable. You could differentiate the groups easily. They talked differently, they walked differently, they dressed differently: They were like chalk and oranges.

Consider the cast members in this little drama in front of me.

At the center of the action we had the active radicals. They're serious people, covered in ISIS-style black from head-to-toe, fully masked, and equipped with bags of tools to hurt people and create destruction. They are extremely organized, informed, financed and digitally connected. They were able to dismantle railings, undo bolts, break through gates, and so on, at high speed. They told you they were "leaderless" so frequently that it became obvious that this was an instruction from their leader.

The second circle consisted of the close supporters. They were mostly reduced these days to being umbrella wielders, whose job it was to shield the law-breakers from people using cameras.

There was also often an outer circle of general supporters who stood at a wider distance. These were the inbetweenies, who were radicalized enough to generally support the vandalism, but who were perhaps too squeamish or law-abiding to get involved themselves.

There was always the nice one, who watches for members of the public (but not the police) being beaten up and rushes to try to stop the violence. This layer often included a cluster of Christians, looking worried about the vandalism, but unable to do anything about it.

Further out, there were the "medics", a dozen or so young people with first aid bags. Some of these seemed to have had a little experience in first aid, while others seemed to have none at all.

When you talked to the "medics", you found that they often genuinely wanted to help. When actually needed, their efforts tended to be rather rudimentary—often amounting to little more than providing Band-Aids and basic disinfectant. In practice, their main function, it seemed, was not so much medical as cosmetic: Because they were embedded with the gangs committing the vandalism or beating up mainlanders, they almost always got to the wounded people first.

The Western media loved to feature them, as they gave substance to their Hero Teens narrative. They filmed these young people offering to bandage the wounds of the people who their colleagues have beaten up — and then stopped filming as real emergency workers (nurses, ambulance staff, police officers, fire fighters) arrived on the scene seconds later to do the real work of setting broken bones or taking people to hospital.

And if one of the amateur "medics" was ever arrested, reporters could report a fresh outrage: Now the police were grabbing "doctors and nurses".

In corners and alleyways, watching from a distance, were mysterious individuals who seemed to do nothing but make endless phone calls. These were the paymasters—the connection between the radicals committing the crimes and the committee pulling the strings.

And of course, at the outside circle of the events, usually standing some distance away, were the police officers. They were generally taller, stockier, and moved more slowly—watching, waiting, talking with each other, or using their communications equipment.

The media tends to take pictures only of the police officers who look most faceless, males in full riot gear. But this was summer in Hong Kong. Most police were lightly dressed. Some wore light blue shirts, and several wore a sort of t-shirt and vest combination. There were several young female officers present. These were almost never shown in the Western media.

Today, as usual, police were on maximum restraint, which meant they were not interfering unless lives were in danger.

It was interesting. You'd think that in a place like Hong Kong, painted as a soulless commercial town, people would value property more than lives, especially multi-million dollar scientific constructions.

But Hong Kong police action consistently indicated the opposite. They repeatedly showed themselves to be reluctant to curtail protesters' activities until there was serious danger of people being hurt.

Next to me were a pair of reporters from the Wall Street Journal. They surprised me. I worked for that group for 11 years, and their journalists had tended to be older people with a long history of covering Asia, and a tendency to identify with Asian communities.

But these reporters looked to be in their 20s, and in conversation they come across as strongly supporting the radicals and their "fight against the communists". They worried me. Neither the police nor the Hong Kong civil service could accurately be described as communists in any way. People using the word in this way sent up instant warning signals.

* * *

My sources among the protesters told me that their main target on Saturday morning this week was tourists arriving at the airport. But so few protesters turned up at the meeting point that the whole plan was postponed until the following weekend.

Looking over video clips, I could see that the roaming groups at the weekend were just a few hundred strong. Even the previous Sunday's "big" march was clearly far smaller than the earlier ones (notwithstanding the organizer's "estimate").

But there was bad news too.

Since "good" protesters were abandoning the hardliners, the violence level was rising: 15 police were hospitalized on Sunday alone, and shops and a Cross Harbour Tunnel toll booth were badly vandalized.

That evening, we had a joint Internet chat between ex-protesters plus Hong Kong moms and dads—and we tried to guess how the Western media would report that excessively violent incident, and guessed they would find a way to point the finger at police with something like: "Hong Kong Police Firing Tear Gas at Protesters Again".

The actual BBC headline the next morning was "Hong Kong Police Fire Tear Gas at Protesters in Fresh Clashes".

We were sooooo close.

Later, reader Billy Leung wrote to me saying that he too had been caught up in the problems in the lamppost testing area at the same time that my family had been.

"I took the family to Megabox last Saturday morning not knowing that we were actually part of the war zone," he wrote. "Luckily we left before the protesters pretending to be rioters/rioters pretending to be protesters/police pretending to be protesters/rioters pretending to be whatever arrived."

Ten Telling Anecdotes At August's End

1) It's August 28 and youngsters are in a state of shock. Jackson Wang, the impossibly perfect Hong Kong-born K-pop star has suddenly dropped off the map.

Twitter was yesterday buzzing with the news that protesters had found his family address and posted it on a black shirts forum.

The singer has been receiving threats after he expressed regret that the protesters had chosen to trash China's flag. It isn't that he was particularly "pro-Beijing", but just that he was a polite young man who doesn't believe that any country's flag should be desecrated in public. Still, the punishment was severe. Jackson's recent US gig was cancelled, and his band, Got7, had to abandon plans to play two concerts in Hong Kong this coming weekend. "Thank you for cancelling," worried fans wrote beneath the Internet announcement, fearful of the safety of the whole group of impossibly perfect looking boy singers.

But there was no sympathy from black-clad radical protesters, who added comments to Internet discussions with a dark, threatening tone: "The time has come for Got7 to become Got6."

It feels wrong to brand Wang as being anti-Hong Kong. He has always been Hong Kong's biggest booster on the celebrity circuit, wearing our 852 area code on his clothes and carrying an SAR flag.

Still, I find it REALLY HARD to feel sorry for someone that handsome.

2) Reader Gopi Maliwal was happy to read that Twitter had cancelled the accounts of automated "bots" distorting discussion of Hong Kong protests.

Until he discovered that his own account was among the frozen ones.

"But I'm not a bot," he complained. He told me he had been sending out tweets "against anarchism and one-sided media coverage."

Twitter responded by making the imbalance worse, silencing one of the few voices offering balance.

3) It was no surprise that radical protesters chose to focus on To Kwa Wan on Saturday: That's the district where mainland China tourists like to disembark.

Blasted tourists! They come here and support our retailers and pump billions of dollars into our economy.

It's disgusting. We won't stand for it any more!

4) Protesters tried to cause an economic crisis in Hong Kong by calling on everyone to withdraw all their money in cash this weekend.

"It was a cunning plan," said a banker named J. Chiu who works at the ICC building in West Kowloon.

"Except for the fact that they tried to do it by ATM, as if all the cash machines were connected by tubes to a huge underground bunker where all Hong Kong's money was kept."

It doesn't work like that. The attack had no effect.

5) Hong Kong MTR staff became targets for protesters at the weekend.

Posters denouncing the MTR as "the Railway of the Communist Party" were put up at stations—and some said they'd attack the MTR HQ today.

If the MTR really was a communist train it would take hours to get anywhere. Actually these days it often does, thanks to people in black standing in train doorways, preventing them from closing.

6) Which reminds me:

Conversation I once had with an ACTUAL communist official.

Him: "Can I be honest?"

Me: "I doubt it."

7) A reader who witnessed the brick-hurling in Mong Kok on Saturday, August 17, was handed a leaflet of "five demands" as he ran to safety. "They are LITERALLY rioting to protest against being defined as rioters," he said, amazed. "You can't make this stuff up."

8) I'm writing this note on August 30. On this date, the Hong Kong government announced that it is setting up four giant inflatable rabbits at the Kowloon waterfront as mid-Autumn festival approaches.

Giant inflatable rabbits! Be still, my beating heart.

Now we must all stop saying that our government is doing nothing.

9) This is a REAL conversation overheard between people pushing wheelchairs and protesters blocking Hong Kong Airport by a father of two girls on my network.

"Please allow these elderly people in wheelchairs to come through."

"Where are they from?"

"Australia."

"No. If they were Americans, we'd let them through. The Americans will save us."

Wicked thought: One side was disappointed, and the other side is going to be severely disappointed later.

10) Pro-Trump reporter Emerald Robinson wrote on Twitter yesterday:

"Capital flight from Hong Kong has reached over US$1 billion per day: Trump is winning the trade war with China!"

Hong Kong protesters on Twitter celebrated, sending the love right back, showing pictures of their Trumpian banner saying *"Make Hong Kong Great Again."*

How can losing a billion greenbacks a day make Hong Kong great?

Rationality is officially dead.

But the discussion is also yet another slice of evidence that some people behind the protests are not even disguising the fact that they are actually anti-Hong Kong and pro-USA.

Know this for sure: The secret organizing committee is not fighting to save Hong Kong, but to destroy it.

CHAPTER 27

Mayhem Comes To Causeway Bay

In Which A Mob Comes To Our Neighborhood—Frightening Altercations—One Man Starts To Clear The Road

WHAT DO NORMAL people do on Saturday nights?

I no longer know. I live in Hong Kong, and on this Saturday night, August 31, I was watching a group of about 220 masked people swarm into Causeway Bay.

Many carried sticks as weapons, while others periodically lit fires in the middle of the street. This has become our new normal.

This reporter was standing with a group of local residents opposite St Paul's Convent School on Irving Street.

Right in front of us, a frightening group of masked men descended on the steel safety railings and started yanking them out of the ground with special tools.

From our ranks, one incredibly brave middle-aged local woman ran up to them and put her hands firmly on the railings. "What are you doing?" she said. "You can't do that."

You know how when someone does something brave, you can sort of suck up some of the sudden outflow of courage yourself? I ran up and stood next to her. I also lifted my camera to document what was happening.

The reaction was instant. Someone shouted "trouble" and a large angry group of people turned in our direction.

A group of men were looking at the woman and at me—and then moving swiftly towards us.

Uh-oh. Not again.

* * *

The latest weekend mega rally took place this Saturday. Numbers, by Hong Kong standards, were small.

The main mass was a group of a few thousand people in Central, and several hundred in Tsim Sha Tsui. Elsewhere, other groups, so small you could just stand there and count the individuals, randomly blocked roads.

I counted just about 220 protesters in Causeway Bay, and there was a smaller group in the next district, North Point. (For comparison: a single Hong Kong housing estate such as Tai Koo Shing on our side of the city houses SIXTY THOUSAND people. In this city, 220 people is just a Hung Hom station bus queue.)

Even the mid-August "mega rally" was far smaller than the earlier ones (despite the organizers' claims of "more than a million").

The disappearance of the peaceful protesters is becoming impossible to hide. Last week's airport attack was postponed because so few protesters turned up.

Yesterday's Tin Shui Wai protest was called off too. Numbers are falling fast. The radical movement is shrinking. The people of Hong Kong are voting with their feet. I'm going to win my bet. Numbers will be below 2,000 by December.

* * *

That night in Causeway Bay, a frightening crowd was on the complaining woman and myself in seconds.

A group of young women physically took hold of the brave middle-aged woman by the shoulders and gently but firmly moved her up against a wall, explaining that the men need to steal the railings for important reasons.

A group of young men forced me to turn my camera off and keep it lowered. The woman trying to stop the vandalism argued back. You can see why. The safety railings were important—Irving Street is a busy, dangerous, five-way junction next to a school, and the children's autumn term started in just 36 hours.

But confronting the protesters was very dangerous.

Some of the men were furious at the woman, screaming at her, trying to reach her, wanting to hurt her.

One of the men was shouting "Chinazi" at her, and he was spitting with fury, his fists clenched. Women protesters struggled to hold him and his violent companions away from us. They succeeded—this time.

But this was a genuinely scary moment—those young men would have physically attacked the innocent woman had they not been stopped, and probably me too.

Group beatings of individuals who are perceived as unsupportive individuals happen regularly.

In minutes, it was over. All the safety railings were gone, and were quickly turned into a barricade in the middle of the road. The woman and I were released. But the public and the motorists had fled. By that time, there was only one vehicle to block.

It was a fire engine, lights flashing, which had turned up to try to put out a fire that the protesters had started.

* * *

And how was the media covering the nightmare that was unfolding in our district?

It wasn't covering it at all. It was busy making our problems worse.

On our phone screens, the media reported that the big story was that "Hong Kong's pro-democracy leaders" had been charged with crimes.

The BBC report, just like most media, referred to Joshua Wong, Agnes Chow and Andy Chan.

I saw not a single report which mentioned that all three of these individuals were openly campaigning for independence against the wishes of the Hong Kong people. How that qualifies as "pro-democracy", I have no idea.

Standing there with other residents, I found myself wishing we had the BBC and the New York Times and the Wall Street Journal reporters in front of me, so that we could ask a simple question: You continually tell the world that Andy Chan is a democracy campaigner—but isn't democracy listening to the majority rather than a tiny minority? Andy Chan was clearly one of the least democratic people in the city.

But someone started to shout and my attention returned to the scene in front of me. We slipped into the protest crowd and moved with them. Listening to the black-clad protesters interacting with local residents turned out to be an interesting education.

As usual, the protesters' chants and graffiti were not about the dead extradition bill, nor were they asking for democracy. Residents and I decided continue walking with them, writing down what we saw and heard.

In rough order of frequency, we saw:

1) Displays of a ferocious hatred for China;

2) Demands for Hong Kong independence; and

3) Angry assertions that the police force was a unit of the triads.

As we watched, the protesters ran to a large wall next to the Central Library, which was used by thousands of children every day.

We followed from a distance.

They wrote their messages in massive graffiti letters:

PoPo suck my dick

Resist Beijing Liberate Hong Kong

Police Is Triads

Fuck the PoPo

Very pro-democracy messages, right, BBC?

After a few minutes, I joined some other residents to walk to the neighboring district of Tin Hau where we saw that protesters had completely blocked the main road, mostly with materials stolen from a nearby building site.

We watched as one brave local resident, a thin local man, marched into the road and started quietly dismantling the barricade, picking up a single piece at a time, carrying it away, and then returning for another.

Neither protesters nor police interrupted him. They just stared.

This battle was supposed to have only two sides! How dare a Hong Kong resident act reasonably outside his own house!

Shouting and the sound of running groups draw us back to Causeway Bay, where I noticed a bottle of beer at my feet as I stood outside the Wellcome supermarket. But wait—I took another look and noticed that it wasn't beer. It was a petrol bomb that had failed to go off.

I looked at my companions and we reflected grimly on the fact that radical protesters were becoming increasingly addicted to arson—and that worried us in a tightly packed place like Hong Kong. This was not a place to play with fire. Someone was going to get hurt.

Minutes later, in the heart of the world's most expensive shopping district, we noticed a new phenomenon.

A cluster of people in green helmets and green vests labeled "Neutral Legal Observers Group" were running around, following the action.

They spoke English, none with local accents. They sounded like Americans or Canadians. We watched them for a while.

It was puzzling. Despite claiming to come from the legal sector, I didn't see them take any interest whatsoever in the clearly criminal acts that were taking place almost continuously.

They studiously ignored local residents trying to stop the vandalism, never trying to help us.

But every time a particularly violent protester was arrested, the green helmets raced to start filming, focusing on the police officer's treatment of the arrestee.

Nor were they just observing, despite what their helmets said. In each case, they tried to get the arrested man's name and talked openly about how they could arrange free defense lawyers for them.

It would be very hard for an unbiased observer not to realize that they were deliberately turning a blind eye to criminality and actively aiding the perpetrators of violence and vandalism.

The Neutral Legal Observers Group appeared to be about as neutral as the People's Daily.

I walked up to talk to one of them, but he brushed me aside, saying that he was not authorized to talk to reporters, and handed me a slip of paper with the group's website address.

Going back to the main road, there was a surreal moment. Some of the burning barricades were on the main road through Causeway Bay, in full view of the tall glass frontage of the Regal Hong Kong Island Hotel, a five-star hotel.

I could see people sipping drinks as they stood in air-conditioned splendor, watching the radical protesters marauding along the main roads, transformed into live entertainment.

My phone dings. A source, Mark K. Lin, tells me that firebombs are being thrown in Tsim Sha Tsui—the battle is turning ferocious there. He says he has a really bad feeling about the evening. This was about 9.40 pm. I decided to leave Nathan Road to him and other members of the network and stay in Causeway Bay.

At 9.59 pm I got a text message from another Hong Kong resident, Janice Leung.

"Are you anywhere near Tin Hau?" she asked. "There are civilians clearing the blockade despite protesters. This is what needs to happen!"

Janice is right. This is what needs to happen. The people of Hong Kong, a peaceful, intelligent, pragmatic, non-violent, law-abiding, and not overly politicized community, need to calmly, quietly, gently take back control of their streets and their lives. And it will happen. This was Saturday night, and the 2019-2020 school term would start in 36 hours—or that was the plan, anyway. For the sake of all our young people, we needed peace to return, as soon as possible.

But before this evening was over, another nightmare was about to start.

CHAPTER 28

The Prince Edward Station 'Murders'

*In Which We Review A Misleading Synopsis—
Trouble On A Train*

THERE ARE TWO versions of the story of what happened on the other side of the harbor, at Prince Edward Station in Kowloon, late on this particular night, August 31.

Again, we have the short version popularized by the radical protesters, the pandems, and the media, and a longer version featuring more detail, complexity, and rather different implications.

In the short telling of the story, brutal police officers attacked innocent members of the public at the station, injuring many of them seriously — and in many versions of the story, killing several people. They then ordered all journalists and photographers out of the station to cover up their crime, and prevented ambulance staff from reaching the wounded or dying. Once dead, the corpses were whisked away in a special train and have not been seen since.

Political activist Alvin Yeung would later tell this version of the story, in somewhat formal language, in a Legislative Council written exchange: *"According to the footage captured by the media, on the night of August 31 this year, some police officers attacked members of the public, who did not put up any resistance, with batons and pepper spray and pointed guns at them on the platforms of MTR Prince Edward Station and inside the train compartments thereat. It has been reported that on that night, the Police evicted journalists and volunteer first-aiders from Prince Edward Station and then, by claiming that there were no injured persons in the station, hindered the entry of ambulancemen of the Fire Services Department to the station to perform rescue work, resulting in the delayed treatment of quite a number of injured persons."*

Notice something?

Yep. There are no protesters present in the story at all. It's all about the police and their victims.

Mr. Yeung added dark hints that the refusal to make public the security footage from the station made *"quite a number of members of the public"* suspect that the worst allegations were true, despite *"the Government's repeated denial of the death of any person during the aforesaid confrontations"*.

In summary, the main event was an attack on the public by police officers on innocent train passengers, resulting in multiple serious injuries and or deaths—which were then covered up.

Was that the story?

It certainly fitted the revolution advisors' strategies, of making sure the police are the heart of the story, and the protesters are removed.

* * *

Radical protesters created mayhem across the city on August 31. Groups in many trouble spots in Kowloon and the New Territories had a modus operandi basically the same as the ones I was with in Causeway Bay, mentioned in the previous chapter—they blocked roads, lit fires, sprayed anti-China graffiti on walls, and smashed shops or restaurants that were perceived to have a connection with mainland China or belonged to a relative of someone who had called them "rioters".

ALL my peaceful protester friends stayed well away—and that meant the vast, vast proportion of people who had marched in June.

Police who tried to stop the trouble were greeted with showers of petrol bombs, iron rods and bricks.

MTR staff and passengers were also a target, with numerous attempts to stop the rail system functioning using objects thrown onto the tracks.

At 9.37 pm, protesters threw a petrol bomb on Humphreys Road in Tsim Sha Tsui, on the Kowloon peninsula. At 10.05 pm, radical protesters retreated north along Nathan Road to Mong Kok, where they moved onto the middle of the main road to create a blockage. At this time, one group of protesters broke away and entered Mong Kong MTR station with the aim of destroying the machinery and disabling the service. They used hammers and an iron pole. They then located the control room and smashed the main glass panel with a hammer they had apparently brought along for the purpose.

Within minutes, the vandals had attracted supporters, and there were soon more than 100 people in black at the station.

MTR staff called the police, but the protesters ran for the shadows. Police arrived minutes later, but the trouble appeared to have evaporated.

By 10.30 pm, the station was quiet again, with staff emerging to sweep up the debris. What rail staff didn't know is that some or all of the members of the violent group which had smashed the facilities hadn't left—they had simply moved down the escalators, onto the platforms. They slipped onto a train.

For passengers already on the trains, heading home from work or play, the radical protesters were easy to spot, exhilarated young people dressed in black with masks and helmets and backpacks filled with clinking objects.

At 10.42 pm, members of the Hong Kong public got into a verbal altercation with the protesters on one particular train in the tunnel approaching Prince Edward Station.

A young male protester slapped the face of a middle-aged man who had scolded him. This incident was caught on camera by someone else in the carriage.

A few other passengers in the train remonstrated with the radical protesters, who responded angrily. This quickly devolved into a physical brawl in that carriage.

Other passengers, horrified by the violence, could be seen quickly leaving the train as soon as it had arrived at platform number three at Prince Edward Station.

Normally, train stops are very short—but the driver found himself unable to close the doors. His equipment told him that someone was holding the doors open.

Witnesses saw that some protesters had left the carriage but were holding the doors open while continuing the fight they had had with the passengers.

Several protesters then re-entered the carriage to hit the passengers with umbrellas. They also used iron poles and fire extinguishers. One was waving a hammer. They then stepped out of the carriage a second time, but turned to throw water bottles and umbrellas into the train at the passengers inside.

The verbal dispute continued, with the doors still being jammed open, and the driver frantically calling his colleagues on his intercom for help.

At this time, some protesters again entered the carriage, focusing their attention specifically on the middle-aged passenger they had slapped earlier in the fighting. He fought back, but most other passengers had fled by this time. He was badly outnumbered.

At one point, a female protester separated herself from the group to use her hand to cover the lens of a reporter trying to film the beating.

After administering this punishment, the protesters left the carriage yet again. One person was seen taking a fire extinguisher and standing on the platform, discharging the contents behind him into the train compartment, which quickly filled with fog.

At this time they noticed a woman standing on the platform recording what was happening on a mobile phone. They surrounded her and grabbed her, video records show. One report said they took her phone.

Many passengers dialed 999.

The protesters, after some discussion, moved to the far corner of the platform, stripped off their black clothes, and put on ordinary clothing in a variety of colors to appear as regular passengers. They did this behind a makeshift wall of umbrellas. However the scene was captured by video cameras.

Also by this time, members of the public were hurrying to the escalators to get as far away as possible, while others moved to the opposite end of the train from the protesters.

Someone entered the train on the opposite platform, number four, and pulled the emergency alarm.

MTR staff noticed smoke or gas of some sort coming out of a carriage and feared for the worst—and they again called the police and fire service.

All this took place in a chaotic eight-minute period between 10.42 and 10.50 pm.

Also at 10.50 pm, police chiefs gave orders for riot officers in the vicinity to head to Prince Edward Station immediately, go downstairs to the platform to arrest the radical protesters, and render whatever assistance was needed to passengers who had been beaten.

At about this time, a police officer suggested to MTR decision makers that the service, despite it being one of Hong Kong's busiest lines, should be halted. But staff were reluctant to do so, and instead said they would prefer to maintain service on the line but get trains to bypass Prince Edward Station, so no innocent passengers could end up at risk.

At 10.53 pm, the MTR staff used the public address system to ask any remaining passengers to leave the trains and the station immediately. Many of the travellers disembarked at this time and headed to the escalators that would lead to the surface. Minutes later, once the travelling passengers were out, station gates were locked and or guarded to prevent people entering or re-entering. The place was quickly secured.

Inside the station, police moved rapidly down the escalator. Three minutes later, at 10.56 pm, they reached platforms three and four.

Protesters, some of whom had not fully changed clothes, spotted them arriving and started running, some along the platform, and others moving into and through the trains. Officers used foam weapons and batons to try to catch the fleeing protesters.

Some would later complain that officers grabbed them roughly, but there is really no other way to seize someone running away from you.

Officers succeeded in detaining a number of protesters, and assembled them seated on the ground. One young man in a black t-shirt leapt to his feet and ran along the platform. Police tried to give chase, but a young man in green attacked them with an umbrella, distracting them just long enough for the youth to jump over the side of an escalator and run up it.

From the train that was stationary on platform four, at least ten protesters attacked police with "sharp objects" and umbrellas.

Police ordered protesters out of the trains on both platforms. While some protesters were now in regular clothing, appearing to be normal passengers, officers could see a number still dressed in black clothes, with the tell-tale masks, helmets and backpacks.

Some of the protesters flatly refused to leave the trains and altercations followed, in which officers used batons and pepper spray. One pointed a rubber baton-launching gun at protesters on the train at platform four. In some cases, police had to enter the carriages to pull the protesters out.

Some critics of the police would later say that the police did not limit their actions to people dressed as protesters and behaved very roughly. This may well be true—in this chaotic situation, with many protesters having changed clothes, officers had to make split second decisions. In hindsight, mistakes may well have been made. It was impossible to confirm that all ordinary passengers had left the train, nor was it easy to differentiate between protesters who had changed clothes, and regular passengers who may have chosen to remain.

Protesters would later distribute short video clips showing police subduing people in the train, painting the incident as an outrageous "terrorist attack by police" on ordinary passengers—editing the protesters entirely out of the story. But it was clear that a large number of passengers had left, and a significant proportion of the people still at the scene were actually part of the group of radical protesters, however they were dressed.

Given the amount of fighting that had taken place, and the potential for injury, officers decided to declare platforms three and four to be a crime scene, and asked reporters to leave. They also called the ambulance service, in case anyone needed medical help.

At 11.04 pm, the MTR train on platform four finally left the station to continue on its journey.

Two minutes later, fire service officers arrived in response to calls about the smoke seen on the platforms. They arrived at Exit B1, which was locked, and, having cutters with them, simply broke in.

One train, which still contained some protesters who had been involved in the fight on the train, arrived at Yau Ma Tei Station at 11:09 pm.

At 11.10 pm, MTR chiefs made the decision to suspend all train services on both the Kwun Tong Line and the Tsuen Wan Line.

Two minutes after that, fire officers reported back to their headquarters that they were satisfied that there was no fire at Prince Edward Station.

Ambulance people arrived at Exit B1 at 11.14 pm, but the police guarding the gates said (inaccurately) that no one had been injured inside the station. There was certainly a great deal of confusion about the precise situation at that time.

Separately, an ambulance crew responding to calls from people who had seen protesters beating passengers on the train, also arrived at the station—reaching Exit E at 11.17 pm. MTR staff were guarding that gate, but allowed the ambulance staff to slip inside.

Down on the two platforms, there was continued confusion for some time about the number of injured people and seriousness of the cases. Estimates differed among the different branches of the emergency services. At first, they thought it was seven, but then added two, taking the total to nine.

Soon after midnight, fire service officers, police, ambulance staff, and MTR staff met for a discussion near the gate. A probationary ambulance officer wrote down that the number of individuals needing attention was 10.

Meanwhile, above ground, a large crowd of protesters had gathered outside Prince Edward Station, having read on the LIHKG online bulletin board about problems on the train. The posts did not mention the fight between protesters and passengers, mentioning only the arrival of the police, and painting the incident as a repeat of the "gangster attack" on innocent passengers at Yuen Long MTR station on July 21.

"Crazy, after getting into Prince Edward Station, police officers hit whoever they saw," an LIHKG user wrote. Attempts to arrest protesters had thus become a random attack on passengers.

The presence of so many hostile people above ground meant that emergency services decided it would be unsafe to transfer any injured people by normal means from the station to ambulances.

So a decision was made to transport them to another station, where the ambulance crew could meet them and take them to hospital. Lai Chi Kok station was chosen for this purpose.

The ambulance officer inside the station did a recount and found that the final count of people needing medical attention was actually seven—which was the figure he put down on paper in the end.

The MTR staff did their part by organizing a special train to carry 45 arrested protesters in their custody, including the seven injured parties. It arrived at Lai Chi Kok Station at 1.28 am. Escorted by police and ambulance officers, the seven injured protesters were taken to Princess Margaret Hospital and Caritas Medical Centre, while the other 38 were taken to Kwai Chung Police Station.

But, in the description of events that was now circulating on LIHKG, the fight was no longer an altercation between protesters and the travelling public but was presented as a spontaneous attack on the public by the police.

The protesters were written entirely out of the story, as if they had never been present at all. *"Police officers assaulted and arrested civilians inside Mong Kok [sic] MTR Station, which was violent and an abuse of power,"* an LIHKG user reported.

"Police officers rushed into the train compartment to hit people vigorously, like what the people dressed in white had assaulted others in the 721 Yuen Long Incident," said another.

The distortion got worse.

"The Police launched terrorist attack in Prince Edward Station, must seek international assistance," said another post, widely shared.

That was bad enough. But the fake narrative was about to get much, much worse.

At 2.21 am, a netizen (a keen internet user) wrote: *"People at the scene claimed that someone had been beaten to death. Haven't fact checked yet!"*

LIHKG allows anonymous posts, so it was impossible to locate who was planting these fake stories.

At this time, the rumor about "murders" at the station was still not widespread. And no one at the scene was pushing that story.

At 3.00 am, police officers held a stand-up press conference at which they described the events of the evening.

There were no discussions about deaths, or even injuries, and no questions were asked by reporters about such subjects. At that time, both police and reporters were focused on the original story: protesters smashed up Mong Kok station and fought with passengers on a train at Prince Edward station until police arrived and made arrests.

It wasn't until the next evening, at 5.15 pm (on Sunday, September 1) that the "alternative facts" started to take wing.

A LIHKG writer wrote: *"The reason for closing the station was that the Police had killed several citizens, so the Police had to tidy up the scene."*

His allegation continued: *"If the evidence could not be destroyed, the scene had to be tidied up to create an impression that the deceased died of their/ his own mistakes or attacks by protesters."*

This was pure fantasy, but it was posted as if it was an informed report.

It was followed by many other comments and posts on the same lines, including this one, which appeared at 8.19 pm: *"Seriously suspecting that someone had died at Prince Edward last night... The station ended up being closed for one day. Undoubtedly destroying evidence."*

The planted story worked. Within hours, there was a widespread belief among some radical protesters that six people had been murdered by police at Prince Edward MTR station.

The following day, Monday, September 2, a reporter at the government press conference asked Chief Secretary Matthew Cheung to respond to the accusations of deaths inside the station. Cheung blandly replied that there were no deaths at that place on that date.

But the rumor was now soaring. Funeral flowers began to appear in huge piles at the station. Opposition members of the Legislative Council took up the cry. This would continue indefinitely, with video allegations of the "murders" receiving hundreds of thousands of views, month after month.

On the last day of each month from then on, there would be funeral services for the "six killed by police" at Prince Edward Station.

Lord David Alton, a British peer with an astonishingly high gullibility level, decided that the reports that the Hong Kong police were murdering large numbers of people were "credible".

But let's move back to that Monday morning, September 2.

For most Hong Kong people, an important event was taking place. It was the first day of the 2019-2020 school year.

CHAPTER 29

The Education Strike Flops

In Which Students Blow A Raspberry At Radicals—
Shue Yan's "Sunday School" Protest

THE LONG SUMMER break was over. For families, it was time to get back to school. Or, for the political opposition, it was the moment for Hong Kong's million or so students to stand up and show which side they were on.

Early on Monday, September 2, this reporter stood with education administrators who were anxious to see if students would follow protest leaders' demands to boycott classes.

Would ANY young people turn up?

Eight o'clock came. The buses pulled in—and a mighty river of students poured off them.

After the buses had disgorged their contents, an international school teacher said: "I don't think a single student was missing."

Teachers at local schools said the same, with most reporting 97 to 100 percent "normal" attendance.

Indeed, there were so few students boycotting classes that reporters could count by hand the number of protesters choosing to stand outside (for those who had not lost this technology).

At La Salle College, some 80 followed radicals' orders while 1,600 defied the call.

At St Mary's Canossian College, about 40 boycotted classes while 1,400 defied it.

Even at HKFEW Wong Cho Bau Secondary School in Tung Chung, the alma mater of Hong Kong independence campaigner Nathan Law, only 30 were seen protesting—and a number of those were clearly adults rather than schoolchildren.

At Chief Executive Carrie Lam Cheng Yuet-ngor's alma mater, St Francis' Canossian College, just eight students protested.

Many Hong Kong schools have thousands of students – on my author tours, I remember going to one large school with more than 5,000 pupils. So the numbers of protesters was tiny.

The strike call, at a secondary school level, had been completely ignored by upwards of 90 percent of school pupils.

* * *

What about university students? At the city's biggest educational establishment, Hong Kong Polytechnic University, a majority of students turned up for lessons as normal.

"I'm thrilled," said one of my colleagues, his tone of voice suggesting the opposite. "I didn't want an extra couple of weeks off, honestly."

In the media, boycott organizers were rather unbelievably claiming that 30,000 students skipped classes across Hong Kong—but a review of reports shows that the only big crowd of protesting students was one at Chinese

University in the New Territories. Clearly the violence and disruption had pushed the vast majority of Hong Kong people, young and old, to the center—away from the extreme edges of the debate.

At Baptist University, a senior administrator told me he was surprised by what had happened. "Attendance is actually better than normal," he said. Almost everyone had turned up first thing in the morning on the first day of the semester—it had been a long time since he had seen that.

The data allowed only one conclusion. In excess of 97 percent of students did NOT boycott classes on their first day back, to the delight of their parents around the city.

What did the media report?

Headline on BBC World News report: *"Students boycott class on first day back."*

Thanks to the power of broadcasting, the shameful BBC newsroom literally fulfills the first part of the old proverb: "A lie will travel around the world while the truth is still putting on its boots."

* * *

There are four things that Hong Kong's radical protesters are violently attacking this month:

1) The MTR.

2) The airport.

3) Logic.

4) Their own reputation.

And that was the opinion of Hong Kong undergraduates, who in general are peaceful, reasonable people who are so non-violent that they carefully walk around ants.

This writer spent most of this week with students and was cheered by what he saw.

Have faith, brothers and sisters, I wrote to my network. Hong Kong's good-hearted, thoughtful young people vastly outnumber the violent, radicalized ones.

Even the recent viral news report that "valiant" male black-shirt protest leaders were getting multiple girlfriends could not persuade one Hong Kong Polytechnic University student to boycott classes.

He turned up to lectures in a t-shirt yesterday that said: "GRADES NOT BABES."

* * *

Checking my messages using the WiFi at the Block X coffee shop, I noted that Tom Guendert had commented that many Westerners don't see beyond the US flags to notice that a significant number of key participants "are really just angry localists with very, very unliberal beliefs of kicking out immigrants and closing borders".

Mother-of-two-children-and-three-enterprises Mrs. Ho strongly agreed. She said: *"One day a member of the Western media will finally look beyond their own preconceptions and realize that the actual people of Hong Kong are definitely not pro-independence and not even particularly anti-China. Why can they not see this?"*

* * *

Two weeks have passed since the total flop of the education strike. It was now September 16 and news outlets were continuing to show escalating violence in Hong Kong—but missed the bigger story that protester numbers were continuing to crash.

Truth is, these two facts were clearly linked.

This weekend's reports omitted overall crowd size, which made it hard for number-crunchers to make their own comparisons—people like KS Chiew, whose message I was reading as I sat in my Block X coffee shop office.

"We seem to have mislaid two million people," wrote the Wan Chai resident. *"Ninety-eight percent of us are no longer joining the weekend rallies. The violence is ridiculous."*

He sent me his notes. The biggest summer turnout was a claimed "two million" on June 16 while yesterday's rally, which took the exact same route, was 30,000 at most, he reckons—a figure which was 98.5 percent smaller than the claimed figure.

In North Point yesterday there were maybe 300 people, he said. At the British consulate yesterday there were barely 100.

Several protests were cancelled because too few people turned up.

"Since when does a 98 percent fall in support not count as a news story?" he asked. It was a reasonable question.

At the universities, lecturers said that most students ignored the whole of the "mandatory" two-week boycott call and now, after that period, classes had normal levels of attendance.

Today, just a few steps from the coffee shop at which I was writing this, another rally of black-clad radicals was taking place. I got up and strolled over to it. There were 76 people declaiming their five demands while the rest of the university (enrollment is 16,000) walked past.

I stopped a few students and asked young people why they were walking past. Most said they were focused on their work. A few said they supported the protests in spirit, but no longer wished to join in for various reasons.

Others said their participation had moved from "daily" to "weekends only" to "special dates only".

Who could blame them? Statisticians said that the percentage of protests which became violent was 85 percent (at least 112 out of 132) overall. In recent weeks, the proportion had risen: I was not aware of any recent demonstrations that hadn't ended in violence.

For the majority of Hong Kong people, politics fatigue had set in. Even the most cursory study of newspapers showed that protests were no longer the dominant local subject.

The same was true for social media. Many Hong Kong Facebook users were returning to traditional soft topics, such as pictures of family, friends, and (among my family members at least) puppies.

In coffee shops and bars, the protests no longer dominated every conversation, thank God.

* * *

The following day, things looked like changing—in my home patch. I received a warning that the trouble may be back.

It was Tuesday, September 17, and fearful school administrators were having unwelcome visions of violence near their premises.

Police tipped them off that there was going to be a black-clad rally at Shue Yan University in North Point, on Hong Kong Island the following afternoon.

Aiyeeah! That university shared the top of Braemar Hill in North Point with SIX primary and secondary schools, so the area was always awash with children. It was my home district, so I knew it well.

What to do?

Some schools cancelled all classes, giving children and teachers an impromptu holiday. Others sent children home earlier, or warned everyone to give the university a wide berth.

School buses were cancelled or rerouted, and road blocks set up to stop drivers turning into Wai Tsui Crescent, where the university was situated.

Families kept well away—but your correspondent of course turned up to see what was going to happen.

Since the flop of the students' strike at the beginning of September, I was beginning to realize that the way students were portrayed as the main body of protesters was wrong.

The number of radicalized people in the universities was much, much lower than people thought. Most students were law-abiding, quiet people.

I had not seen any violent radicals at Shue Yan University. Instead, there was a small coterie of people who graffitied the walls and stuck up posters, but that was it.

And how did the actual rally go?

In the event, it was a bit limp, to say the least. Out of the university's 5,200 students, only 194 turned up. They congregated on the road outside the university and listened to a few speakers who told them that the Hong Kong civil service was actually a secretive communist organization working for Beijing.

Then they sang their hymn-like anthem, Glory to Hong Kong. It's actually not a bad song, but unfortunately includes the pro-independence lobby's slogan about freeing Hong Kong and having a revolution.

Then they went off to the nearby 7-Eleven to buy snacks.

It was a bit like a church youth group on an outing.

In fact, it was a LOT like a church youth group on an outing — the sermon, the exhortation, the warnings, the hymn.

* * *

Eight Vignettes From September 2019

1) The bus of my eagle-eyed contributor Gerry Em was stuck in the huge airport road traffic blockade.

As phone apps showed police approaching, a male passenger asked the driver to open the door because he had "some rubbish" that "needed to be thrown away".

Gerry was puzzled — until he saw that what he described as "thuggish young men" were passing numerous items from every corner of the bus to be thrown away: Helmets, black shirts, spanners, items that could be used as weapons.

If you need equipment for a revolution, head to the airport road. "You'll find an impressive stack of discarded items by the roadside," Gerry said.

2) On a Monday evening, a colleague watched aghast as a group of students marched over to the garrison of the People's Liberation Army in Central and started shooting high-powered laser beams into the compound, trying to damage people's retinas.

Guys: Don't do this. Thanks.

I think this may be another thing that people on all sides of the debate can agree on.

3) Protesters smashed up 32 MTR stations on Saturday and 12 on Sunday, the first weekend of September. They destroyed control room windows, ticket machines, cameras, gates and platform safety doors.

One protester was seen painstakingly wrecking the carved braille map that blind passengers use to navigate the station.

The MTR is Hong Kong's pride and joy. I withdraw my earlier assertion that the protesters had excellent marketing skills.

4) An interesting comparison has come to light this week, with similar incidents taking place on both sides of the planet.

In Hong Kong, protesters plotted to illegally take drones to the airport at Chek Lap Kok.

In London, protesters plotted to illegally take drones to the airport at Heathrow.

In Hong Kong, the authorities sprang into action.

In London, the authorities sprang into action.

In Hong Kong, the authorities placed a reminder on the government website saying: "Aviation safety is crucial to the public and passengers." (translation: "Let's not crash planes and kill everyone").

In London, the authorities in London sent out a squad of officers, three police vans and a police helicopter, and "pre-emptively" arrested nine people for simply thinking about committing such a crime.

What a difference.

And guess which set of police officers get painted as heavyhanded? Hint: Not the London ones.

5) The Hong Kong government paid for 20 young local designers to enjoy a junket to a major London fashion convention in mid-September.

Just before the presentation on Saturday, 14 September, designer Yeung Chin got ready to bite the hand that fed him.

He told his models to wear only one shoe so they would limp, gave them clothes with gory images of body parts on them, and set off a smoke machine. The presentation would send an unmistakable message to the world about all the nasty secret murdering taking place in Hong Kong! Mwa ha ha.

Just before the show began, Chin's smoke machine set off the fire alarm—and designers, models, and the entire audience had to evacuate the building.

Clearly, the God of Karma was watching.

6) The committee was back in action, becoming ever more blatant.

At one march, they got the young people to carry a shiny new banner. It said: "Trump 2020".

That was all. The banner didn't mention Hong Kong or China at all.

The funny thing was that all the Westerners I know who still actively support the protests are extremely left-liberal—and surely hated the thing.

And the remaining individuals still unconvinced that American sources are working with local subversives dropped their objections. It had all become too obvious to argue against.

Separately, reader Doreen Jaeger-Soong spotted a problem with the protesters' demands for Trump to come and free Hong Kong from China. "He probably wouldn't be able to find Hong Kong on a map," she pointed out.

7) On RTHK Radio III's Backchat program, Claudia Mo said radical protesters only vandalized inanimate objects.

This writer, who also appeared live on the show on September 12, pointed out that "a police officer is not an inanimate object".

She responded that the protester I saw attacking the police officer could have been a police officer in disguise.

I wonder how she imagines conversations at police stations go?

Officer Chan: "How about I throw a petrol bomb at you, giving you first degree burns and very possibly killing you?"

Officer Wong: "Good idea! Let's do this thing."

8) A mother-of-one named Luk pointed out that every newspaper article divides people into the "protester side" and the "pro-Beijing" side.

"Where are the ordinary Hong Kong people?" she demanded.

The typical Hong Kong person (she said) is pro-democracy while strongly against violence, against Trump, against localism, against self-determination, against anti-China slogans, against flag-burning, against colonialism, against conspiracy theories, against the media's demonization of police officers and civil servants, against petrol bombs, against arson, against the blocking of the airport, against the vandalizing of MTR stations and police premises, etc.

In short, the majority of Hong Kong people are reasonable people who appear nowhere in the only two groups featured in media narratives.

Exactly.

CHAPTER 30

Child Labor

In Which We Learn About Child Labor—A Poster War—Critics Of The Protests Fight Back—Violence Escalates As Numbers Fall

"THEY'RE JUST CHILDREN," he said.

"I know!" I said. "They're incredibly childish."

"No," the police officer said. "I'm not saying they are childish. I'm saying they are children. They are *literally* children."

Officers had noticed a curious fact—the violent radicals were getting increasingly short of stature in recent weeks. They'd been physically shrinking, like washing left in the rain.

After close-up tangling with some violent ones, and a rush of arrests, the masks came off and the truth was out.

The groups were now bulked out with youngsters, he said.

As adults and university students had abandoned the protests, whoever was organizing them had gone around collecting children from schools to keep the numbers up.

It was easy enough. They could be paid a fraction of what you'd need to pay an adult. And some you didn't even need to pay. Children have a powerful sense of right and wrong, and if you ask them to dress up and save the world for justice and democracy against a Nazi-like oppressor, they will do it. Children are good people.

"High school kids?" I asked.

"Mostly. They tend to be teenagers. Perhaps 40 percent of some radical groups are minors. But some are younger. They are ten or eleven, so upper primary school age."

This must be a real worry, considering the amount of violence out there, I said.

"Too right," he replied.

A day later, another police officer confirmed the story over a double espresso in my Central coffee shop/office.

"We even discussed changing the wording on the banner we raise," an officer told me. "The one that says 'Disperse or we will use tear smoke'."

"To what?" I asked.

"The revised version would say 'Disperse or we will tell your parents," the officer said with a laugh. "That's a much scarier message for children of that age."

But although we were smiling, we were both sad. We both have children of our own—and it was terrible to hear that so many were being radicalized by a secretive consultant-driven movement that was blighting so many lives.

* * *

I got up at 6:00 this morning, September 22, to check the results of a rather genteel battle on a wall opposite my home.

For some weeks, the rather mild, church-youth-group-style protesters among the Shue Yan University students had been putting up political posters on a "Lennon Wall" on the road, plus painting graffiti on all the walls and pavements nearby.

The posters and slogans revealed to passers by that the police had now secretly killed more than a thousand people. They were just silly, and only the most radicalized people could have taken them seriously—people like British parliamentarian Lord David Alton, perhaps, who we now heard was working with Benedict Rogers, the right wing UK activist who would later be memorably and accurately dubbed "a serial fantasist" by Grenville Cross, an elder statesmen of the Hong Kong legal community.

In the opening days of the poster war, local residents left the posters unmolested.

But recently a bit of a war started. Residents, running out of patience, took down a whole set of posters.

The next day, students replaced them.

Residents removed them.

Students replaced them.

Residents removed them.

Students replaced them.

I decided that I approved of this battle, both sides. If the alternative was vandalism and petrol-bomb-throwing, I would take The War of the Posters any day.

Actually, fighting-by-wall-posters is a celebrated mainland Chinese communist tradition with a long history, although I wouldn't tell the protesters that. It was certainly very prevalent during the 1967 pro-Communist riots in Hong Kong. Then, university students would scrawl messages on paper (then known as Big Character Posters) and stick them on walls around the city.

These praised Chinese communism and denounced Western capitalism—in other words, they were the diametric opposite of what we see today.

In the 1960s, China-friendly people would create huge examples of what we now call Lennon Walls, while anti-China groups would tear everything down—the opposite of what we see today.

One reader, Benjamin Rees, told me he was old enough to remember the original poster war—and thought it remarkable that the two sides had swapped places.

It was now Sunday morning, the end of the week-long poster war, and I noticed that there hadn't been much activity at the wall at all the previous day. I wondered who won, the residents or the activists?

At the crack of dawn, I slipped out of the front gate and crossed the road to check.

Answer: Neither group had won. There were several posters left, but a day of blazing tropical sunshine yesterday had faded the posters to illegibility. So nature won, I guess.

* * *

Still, it's a funny thing: I keep finding that the activists, even the violent ones, are far more honest than the media.

The black-clad protesters are completely straight about their hatred for all things Chinese and their desire for a revolution that brings about self-determination for Hong Kong. You just have to talk to them for one minute or watch them for 10 seconds.

This weekend they drew huge Nazi swastikas in red, damaged China flags and physically attacked shops (and humans) perceived as having sympathies towards the mainland.

But most Western reporters don't notice any of that, preferring to characterize them as Brave Soldiers on a Noble Jihad for Democracy.

I still believe that most journalists are not paid to push this line. They just do it naturally. Confirmation bias is strong in this group.

Ten Vignettes From Late September

1) In a rare lifting of their Xi-Jinping-like press censorship program, radicals on Saturday withdrew their umbrellas to allow us to film them setting the flag of China alight.

But the flame wouldn't catch—they'd accidentally bought a fire-proof flag! (What a pain are the government's mandated fire safety regulations!)

As embarrassment mounted, the umbrellas were opened again to hide the scene.

After that, they promulgated a new policy.

China flags were to be stomped on, torn, or thrown into the harbor instead.

2) Meanwhile, the knowledge that there are US forces involved in the protests is now so widespread that both sides are making jokes about it.

BOOM!

A tear gas canister flies towards the protesters.

Protest leader: "Everybody get down!"

(Brad, who is a US infiltrator, starts doing his best hiphop moves.)

3) Reader Jupy Chow pointed out that "democracy" sounds like "demo-crazy".

That may not be the official etymology but in Hong Kong it makes sense.

Many people on my network said they were irritated by people (particularly Westerners) endlessly pontificating about what Hong Kong police officers were doing wrong. A retired reader named Ng said he responds by pulling out copies of civil service Application Form GF340. "Fill this in and you can become an auxiliary police officer on the front line he tells them. "Instead of complaining about whatever police officers do, you can show us the right way to do it."

He said critics of the police back off so fast they cause a vortex in the spacetime continuum.

4) We're becoming horribly inured to petrol bombs. Who'd have thought it possible? I saw one guy with a Molotov cocktail and a Pacific Coffee chillino and wanted to shout at him: "Do you have any idea how bad plastic straws are for the environment?"

5) Behind the scenes at the MTR, staff say their spare part inventory is down to just five percent—and that was before another batch of ticket machines was ruined on Sunday.

"It's so ironic," says a Hong Konger who has a factory in Guandong. "Our MTR is wrecked, but the exact copy in Shenzhen, built by the same people to the same design, is gleamingly new and works perfectly."

Well, one is an industrious and law-abiding Chinese community and the other is Hong Kong.

6) Okay, okay, that's not fair. Hong Kong is ALSO an industrious and law-abiding Chinese community, but cursed with too many US-backed activists openly encouraging radicals to use metal poles to smash our shopping malls, train stations, travel trade, reputation, hearts, etc.

I'm used to ultra-nationalistic people being highly annoying, but never expected the other side to be just as bad.

7) Political activists tried to stop Hong Kong students lunching at university canteens on Friday, September 27. This follows a claim by activists that a relative of the catering firm's founder used the word "rioters" to describe a mob hurling stuff.

At Hong Kong PolyU, I watched black shirts stand outside the canteen entrance with a megaphone, telling students about this person who had committed the unforgivable crime of exercising her right to free speech.

But young Hong Kongers were having none of it. They were fed up of radical politics. They streamed past, and the huge restaurant was packed by noon. On some tables, Hong Kongers and mainlanders lunched together.

Angry black shirts then marched in to face down the canteen serving ladies and the young people BLATANTLY eating lunch in defiance of what they had been told.

Then a professor, a tall Westerner, stood up and delivered an impromptu lecture, scolding activists for almost ten minutes.

He said there was a world of difference between peaceful protesting, and the behavior of "yobs" with zero respect for the law or their fellow Hong Kong people.

Black shirt activists, caught off guard, listened in stunned (and mostly surprisingly polite) silence.

8) Hong Kong residents regularly accuse RTHK news staff of extreme pro-activist bias by the use of curious semantics and anonymous "quotes", and a reader showed me a hilarious example today.

When thousands of angry citizens had their bus, car and taxi journeys blocked by road-barricading activists on Saturday night, September 28, the RTHK report summed up their mutual fury with just one single anonymous quote: "One motorist RTHK spoke to said he wasn't bothered about the inconvenience and what the protesters were doing was more important than his journey." Hit me! Hit me harder!

On Sunday, 6 October, there was an outbreak of vandalism and dangerous road-blocking that stretched from Wan Chai to Admiralty. Again, thousands of people ended up trapped in buses and cars, before police, after their usual annoyingly lengthy display of patience, intervened to get Hong Kong moving again.

The opening of the RTHK news report made it sound as if police, rather than being latecomers, were the root of the problem. The lead paragraph of the report said: *"Police shot rounds of tear gas at anti-government protesters in Admiralty and Wan Chai late on Sunday afternoon, before beating, pepper spraying and subduing several people a short time later."*

9) Hong Kong's apolitical majority is starting to get antsy about the constant stream of polarizing stories from Apple Daily, Hong Kong Free Press, some reporters at RTHK, and most of the Western media.

A group of Hong Kong doctors put out a joint statement saying: *"Our law enforcers, police, have been demonised. Some citizens carry an unnecessary sense of enmity to the government, police and public organisations. They have even destroyed and obstructed public transport."*

But they added that we should not just blame the young. They wrote that they regretted the way some people "provoke youngsters to pervert the course of justice."

It was actually a well-written and intelligent plea.

The doctors inspired other professionals to follow suit.

Senior Hong Kong lawyers wrote to me to tell me to watch out for a full page ad they put into the Standard newspaper this morning saying that they had "watched in alarm and dismay as our beautiful city has faced mayhem, destruction and chaos over the past 100 days".

But, they wrote, the people of Hong Kong will not abandon our community's core values–and these include the rule of law, the condemnation of violence, and respect for the personal safety and the property of others.

Even bankers, who are not famed for being paragons of virtue, were publicly shaking their heads at the lack of ethics on show at the protests.

HSBC said that "only in a peaceful and rational environment" could problems be resolved. British bank Standard Chartered said it staunchly supports Hong Kong's government and the principle of "one country, two systems".

Bank of East Asia said: "We condemn all forms of violence and hope the city can restore peace and order as soon as possible."

Interesting. The Apoliticals are finally speaking out.

10) Senior MTR staff told me they were unhappy with violent protesters and disappointed with the media.

The local and international press, including the New York Times, gave the police a hard time for days when they once used tear gas in an MTR station, complaining that the canisters were a "potential lingering irritation".

But the media showed zero interest when protesters threw a lit petrol bomb underground, infinitely more dangerous.

The fire, put out by a brave staff member, could have killed thousands (a single MTR train carries 3,750 people). The protesters also smashed all the safety cameras in several of the station.

Surely getting killed on the way home should also count at least as a "potential lingering irritation"?

CHAPTER 31

Color Revolution

In Which We Learn Of The Smallest Rally Ever—
Ted Cruz Visits—An Office Is Vandalized—Blue Water—
Wisdom of the Ethnic Minorities—Clean Up Groups Proliferate

A MASKED PROTEST RALLY in Central Hong Kong in mid-October had an extremely low turn-out: One skinny youth.

True story. "No one showed up! Only me! Wearing a mask to show off! This is quite disappointing," Ronald, 20, told Associated Press reporter John Leicester.

The worst thing was that Ronald had also gone to the Tsuen Wan protest the previous night which drew a grand total of only FIVE protesters. Shocking!

The reporter described Ronald as being "confused, shocked and more than a little sad as he gazed unbelieving around the empty park".

Where was everyone?

AT HOME, getting a life, Ronnie baby. The numbers of radical protesters are shrinking like Trump fans who actually get to spend time with Trump.

Hong Kong's main Saturday protest rally, a march starting from Tsim Sha Tsui, attracted only a few thousand people.

But they made up for smaller numbers with extra violence. They trashed shops and the Kowloon Government Offices, a facility that serves people living in one of the poorest, most crowded parts of Hong Kong.

* * *

Disaster. No sooner have we, the Hong Kong moms and dads, really started to work out the links and connections between the various hidden forces behind the protests, than we discover that the secret edifice is splintering. Our sources are reporting that lots of arguments are taking place.

Many behind-the-scenes people are finding the Americans hard to deal with, especially the less informed arrivistes. Their extreme focus on Trump, the US flag, and the 2020 US election are seen as doing more harm than good, but everyone is trying to be nice to them as they have multiple funds with which they can finance anti-government activists.

There's also a sense that the US agents will go their own way whatever members of the committee say.

As a result, the unity that served the anti-government movement so well up till now is disintegrating.

There is also tension between the unashamedly illiberal localists, who hate mainland immigrants, and the Hong Kong students—who take the more politically correct line that it's okay to hate the Chinese government but not okay to hate mainland Chinese people.

As for the Taiwanese, the social engineering in their territory appears to have been achieved, but some of them want the pressure (and finance) to be maintained until the actual election in January.

Then there is tension between some of the radicalized youngsters and the traditional "pro-democracy" politicians. Some of the first group genuinely believe they really can topple the Chinese government, make Hong Kong independent, and became rulers of a new nation—with the help of the Americans. The second group, generally older and better informed, are skeptical about the achievability of these aims and very cynical about how far the US will actually go to help.

Related to that, US President Donald Trump has expressed a lack of interest in both Hong Kong and Taiwan, considering them small fry, and willing to sacrifice them instantly if better options come along.

But from the point of view of people living in Hong Kong, most worrying is the growing presence of a subset of serious revolutionaries who are talking a no-holds-barred approach, anxious to move into the stockpiling of explosives, with a vision of a future that is "noble" guerilla warfare to them but would be classified as terrorism by anyone else.

Part of the problem is China—not because of its reaction, but because it still hasn't reacted. It appears to have done literally nothing. Everyone assumed the Chinese army would have been sent in by now, or there would have been a clampdown in some other way. That would have meant a key objective, the destruction of "one country, two systems", would have been achieved. But none of that has happened.

Yes, there are Chinese agents in Hong Kong too, and yes, there are Chinese soldiers in Hong Kong, as nobody denies. But they have clearly been asked to stand by and allow the local people to handle this situation. It's a surprise to everyone that they have successfully managed to be so restrained, despite decades in which the Beijing leadership has been painted as ruthless and heavy-handed.

* * *

But lo, what light from yonder window breaks?

'Tis the dawn and US Senator Ted Cruz ("Great American Savior") has flown into Hong Kong.

Mr. Cruz recently slammed an American company called NonLethal Technologies for selling non-lethal crowd control equipment to the authorities in Hong Kong, where it was used to kill nobody.

Mr Cruz COMPLETELY FORGOT to slam American gun makers for selling highly lethal crowd control equipment to the authorities in the US who used it to kill 996 of his own citizens last year.

Strange that.

* * *

Some of the Hong Kong black-shirts carried US flags on Saturday. As they walked, the news flashed up on all our phone screens that Trump had made a deal with China.

Suddenly America loved China. The US even praised what the mainland was doing in Hong Kong.

"I think great progress has been made by China in Hong Kong," Trump said. The numbers of people involved in the unrest had dropped, he added.

Traitor! Pontius Pilate! Turncoat! (I'm surprised they didn't start hitting people with the US flags, as they did at the airport on one occasion.)

* * *

The main event on Saturday night, October 12, was in Sha Tin, and involved only about 300 people. The majority chanted slogans against China and the police at a shopping mall.

About 12 went downstairs to the Sha Tin MTR station and promoted Glorious Western Liberal Democracy by smashing turnstiles and destroying the glass-walled office used by railway staff, as one does.

A South China Morning Post reporter asked one of the vandals, 16-year-old Logan, for his motives. He was just expressing his anger, he said. He knew that what they were doing would likely achieve nothing — but he "didn't care much".

He clearly hadn't read the Western media editorials telling him that he was the world's "last hope" for liberal democracy.

* * *

Meanwhile from our former colonial overlords: UK politicians criticized Hong Kong police for arresting 2,379 people, mostly for violent crimes, over a five-month period.

At the same time, UK police arrested 1,300 people, mostly for non-violent crimes, in less than a week.

Not that UK politicians are hypocrites or anything.

When Extinction Rebellion started disruptive protests in London, the Metropolitan police simply banned all protests in that city at a stroke of a pen.

So let's get this straight. If they ban all protests with a single utterance, that's not a problem. But if we ban one out of a hundred, our community is an evil place that is crushing free speech.

Free London!

* * *

On Sunday afternoon, an even smaller group of vandals (fewer than 100) hit Cityplaza in Tai Koo Shing.

There and in other places they continued with actions that the media describe as "calling for democracy" but which honest Hong Kong people would describe more truthfully: They set off a fire bomb at a shopping mall, slashed a police officer's neck, and smashed up a branch of Starbucks, spray-painting foul language on the walls.

"Nobody agrees with this," a Hong Kong mother-of-two told me. "This is just wrong."

What to say? I hate to admit to people that I am a reporter these days.

I feel guilty about the way the media treats Hong Kong people. These citizens are a group of literally millions of law-abiding people trapped in the middle of an awful argument. Yet the world's media ignores them, seeing only those at the extremes—and refusing to see the manipulators behind the scenes.

But things are changing. People on all sides of the Hong Kong debate are hungry to counterbalance the actions of the violent radicals who are spoiling things for everyone.

On the evening of Wednesday, October 16, I was with friends, mostly Hong Kong-born, and found we all shared a feeling that there must be positive things we can do, like help clean and rebuild the place, clear barricades, and encourage respect for others.

Many have already started, such as some people with a Facebook page named Save HK, and a nice cluster of old folk in Wan Chai.

People experienced at cleaning advise that volunteers can sweep up broken glass and remove profane graffiti but should be aware that touching flyposted material can be dangerous.

* * *

The next event I'm going to mention was a telling one on several counts. It took place on Sunday, October 20.

Police REFUSED to issue a permit for a Tsim Sha Tsui march because of the huge risk to innocent people and property—and they now had more than 100 case studies to prove it.

Leaders of the Civil Human Rights Front had a rare attack of truthfulness and AGREED with the police to withdraw the application, so as to avoid mob violence.

And then came the bad news.

One of the leaders, Figo Chan, broke away from the team decision and called on black shirts to march illegally, damn Hong Kong's rule of law.

Chan said he wasn't afraid of any violence. That made sense, since his followers would inevitably be the cause of it.

And that is exactly how it turned out.

Without even waiting for the evening, the violent radicals attacked on multiple fronts.

The horrific outcome was just as the police AND the peaceful protesters feared—petrol bombs thrown, shops smashed, banks and restaurants burned, public transport facilities vandalized and so on.

Hong Kong families and old folk were in serious danger as ground floor premises associated with mainland Chinese individuals were set alight without the slightest regard to the homes above them.

Bomb disposal staff dashed to the scene to safely detonate an IED (improvised explosive device) in Lai Chi Kok. A portable firebomb factory was found in Tai Po. Burning petrol bombs were dropped from skyscrapers directly at police officers' heads.

A mob of men in masks beat up a Putonghua speaker who called on them to stop the vandalism.

Protesters used a chain saw to remove a security camera at Yau Ma Tei MTR station. They also threw petrol bombs into at least four MTR stations.

A Chinese medicine shop was wrecked and ransacked purely for the crime of being Chinese.

A Winnie the Pooh doll was ceremoniously impaled on a stick and set on fire. Take that, Xi Jinping!

Police manning the water cannon paused on Nathan Road when they saw the Civic Party's Jeremy Tan standing with press and protesters outside the mosque and gave them a blast of water. Almost immediately, black shirts started sending messages that police deliberately attacked the mosque as part of China's clampdown on Xinjiang!

People are SO consumed by suspicion, they genuinely think like that.

Videos clearly showed the stream of water aimed downwards at Tam, rather than upwards at the mosque. However, that's not what was reported. The baleful Hong Kong Free Press said: "Eyewitnesses said that there were no protesters nearby at the time of the incident."

At the same time a short distance away, elected politician Edmond Chung had his office vandalized by black shirts as punishment for the crime of being a member of the "wrong" political party.

Chung is vice president of an organization that helps young people. He's a bit too pro-Beijing for me, so I wouldn't rush to vote for him—but I strongly believe that attacking him is the direct opposite of democracy.

Prediction: The shockingly anti-democratic attack on the elected politician's office will get virtually zero coverage, while the police blue water "attack" on innocent South Asians as "representatives of Xinjiang" will be widely covered and discussed, locally and internationally.

Next morning: The shockingly anti-democratic attack on the elected politician's office got virtually zero coverage, while the police's "attack on innocent South Asians" as representatives of Xinjiang was widely covered and discussed. Aieeyah!

* * *

In the following days, Protest leaders decided to capitalize on the success of the fake "attack on a mosque" story by organizing a special extra protest for Brown People.

So they told reporters that there was going to be a joint demonstration of Muslims and Hindus and their supporters.

It took place the day before I wrote this. It was a flop. By the evening of that follow-up march, it was clear that very few Brown People joined in the mayhem, which centered around the burning of Mong Kok MTR station.

Brown People are not dumb. We saw the video: The water was clearly aimed diagonally downwards at Mr. Tam and his followers at the illegal protest. (Besides, in our countries of origin, police fire guns, not water.) Hong Kong's 300,000-strong Muslim community is too smart to be tricked like that.

Organizers added Hindus to the list of people called to the demonstration because brown people are Brown People, right?

Hong Kong's 100,000-strong Hindu community are also intelligent, non-violent people, and chose not to flock to the event. They were busy celebrating Diwali, a beautiful festival in which love is celebrated and candles are burned–not MTR stations, thank you very much.

Who else stayed away? Almost everyone. Even my lovely huggable devoted protester friends who go to absolutely everything stayed home on that occasion, because of the insufferable number of thuggish people now dominating the protests.

So last night it was pretty much ONLY the worst of the thugs—fewer than 1,000 of them.

And boy, could you tell. With no one to hold them back, they set fire to Mong Kok station, smashed up a Tsim Sha Tsui branch of Starbucks, beat up a man who committing the crime of speaking Mandarin to them, used hammers to smash the head of a guy taking pictures, etc.

Oh yes, and the theme of the protest was "anti-brutality".

SOMEBODY NEEDS TO SAY THIS.

You can't denounce brutality by beating up people.

You can't ask people to stop calling you "rioters" by rioting.

You can't call for democracy by trashing the offices of elected politicians.

You can't ask for free speech by silencing anyone who disagrees with you.

You can't ask for the right to govern your city by destroying it.

You can't improve our relationship with mainland China by abusing every symbol of China.

You can't improve ANY situation by calling in Donald Trump.

And you can't say the police are heavy-handed while trying to burn officers alive.

It's that simple, really.

* * *

On Wednesday, October 30, I woke up to find that the protesters who live opposite me, the ones that seemed like a church youth group, had plastered walls and railings with a Hello Kitty style cartoon guide to committing arson and vandalism. It was SO them.

Cute cartoon figures holding a hammer illustrated the instruction to "Renovate" (vandalize and set fire to) businesses.

Cute cartoon figures holding spray paint illustrated the instruction to "Decorate" (deface with flyposters and graffiti) stores.

Vandalism has never been so adorable.

When I got to PolyU, I found walls adorned with calls to rally for autonomy for Hong Kong. As usual, the posters didn't mention democracy at all.

* * *

Renovators were busy this week. Two restaurants were smashed up in recent days, one in Hung Hom and one in Tuen Mun.

A report said that one belonged to an unfortunate Hong Kong person with Fujian roots (and thus "deserved" to have his business firebombed) while the other belonged to a Hong Kong person who supported the black shirts and was hit by mistake.

An alternative report said that the second restaurant was attacked by critics of the protests who copied the renovation idea.

Who's right? I don't know.

But I have a wild and crazy idea.

How about we don't trash ANYBODY's restaurants?

* * *

A Hong Kong resident named Paul was annoyed to see renovation posters appear on his local branch of Starbucks.

People passing by paused to take pictures of the signs but didn't touch them. Paul eventually decided to rip them down. As he did so, he heard abuse shouted at him but he didn't stop.

"You have to do what you think is right," Paul said. "But screw anyone who thinks that defacing and destroying property is about 'loving' Hong Kong."

* * *

On my screen, I see that Newsweek is telling the world the news: "Hong Kong Protests Turn Violent After Five Months".

After five months? So more than 100 violent incidents between June and this month NEVER HAPPENED?

"How could Newsweek get it so wrong?" Lucy Luk asked me.

"Easy," I said. "Journalists believe their own myths."

This reminds me of a quote from Andrew Cline, a professor who studies this subject, who explained: "Once a master narrative has been set, it is very difficult to get journalists to see that their narrative is simply one way, and not necessarily the correct or best way, of viewing people and events."

* * *

The next day, I arrived on the walkway in Hung Hom just after agitators had pasted fresh "name and shame" posters adding Disney, Marvel, ESPN, NBA, Nike, Vans and Lancome to the list of enemies.

Staff working at those firms need not panic yet. (Calm down, Hulk.) They were not color-coded for Renovation or Decoration. Hopefully it will be the least violent punishment on the list, which is boycotting.

Luxury jeweler Tiffany and Co was on the list, so radicals will have to try to get through the week without buying HK$100 000 diamond rings.

Oh the suffering!

Puzzled, I note that US clothes store Gap is on the list. What was its crime?

The poster says: "It apologized after a T-shirt showing China without Taiwan was sold at a store in Canada, issuing the statement 'Gap Inc. respects China's sovereignty and territorial integrity'."

Gap respected China's sovereignty and territorial integrity!

How could they do such a thing? I'm shocked. Shocked.

* * *

Meanwhile in cyberspace, I see that radicals are discussing the Renovation of the Hong Kong branches of two Singapore banks, DBS and UOB, plus the Singapore High Commission.

This would be to punish Singapore Prime Minister Lee Hsien Loong for saying negative things about the protesters.

Hey, violent radicals, why not fly to Singapore and try your antics there?

That would be a learning experience for everyone.

I also found a note from resident Shaun Dove. "I heard of a Harry Potter trick," he said. "Rioters stop the violence and destruction, and the police stop using force. It really works. It's like magic."

Among people on my network, both yellow camp and blue camp members loathe the Renovation trend.

I wish someone on the committee would gently teach the Renovators the free speech dictum of Noam Chomsky: *"If we do not believe in free speech for people we despise, we don't believe in it at all."*

Five Notes From October

1) Talking of South Asians, as we were earlier, I heard that a decision has been taken in China to allow Bohemian Rhapsody, the bio-movie of Farrokh Bulsara (Freddie Mercury), to be shown with just a little censorship.

I suspect it's the line in the song which goes "I'm just a Pooh bear from a Pooh family."

Ba-dump. Tish!

2) Part of one of my recent articles has gone viral, with lots of people making copies of it, turning it into memes, translating into Chinese, and reprinting it widely. I'm happy to have been of use.

3) Joshua Wong revealed that he would no longer be mentioning Demosisto, the pro-independence political party he founded. By ceasing references to the group, Wong hopes to stand and win a seat in next month's district board election. (Not sure if he realizes that we can all still access his Demosisto website, which still calls for self-determination for Hong Kong, in Chinese and English. The Internet is kind of public, Josh old buddy.)

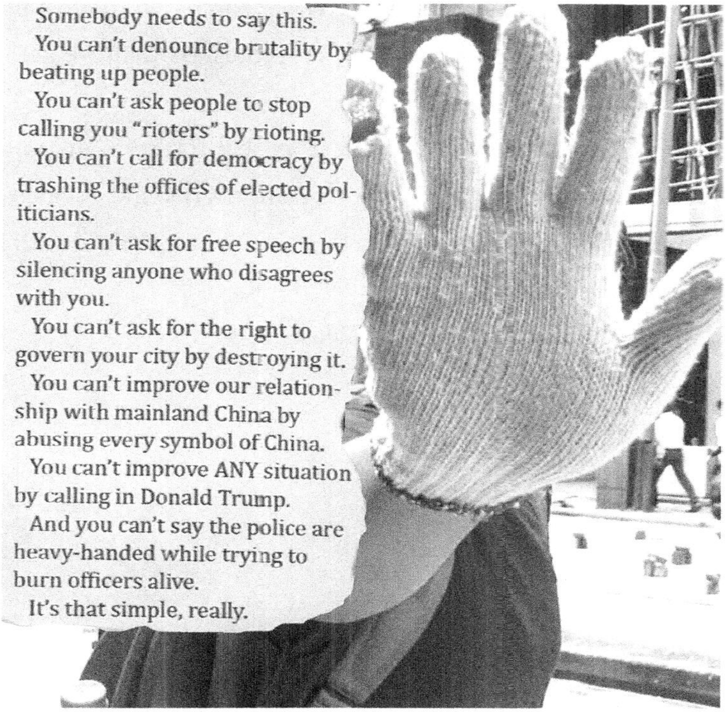

4) Video circulated of a fight which broke out between a black-masked youth and an old man taking pictures.

The tall young man sent a flying kick at the 60-something citizen, but the wiry oldster grabbed his foot, and then fought back with his fists. The youngster eventually ran away.

A woman made excuses for the boy. "The old man kicked him first," she told a shocked crowd of onlookers.

But the video showed this was not true. The old man's feet stayed on the ground.

"Waah!" joked Ho Yin-ng. "The old uncle's kick is so fast, it was invisible."

Alan Chiu said: "This must be the legendary 'shadow kick'."

5) Yes, people are a bit passive in Hong Kong, compared to most places. In UK, police and citizens are far tougher on protesters than we are, despite ours being significantly more dangerous.

"London commuters went batshit crazy at protestors disrupting our transport systems here," Lisa Lai Roberts from UK told me. A video showed them grabbing protesters and heaving them away. "Don't mess with London commuters."

Can we borrow a few Londoners, please, Lisa?

CHAPTER 32

The Wedding Party

In Which Violence Erupts At Malls—Intimations Of Balance—A Wedding Party—Car Park Tragedy—The Active And Passive Trick

A FEARLESS MIDDLE-AGED man marched into a Wan Chai street on the afternoon of Saturday, November 2. He single-handedly removed barricades near the Hopewell Centre, ignoring the objections of angry masked men in black.

They poured petrol onto the barricades and set them on fire to make his job harder—but he held the parts of the obstacles which were not burning and continued to patiently drag them off the street.

"Lucky he was Caucasian," said reader Shirny Lau. "He would be beaten unconscious if he was Chinese."

Sad but true. Elsewhere on the same night, several ethnic Chinese people who expressed disagreement with the protesters' views were beaten unconscious. (But again, I repeat, for the umpteenth time: We should not confuse the organized, violent radicals with the peaceful protesters—who today were again much lower in number, but who can still be seen watching from the side, or occasionally filling the role of the nice one).

Talking to Hong Kong mothers and fathers about what's happening behind the scenes in Hong Kong, we note that it fits extraordinarily well with the key principles in the revolution consultants' handbooks about overthrowing governments.

They specify that there are six pillars holding up the government—all of which must be neutralized. Insurgents have to get the people in those pillars on side or make sure they are delegitimized or even defunded and abolished.

First is the police. In Hong Kong, the committee has succeeded in taking one of the best-loved forces in the world and rebranding it as a Nazi-like force of ruthless mass-murderers controlled by people over the border. There are loud calls for the police to be defunded and abolished.

Second is the official bureaucracy through which the government works. In Hong Kong, pandem legislators are using filibuster tactics to bring the work of the Legislative Council to a halt. They have disabled key funding channels, through their disabling of certain committees, and are planning to halt all government work as a strategy after the 2020 Legislative Council election.

Third is the education system. The radicals have performed poorly in primary and secondary schools in proportional terms (there are a million children in Hong Kong), yet the relatively low participation level has not been a problem. The schoolchildren who do turn up have been well-exploited by the media, which has gone out of its way to focus on images of children in school uniform protesting. And as numbers of adults actively participating in public disorder events falls, the proportion of young people is rising. In terms of universities, the committee has pulled in all the student union heads, so feel that they have got that sector firmly in hand.

Fourth is organized religious groups. There are a lot of Hong Kong Chinese Christian groups involved in the protests, plus some English-speaking church people. Yet the Buddhists, Muslims and Hindus have largely declined to participate.

The big international English-speaking churches have stayed out of the political argument, and the Catholics are divided. The majority appear to stand with a leader named Cardinal John Tong Hon, who is known for brokering good relations between China and the Vatican.

A smaller group is actively participating at a high level in the protests. In particular, there is retired Bishop Joseph Zen Ze-kiun, whose flock of anti-government campaigners includes newspaper boss Jimmy Lai and democracy campaigner Martin Lee.

Fifth is the media. Most of the local media and all of the major international media are pushing a single narrative, in which mainland China is the aggressor (despite its non-involvement) and the Hong Kong people are united in their call to Donald Trump for rescue.

Sixth is the business community. There is major work going on by the committee behind the scenes to create a list which shows which shops and services have stated that they are standing with the radical protesters. The idea is that a "yellow economy" will rise up and other shops and services will go bankrupt.

There is a lot of belief in this idea, but old hands say it will fail: It is dependent on its own myth that Hong Kong speaks with one voice and misses the truth that the majority of people in this city lean towards the apolitical and pragmatic end of the spectrum.

The yellow economy will fail to take off, they say. We'll have to wait and see.

* * *

Today, November 2, has not been a good day. People on the network are not happy. For the past few months, police have been following the Carrie Lam administration's advice to continue issuing permits for demonstrations as a default policy. But they haven't been turning them down enough, as far as many people are concerned.

"The Hong Kong Appeal Board on Public Meetings and Processions still regularly gives out permits to protesters who promise their rallies will be peaceful, despite the fact that more than 90 percent of them now turn violent," says Errik Chow, father of one.

He mentions an old English proverb which says: "Fool me once: shame on you; fool me twice: shame on me."

"The Board should have a special version," he says. "Fool me once: shame on you; fool me 100 times in a row: huge, huge, huge shame on me.'"

But I respond that it's hard for the Hong Kong police to deny a single permit—any refusal is greeted with wall-to-wall condemnations on Twitter saying: "See? See? They denied the marchers a permit! This proves that all freedom in Hong Kong is gone. 'One country, two systems' is DEAD."

To fight that lie, permits need to still be widely and easily available, and that's why the board that issues them has taken a highly lenient stance. Truth is, it's far easier to get a permit in Hong Kong than it is in most Western countries. You won't see that fact in print in the media, I guarantee.

But sometimes the likelihood of looming violence is just too great. Then, board members just grit their teeth and deny the permit.

Today was such a day.

No permit was granted, but the radicals simply ignored that fact, and a few thousand held a march anyway—which soon turned predictably violent. At least it wasn't a big crowd. I was watching from a distance and keeping an eye on the media at the same time.

My eyebrows were up as I scanned media reports.

Curiously, I was finally detecting signs of a change of tone overseas. It was no longer 99.9 percent beatification of the protesters—there were voices, just a few, around the world starting to see the other side. It was probably now more like 97 percent biased, and two or three percent straight, balanced, informed reporting.

On Twitter, one black-masked Hong Kong protester sent out a greeting to his counterparts overseas in Catalonia, Chile and Lebanon, where protests were dealt with in a much more heavy-handed way.

"Hello all protesters around the world," the Hong Konger wrote.

A quick reply came from South America: "Fuck you, we have nothing to do with those thugs from Hong Kong."

One of the possible reasons for the change is this: People around Hong Kong and elsewhere on the planet can now access live TV feeds of the violence on our streets.

These show what's actually happening at most protests. You can see the violent radicals rampaging around, sometimes for hour after hour after hour, before the police respond in any way.

And you can then can see how these events are deceptively written up by journalists from the BBC, RTHK, Apple Daily and elsewhere as if the trouble starts with the police.

Hong Kong residents of all cultures are baffled by this. "Maybe they live in some parallel universe where effect comes before cause," says reader Jon Wacom.

Local journalists are certainly getting negative comments on their work from members of the Hong Kong public.

A mother forwards me a report from a Hong Kong man named Antares Au.

Reading the South China Morning Post, Antares saw an image of a woman struggling with a police officer captioned: "A partygoer is arrested near Lan Kwai Fong".

The implication was that one of those oh-so-brutal male police officers had jumped on an innocent reveler, and a female one at that, partying in the bar district.

But Antares knew that was not the case. He'd been right there on the spot at that time. He'd seen the woman screaming profanities and poking police with her umbrella. The police officers simply responded as any police officer anywhere on the planet would respond to physical provocation.

So Antares added a straightforward, factual account in the comment section below the online version of the article.

His story was quickly deleted with a note saying that it "violated" the newspaper's rules.

"This is the nature of the beast we're dealing with: A press which operates solely to advance its bias, to the exclusion of facts," Antares said.

By the end of an exhausting Saturday, I was (for a change) looking forward to Sunday. The protests on that day are often a little calmer, drawing out some of the good protesters to dilute the number of violent radicals.

* * *

But not this time. I didn't know it at the time, but a small announcement presaged the beginning of the end game.

The wires came alive on the afternoon of Sunday, November 3, when radicals passed around what they clearly saw as a shocking piece of news: a police officer was deliberately and blatantly getting married.

Not only that, but the romantic couple was having a FAMILY PARTY, to which their relatives, including old people and youngsters, would be present, and very likely some colleagues too.

The accounts on Telegram, LIHKG and other networks were suddenly alive with outrage.

It's hard to explain to people outside Hong Kong just why such a normal act, two people getting married, could produce such sustained fury from so many people.

But you have to remember that the police were no longer seen as human beings doing a difficult job—they had been turned into two-legged manifestations of evil. To radicals in Hong Kong, and, I am ashamed to say, probably a few of my own friends and students, it seemed entirely reasonable to go and try to wreck the happiest day of two entirely innocent people.

By four in the afternoon, crowds had gathered around the Crowne Plaza Hotel in Tseung Kwan O, on the East Coast of the Kowloon peninsula.

But police could not rush to the rescue of their off-duty colleagues. There was trouble elsewhere they had to deal with.

* * *

But before going there, we should talk a little more about the media here. The change of implied order of events was not the only technique reporters used to distort the truth.

One of the funniest was a writing-editing technique used particularly well by a writer at RTHK news, who people in my network had nicknamed "Mr Pravda". He uses the active tense for police actions, and the passive tense, with the subject omitted, for protester actions. Protesters would simply disappear from headlines and news ledes (journalistic jargon for the opening paragraph).

So, during a typical riot, protesters may throw firebombs and police might react by firing tear gas to disperse them.

But in the write-up, the order of events will be reversed, and police action will be given in active form, subject included: "Police fired tear gas".

The protesters' action would be given in passive form with the subject (the person doing the action) omitted: "Firebombs were thrown."

Sometimes Mr. Pravda would omit mention of the vandals and details of the act of vandalism itself, with vague phrases such as "chaos broke out" or "shops were targeted".

His bias was as hilariously transparent as that of any Communist Party official writing in the People's Daily.

Police fired tear gas!

Police beat people!

People arrested protesters!

In other news, shops were... targeted.

(We have no idea who did this. Probably police?)

There were two other curious Mr. Pravda characteristics, which were clearly on display in coverage of news items this particular afternoon.

Compare what actually happened with what was reported.

Clusters of residents, many of whom were families with children, were shopping and eating at one of Hong Kong Island's most popular malls, Cityplaza in Taikoo Shing, on the eastern side.

A few protesters were leaning over the balconies, singing their hymn.

Then there were shouts and terrified people started running.

Black-masked vandals stormed into the mall, approached two restaurants, scared the diners out, and vandalized both places. They knocked over furniture, smashed plate glass windows, and used spray paint to graffiti the walls with foul language.

And the RTHK report on this incident?

"Riot police stormed into the Cityplaza mall in Tai Koo on Sunday evening", was the opening phrase.

You do get some reference to what the police were responding to further down, described in vague terms. "But the trouble started after 6 pm, after two restaurants were targeted," it says.

Who "targeted" them? It doesn't say. In what way were they "targeted"? It doesn't say.

What happened to these restaurants? How did the workers feel? Or the families eating in them? We're not told any of this.

There is mention that "a small business was firebombed".

By whom? It doesn't say.

Did the firebombs throw themselves? Apparently so.

Why that business in particular? Was the shopkeeper or owner a mainland Chinese immigrant, by any chance?

The answers to all these questions, which any half-professional reporter knows should be the heart of the story, are completely omitted from the report, which twists the news so badly that it retains only one function — it transfers the criminality from the perpetrators to people trying to stop them.

Mr. Pravda's reports often include quotes from unnamed, unidentified witnesses complaining that everything is the fault of the police, and an anecdote about police officers treating journalists roughly.

In this particular report, the RTHK journalist bizarrely implies that the only unhappiness at the scene was caused was a result of police coming in to deal with the vandals: "Riot police quickly stormed in, rushing past families and shoppers, leaving a woman in tears."

Another example: a frightening attack also took place at a shopping mall in Tai Po this same afternoon.

Masked vandals smashed up a Japanese restaurant in a brutal response to a part owner's relative exercising her right of free speech to denounce violence.

Staff and customers phoned police, who arrived at high speed.

What did Mr. Pravda report?

"Riot police also rushed into the Tai Po Mega Mall in the evening, subduing at least two women." (Note: Not vandals or criminals who committed crimes, but just "two women". Now they are arresting people just for being female!)

After reading about the outrage of the police entering a mall, we learn why. "A Yoshinoya restaurant was vandalised earlier in the afternoon." (Note the passive tense and the omission of the person or people who did the vandalizing. The restaurants apparently vandalized themselves.)

And of course, there were the anonymous quotes. "One witness told RTHK she thought the police were out of line," he writes. The report continues:

One woman who took part in the human chain after watching a movie at the mall was confounded at why the police even showed up.

"We were just standing there holding hands," she said.

"No reason, Not one reason. I didn't see any violence anywhere.

"Nobody was doing anything wrong as far as I can see, and I walked through the whole mall and I saw nothing bad, so I don't understand."

Another woman agreed that the police overreacted.

"They shouldn't be here because all we did is just sing. That's it! Why threaten us? Why hold a gun? Why spray the people? It's absolutely ridiculous!" she said.

You can't make this stuff up.

It wasn't just a few reporters at RTHK doing extremely one-sided reporting, but also counterparts at Apple Daily and the Hong Kong Free Press and several other outlets.

By November, those of us watching the violence would sometimes amuse ourselves by making up reports about how the scenes in front of us would be described by these news outlets.

Headline: "Police Continue Crime Spree".

Text:

Police blatantly arrested members of the Hong Kong public yesterday.

In unrelated news, petrol bombs threw themselves yesterday, launching themselves through the air.

Bricks followed.

Windows of restaurants smashed themselves in an orgy of destruction.

Families with children were fine with all this, but then police arrived.

A resident said: 'How dare police attend a crime scene! That's surely illegal.'

An unnamed shopkeeper said: 'We are delighted to witness the destruction of our livelihood by masked vandals because we support them entirely."

* * *

In the same Taikoo Shing shopping mall, Cityplaza, later the same evening, a fight broke out in a restaurant between an apparently mentally challenged individual and others, resulting in a bloody fight in which a pandem politician had part of his ear bitten off.

All in all, it was one of the worst weekends so far.

Members of my network and myself went to bed that night shaking our heads at the string of horrible events—the besieged wedding, the vandalized shops, the twisted reporting, the bloody fight.

But there was going to be worse news the next morning.

* * *

What we didn't find out until the following morning was that the mayhem had continued in Tseung Kwan O, the site of the wedding party, long past midnight.

As usual, any calmer protesters gradually left the scene as the night continued, leaving only the more radical protesters.

As midnight passed, about 100 remaining radicals had blocked the streets, having built barricades in the areas of Tong Chun Street and Tong Ming Street.

The following morning, Monday, November 4, we woke up to find social media focusing on two new stories.

Police had swarmed into a multistory parking lot in Tseung Kwan O, near where the attempted attack on the wedding had taken place, grabbed one of the protesters, and they had thrown him over the edge of a wall!

Really? *Police had thrown him over a wall?*

That was awful to read. The unfortunate victim had fallen a long distance, three stories, and lay smashed on the ground—but was still breathing at the time. An ambulance was called, but other brutal police moved quickly to prevent it from reaching the injured young man.

About half an hour later, ambulance men finally managed to fight their way past the police officers and managed to reach him—but it was probably too late. He had lost consciousness and was now on the critical list, his head smashed from the fall. He was in critical condition in hospital and might die.

It was a grim and depressing story, and on the Internet, artists were quickly mocking up cartoons or photoshop art showing police officers throwing a young man off a building.

Despite all the cameras at the scene, no one had filmed the officer throwing the young man to his doom, and he had apparently been alone, with no witnesses to the crime. Who was the murder victim? Not even a protester, apparently.

CNN reported that there was no indication that the young man, who had been named as computer science student Alex Chow Tsz-lok, had even been involved in the protest.

He was simply an entirely innocent victim. The implication was that he may even have been a passer-by; a person who didn't own a car strolling through the third floor of a car park in the middle of the night, as one does.

Just think of that. An innocent young man is seized and flung over the edge of a building—it is hard to imagine anything more evil.

The radicals had a simple description for what had happened to him: this was a clear and undeniable attempt at murder by the gang of killers known as the Hong Kong Police Force. They had been telling us that all along, and now here was proof in the broken body of an innocent young man.

* * *

That evening, a reporter named Tse Pui-shan turned up with a large gang of friends at the regular police press briefing wearing anti-police signs on their heads, causing a disruption that led to the event being abandoned.

He was then quoted by other reporters complaining that by halting the event, "the police were depriving the public of their right to know".

* * *

It was all very dispiriting, but one can't stay at home and mope.

This was literary festival week in Hong Kong, and this reporter was visiting a different school every day to discuss various aspects of writing, including journalism.

On Wednesday, November 6, I went to a school at the top of a hill reached by a long staircase and a winding sloped path.

At the school, I gave a presentation, and called for questions–and the children at Wah Yan School turned out to be very impressive.

The subject turned to journalistic ethics, and, with no prompting from me, they said that reporters should be balanced but were failing to achieve that in Hong Kong.

* * *

After the school talk, I got back to the PolyU Block X coffee shop to find readers had sent me a clip of a TV reporter trying to get an old man in Tuen Mun to criticize the police. It made me laugh.

Reporter: Did you feel unwell when the tear gas came in?

Old man: Can't you see how well I'm looking? I'm 80 years old! There's chaos everywhere! Of course, there was a chance that tear gas would end up here. It's hardly a surprise. Not a problem.

Reporter: So you won't be making a complaint?

Old man: Complaint about what?

* * *

There are clear things that the revolution consultants have got right. For example, the Serbian handbook specifies that the protesters should brand themselves as *democratic, honest, popular* and *progressive,* while those who disagree should be portrayed as *dictatorial*, *illegitimate*, *corrupt* and *ruthless*.

Similarly, the protesters should anticipate being called *traitors* and *terrorists*, and prepare themselves for their opponents to describe themselves as *patriotic* and *responsible*.

This describes the situation precisely, right down to the words chosen.

When someone tells you that that there have been more than 100 murders in your town and no one has noticed

CHAPTER 33

The Car Park Fall

In Which We Learn What Happened In The Car Park—
A UK Media Analyst's Observations About International Coverage

OVER THE NEXT two days, a pair of completely different stories emerged about what really happened in the early hours of Monday morning at the car park near the wedding party.

The radicals were mostly clinging to their story that police had moved into the car park and either thrown student Alex Chow Tsz-lok over the wall, or stormed through the car park in a way that scared him so much that he had ended up fleeing from them, and fallen to his death.

Either way, it was clearly the direct fault of police officers, who should be charged with murder, they say.

Furthermore, "everyone agreed" that evil cops had then prevented the ambulance from reaching him, hoping he would die before they got there.

But reading the reports, it became increasingly clear that they had no hard evidence of any kind for any part of their tale.

Ambulance staff were now speaking out too—and they had a very different story, and in particular went into detail about the second allegation. They said that there were so many call-outs that night that five different ambulances from the nearby hospital were on the streets.

One was assigned to go to pick up Alex Chow, the young man who fell from the car park, with the call received at 1:11 am.

But the ambulance driver found the road blocked by buses and private cars which could not move in any direction, since protesters had built barricades in the road, causing traffic to seize up.

Eventually the ambulance driver managed to get round the barricades and the other vehicles, reaching Chow at 1:30 am. They felt that the 19 minutes they took were entirely reasonable, considering the distance from the hospital and the sheer number of blockages on route.

And what about the stories of police deliberately delaying them?

Leung Kwok-lai, Fire Services Department Assistant Chief Ambulance Officer (Kowloon East), said they were not true. The crew did not come into contact with police at all.

So the allegation that police stopped the ambulance from reaching Chow seemed clearly false—the vehicle had been slowed by protesters' barricades.

What about the first part of the tale? What actually happened to Alex Chow in the car park?

One student gave an interview which provided an important clue—he said that a number of the young men were very much into making parkour-style movements, running along passages and rooftops and making dramatic, acrobatic jumps.

But the car park was a dangerous place for that, because some of the outer walls had ledges beyond them, while others didn't.

Had a young man mistaken the third floor for the second floor, tragedy would have ensued. This insight from a student turned out to be the key that unlocked the mystery.

And it was powerfully confirmed later that week, when security videos taken inside the car park were found and put online. They revealed what had almost certainly happened that night.

The videos showed that during the period in question, there were no police officers at all in the car park. But Chow and other young men were inside, moving around.

In one scene, a young man runs towards an outer wall and leaps smoothly onto it in a classic parkour jump—but then realizes there is no outside ledge on this particular floor, and stops himself just in time to prevent himself going over.

In another video clip, a young man makes a similar jump, but does go right over the wall. Fortunately, he manages to spin around, grab the wall, and pull himself back.

A third clip shows Chow in the car park, moving around by himself. But he soon goes out of camera range.

The obvious conclusion was hard to avoid. Chow, exactly like the other two young men, had probably tried to jump the walls on the third floor.

And just like the others, he had discovered that on that level there was no outer ledge on which to land—but it was too late for him, and he had tumbled over the side, falling three stories to the ground.

It had simply been an accident: and one caused by a misjudgment he had made himself, and which two other young men had made in the same car park at the same time. That was the only rational deduction from the security video clips.

But of course, if you were in an entirely irrational mode, as the hardliners were, any assertion that this was a tragic accident could only be seen as a lie.

They continued to insist that police had thrown him over the wall. Drawn images showing that non-existent event proliferated on walls around Hong Kong, just as images of Lost Eye Woman had appeared around the city and around the world in August.

The radicals gave notice to the government—if Alex Chow Tsz-lok dies, he would be considered yet another police MURDER VICTIM to add to the Prince Edward Station killings and there would be hell to pay.

On Friday morning, November 8, at just after 8 am, Alex Chow Tsz-lok died—and the radicals vowed the harshest of revenges.

"They are really, really angry this time," said my source among the still active protesters. "They are going to burn down the city."

My sources in the police and the government said the exact same thing—they detected an unusual amount of fury at the "murder" of Chow and were considering shutting all schools in Hong Kong in a bid to keep children safe.

The prediction was that the city was going to descend into chaos over yet another murder that hadn't happened.

* * *

Parents and single residents of Hong Kong soon reported that there was action on social media too.

Several people who rebutted anti-China tirades on Facebook found their accounts frozen.

Donald Tam responded to a critic of China with a mild comment: "This guy is a troll... ignore him".

Donald was suspended for 30 days by Facebook.

Others had similar experiences. "As far as Facebook is concerned, all hateful posts are okay if they are against China," said John Chow.

"Free speech is only for people with Sinophobia," Yang Chunyang said.

* * *

By the afternoon of Friday, November 8, several media outlets were describing the sad demise of the student who fell from a car park as "the first death" of the protests.

Hong Kong parents in my group disagreed. A fight had broken out on June 16 at the Star Ferry between a gardener, 63, and a salesman 26, both of whom had earlier attended the protests, they point out. The older man died and the younger one was arrested for murder.

"Why does everyone look the other way on that one?" asked my source, rhetorically. "Probably because there's no way to blame it on police."

This weekend, there were several memorial events for Alex Chow, and initially they seemed to be relatively peaceful.

This was Saturday, November 9, and one of Hong Kong's best annual events was scheduled for this evening—the celebration of local heroes at the community awards ceremony on Saturday at Government House.

This year, the list included a British Lord who fine-tuned our legal system to its present world-class standard, three hero police constables who jumped into the sea during a lethal typhoon to save distressed citizens, and a sewage engineer who kept Hong Kong's toilets flushing for decades.

But the event was spoiled by pandem politician Ted Hui Chi-fung shouting abuse at the police officers.

I hope karma stops his toilet working.

Also this evening, I received some interesting news from overseas. A UK-based media center found that the New York Times produced relatively few articles for a wide range of violent protests around the world this summer—but an astonishing 282 references to the protests in Hong Kong.

Fox News produced more than 20 times as many reports on the Hong Kong protests as it did for the other ones.

This is despite the fact that the other protests involved police or army officers shooting significant numbers of protesters dead—unlike Hong Kong. Standard measures of news value ("If it bleeds, it leads") were ignored.

The media's decisions on what to cover has "little to do with their righteousness or popularity, and much more to do with whom they are protesting against", said the study by Alan MacLeod of the Glasgow University Media Group.

The stats he has collected are impressive. They clearly show the Western media is deeply biased against China, a conclusion which will come as a great surprise to absolutely no one at all.

The Fox News reference doesn't surprise me, but the New York Times' egregious performance is a disappointment.

It reveals a grim determination among journalists to add "news value" to any protest that can be manipulated to show China in a bad light, even if half a dozen other protests are far more newsworthy by any normal measure of journalism.

* * *

Talking of media, I took a moment to check Twitter. Our old friend, the discredited prophet of doom Gordon C. Chang, has been sounding disappointed that Hong Kong protests have still not produced the growing death-count of anti-government rallies in other places.

But he has perked up a bit at Alex Chow Tsz-lok's death. "Even a single death creates a cycle of revenge and retaliation that no one will be able to control," he wrote.

He and the people who respond to him sound deeply hopeful.

Unfortunately for Chang, but thankfully for the rest of us, most gatherings to remember the unfortunate student, so far, have remained peaceful. It has actually been a relatively calm day.

* * *

Okay. Disregard that previous line. I spoke too soon.

It is being overtaken by events.

Things are not calm. Today is Monday, November 11, and the press is reporting that there has been a massive uprising among Hong Kong's student population. They are taking over the city's main universities.

There have been "coups" of a sort at Hong Kong University in Pok Fu Lam and City University in Kowloon Tong, and pitched battles are being reported at Polytechnic University on the east side of Tsim Sha Tsui and Chinese University of Hong Kong in Tai Po, a town in the New Territories.

"The students are revolting," says Philip Mo, one of the fathers in my group. "In more ways than one."

But his clunky joke (perhaps I should say Dad Joke) leaves me cold. I am too busy being puzzled.

The story baffles me, and much of the network: Since September, we have been convinced that the vast majority of Hong Kong's university students had stepped away from the radical protests, leaving only a small number of highly politicized individuals to co-operate with the violent radicals' activities—normally the student union leaders and their close associates.

Yet judging by the reports coming through, and particularly the pictures being broadcast from Chinese University, I may have got that wrong. The students of this city en masse are conducting a major uprising, according to the reports. Predictably, it is being touted as "revenge for the murder of Chow Tsz-lok".

But let's go back a few hours, to the very beginning of this tumultuous week.

CHAPTER 34

A Man Is Set On Fire

*In Which Our Narrator Takes Part In A Race—
Feeling Like A Bug—A Man Is Set On Fire*

THIS MONDAY MORNING, November 11, started really badly for Hong Kong with "Operation Dawn", a well-planned and secretive campaign to shut down the city. The committee had done its job extraordinarily well, with detailed planning and a clear strategy.

The radicals were trying to paralyze the city's transport hubs to stop Hong Kong people getting to their workplaces or schools.

But in addition to the usual attempts to halt buses and trains, one group threw objects onto railway lines near University Station in Tai Po: an extremely dangerous act.

Police raced to the scene to try to stop them. But the protesters were armed with firebombs and worked hard to maintain their position.

Gone were the days when daytime protest activities were relatively peaceful and the "witching hour" tended to start after dark, at about 8 pm.

No. This week, by seven o'clock in the morning, a pitched battle was under way at Chinese University, and it continued on and off until 11 am It was basically a fight between Molotov-cocktail-armed protesters and police trying to disperse them with tear gas at a Chinese University access point unromantically named No. 2 Bridge.

But here was the problem. The bridge overlooked the Tolo Highway, one of the most important major expressways through the area, linking the New Territories to Kowloon and Hong Kong Island, and protesters were throwing heavy objects down onto cars. Some called it "the deadly hailstorm".

This again showed impressive planning and co-ordination.

At the same time, an identical group using identical methods had taken control of the over-the-highway footbridge outside the Cross Harbour Tunnel, linked to Hong Kong Polytechnic University. They were dropping objects onto the traffic there, too. Showers of chairs and bins and other objects were falling onto cars, buses and trucks.

The perfectly syncronized actions showed that the instructions had come from the secretive leaders of the yellow coalition.

Both roads were vital arteries needed to keep the Hong Kong community functioning.

The Tolo Highway was one of the main expressways used by residents of the New Territories, the rural "countryside" parts of Hong Kong, to get to work in the densely urbanized areas of Kowloon and Hong Kong. It was also a major route for trucks and other transport vehicles.

The road outside the Cross Harbour Tunnel was literally the busiest road in Hong Kong, filled with traffic 24 hours a day, seven days a week—and mostly as a stop-start traffic queue, because it is so heavily used. If you go at the crack of dawn on a Sunday, you can keep your vehicle moving gently, but even on that day of rest, it turns into a slow traffic jam by 10 am.

The committee leaders had been smart, or well advised by the pro-revolutionary groups providing training: Close down these two roads, and much of the community's activities grind to a halt.

The aim was no less than to bring Hong Kong to its knees.

* * *

I'm writing this at a table in the coffee shop at Exchange Square. The live reports from the scenes continue to refer to the protesters as "students" but the parents are skeptical. The notion that the student population of Hong Kong is rising up against the government doesn't ring true from what we know about the young people of this community.

In reality, people on my network think the real root of the problem is politically motivated violent radicals infiltrating university student groups and causing problems—plus the destabilizing agents from the West, working with anti-China subversives from Hong Kong.

Staff at the coffee shop in Exchange Square I use as my Central office have decided that the chances of them being attacked are now high, since Starbucks is now ludicrously being painted as worthy of destruction.

They politely tell us that we must all vacate the premises by 11.30 am, as staff will be sent home and the premises shut.

Aieeyah! My second most important office will now no longer be available. Not good.

* * *

And back at Chinese University? As is now becoming common, protesters are arguing that the police have no legal right to enter the protest area and stop them.

This makes no sense.

The Chinese University's President, a man named Rocky Tuan, turns out to be an impressively articulate man who sends messages to both sides: to the police asking them to remain calm, and to the protesters asking them to leave their encampment.

Yet, for all his attempts to sound balanced, he has no doubt which side is causing the problem.

In a reference to the throwing of objects down onto the Tolo Highway, he writes: "We condemn such irresponsible acts as it could seriously endanger human life. We understand that the police had to enter our campus and station themselves on the bridge to prevent such acts and ensure the safety of traffic flow on the highway. Although CUHK has right of way to the No 2 bridge, it is officially public property."

* * *

Meanwhile, the city-wide transport attack is causing problems everywhere—and triggers one event that will stay in most Hong Kongers' minds for the duration of the protest.

At noon today, a father-of-two (some reports say three) who works in the construction industry was on his way to hospital for a medical check-up.

A resident of Ma On Shan, he noticed a commotion at the local MTR station. A group of about 20 hardline radicals were actively vandalizing the ticket machines and terrorizing staff.

He chases after the vandals, who run away. He was a wiry man, but not young or strong or fast and fails to catch them.

At the footbridge over On Chun Street, he gets into a verbal altercation with some of the protesters, which turns into a scuffle. The old man is slightly wounded on the head, and bleeding from a small cut. A passer-by tends him.

But the man, who was wearing a rumpled green polo shirt, is indomitable. Seeing some of the protesters watching him from a distance on the footbridge, he walks back towards them, and shouts: "You are not Chinese."

"We are Hong Kongers," the radicals shout.

As the man continues to debate with the couple directly in front of him, another radical protester calmly approaches him with container and pours liquid over the man.

At first, he doesn't react at all.

Then the assailant throws a flame at him.

The old man's upper body is suddenly engulfed in red—and he staggers backwards, slapping at himself. His face, chest and neck are on fire.

He flails around for a few moments, and then manages to pull the burning shirt off.

In a short space of time, a significant portion of the skin on his body (doctors would later estimate 40 percent) has been badly burned. When an ambulance arrives, they rush him to hospital where he is in critical condition.

I put a clip of the attack of the man onto Facebook.

Facebook immediately deletes it.

But other people on the network have picked it up and is it soon in wide circulation.

I put it back up on Facebook, and this time it stays.

* * *

In the evening, the stand-off at the bridge over the Tolo Highway is continuing. Chinese University head Rocky Tuen decides he must physically go to the bridge to try to negotiate.

He talks first to police officers, who tell him that they have no choice but to attempt to stop the continuing reckless endangerment of human life by protesters throwing objects at vehicles moving at high speed. It is only a matter of time before someone is hurt or killed, they point out.

Tuan agrees.

If protesters will cease doing this, officers will retreat from the bridge, the police tell him and his colleagues.

University officials agree that this has to be the way forward, and take this message to the activists—who flatly reject it and refuse to stop hurling objects over the side.

University officials are disappointed but go back to the police, finding them less intransigent than the activists.

The school administrators ask police to move their officers away from the bridge as a gesture of good will to break the deadlock.

Police officers do so—and protesters snatch their advantage, moving in to take complete possession of the bridge over the highway.

The activists then erect barricades to prevent any access to the university from that side, the eastern part of the campus.

They decide to turn this into an "occupation", and make plans to sleep overnight at the site or in the nearby sports field.

While the media continues to paint the police as exceptionally heavy-handed, the force has once again demonstrated its real besetting sin: its light touch means that it is too often taken advantage of.

CHAPTER 35

The Amazing Race

In Which We Take Part In Cross-City Dash—My Office Wrecked

IT HAD BEEN A WARM NIGHT. The next morning dawned cloudy and hazy, and the temperature had dropped slightly. It was hard to see the sun.

But we were all sweating. Everyone was sweating.

Hundreds of thousands of frantic, cross-Hong Kong races broke out spontaneously this morning.

It was like a city-wide episode of TV's The Amazing Race, but with several million contestants, all scrambling to get ahead at once.

That's because today, Tuesday, November 12, was an escalation of what the radicals are trying to persuade the media (largely successfully) to call a "general strike" in revenge for the "murder" of Chow and many others. One group of protesters is pushing the number of secret corpses as 118, while another says it is between 1,000 and 3,000. The committee is having trouble getting everyone on the same page on this one.)

Like yesterday, much of the media is using the protesters' terms, implying that this is a work stoppage in which people put down their tools voluntarily.

But the truth is that this is a concerted attack on what is probably the world's busiest urban transport system, in a bid to force the community to come to a standstill. The people who wrote the training manual for the activists knew exactly what to do.

For me, like countless other Hong Kong residents, the public transport attack presents a practical problem—we have to get to our workplaces, earn our living, feed our children, keep the plates spinning.

And so, as we leap out of bed at 6 am or 7 am, we find ourselves immediately in a real-time competition.

Ordinary Hong Kong residents (let's call them Team A) will try desperately to get to our workplaces or schools.

We will walk, we will run, we will try multiple types of transport.

Radical protesters (Team B), will try to stop us.

Here's my personal experience of that particular commuting trip, to give the reader an impression of how it worked.

Round One:

My paid work assignment on that day is to get to RTHK studios in Kowloon Tong to co-host a live show at 8.30 am

The show is called Backchat and is run by RTHK people who genuinely do make an effort to be balanced.

I set out early in the morning, soon after 7 am.

First, Team B scores early.

They have visited bus stations in the night and slashed the tires of numerous public buses to disable public transport.

(One point to Team B.)

Gah! My bus fails to appear. @#$!

Round Two:

My wife is normally up and out of the house at the crack of dawn as she has a long drive to work to a school in a rural area but I manage to get a lift from her and her car pool—so I am on the way despite the slashed bus tires.

(One point to Team A.)

Yay!

Round Three:

Then comes trouble.

Team B has blocked the main roads through Kowloon, trapping the car I am in.

The minutes tick by and the traffic is completely stationary on the busiest road into the heart of Kowloon, the wide avenue that emerges from the Cross Harbour Tunnel and crosses under the aforementioned footbridge that joins Polytechnic University to the Hung Hom transport hub.

Police, thank God, seem to have stopped protesters raining objects down on us from that walkway.

But nothing is moving. There must be a blockage further down.

Nobody here in this traffic jam is going to get to work or school on time. The live radio show I am supposedly co-hosting is will start in less than 10 minutes.

(One point to Team B.)

Boo.

Round Four:

I decide to leap out of the car, and run across multiple lanes of traffic. I manage to get into an MTR train. I'm moving again. By this time, the radio show is just minutes away from starting.

(One point to Team A.)

You can't stop me!

Round Five:

But Team B is one step ahead of the many of us who have raced onto the MTR trains. They have dropped objects onto the railway tracks, halting the trains, which grind to a complete halt.

(One point to Team B.)

Aieeyah!

Round Six:

I run out of the MTR station and leap unto a green-top minibus which is heading in the right direction, towards Broadcast Drive.

This particular minibus, fortunately, is on a street that is (so far) not blocked, an avenue that crosses busy Junction Road, and vehicles are moving reasonably quickly.

Again, I am back in with a chance of making it to the show, albeit it not on time, as the show will already have started, some seven or eight minutes ago by now.

(One point to Team A.)

I'm hopeful of being less than 10 minutes late.

Round Seven:

But I rejoice too early. Members of Team B spray-paint the front windows of moving double-decker buses on Junction Road, blinding drivers and causing traffic jams which halt all the minibuses in this area, including mine.

(One point to Team B.)

Gaaaaah!

Round Eight:

I get out of the minibus and eventually sprint into the studio.

I am hot, sweaty, exhausted, and 20 minutes late for the show. It was a live show, so being late was a pretty big failure.

Team B, the protesters, are thus declared the winners, in my case. I hope other people around the city had better luck.

* * *

Part of this particular radio show is a live interview with Benson Wong, a former academic who has become the master of the vandals' "Blame Everyone Else" strategy. Here's an extract from our live, on-the-air conversation about how the civil service is being blamed for every bad thing that happens:

ME: If you are part of a gang and you start some riotous event and someone gets hurt, isn't it at least a teeny bit your fault?

HIM: Um.

ME: You blame Carrie Lam, you blame the police, you blame the Chinese government.

HIM: Because they are the powerful people. They are powerful, you know? We cannot put the powerful and the powerless at the equal situation.

ME: Yes, but if you are actively destroying things—

HIM: What kind of things? What kind of things? Destroy the bus? Destroy the train?

ME: Destroying human beings. Throw firebombs at police officers.

HIM: Who are innocents? Innocents, I say? Are the innocent police hurt?

ME: So you're saying that it's fine to blame everything on other people?

HIM: That's fine. That's correct. Why can we not find people to be blamed if he or she is doing something wrong? Otherwise we can do all the wrong things—powerful people—and I can escape all the responsibility if I am actually referring to what you have said.

ME: It seems to me that in a complex situation such as this, it's not as simple as you say. In fact, responsibility needs to be shared between all the people, the protesters, the police, the government, the people encouraging the violence as well—they are all liable for their share of the violence. Surely it doesn't feel right to exonerate all the people and put them blame onto... Carrie Lam, for example?

He goes on to explain that he does blame everyone for the violence EXCEPT the people actually causing it.

I'm talking to a brick wall. We move to a different topic.

* * *

Before I leave the studio, I hear some good news: Train passengers, members of Team A, got a nice surprise from MTR bosses.

At some stations, they set the exit turnstiles to $00.00.

A note flashed up when they used their Octopus cards to leave: "No money has been deducted."

Bad news: People have noticed that the staff of the railway company have been continuously co-operative, and flexible. For this sin, Apple Daily readers declare MTR staff as enemy number two, after the police.

While I had been embarrassingly late for my live show, other members of Team A did have more luck, I heard from contacts on the way out of the radio station.

In several cases, protesters trying to stop trains and light rail vehicles had been sternly ejected by Hong Kong residents.

One retreating protester, finally letting the train doors shut, was quoted to have shouted at the public over his shoulder as he departed: "Okay, you go to work! Make money and buy a flat!"

Who would ever have thought the day would come when someone in Hong Kong would shout "make money and buy a flat" as an insult?

Sheesh. You shouldn't disrespect a community's most deeply-held religious beliefs.

* * *

After the show, I had no choice but to go to my Kowloon office, the coffee shop at Block X of Hong Kong Polytechnic University, since the Central coffee shop was now closing after breakfast every day.

Arriving soon after 10 am, I stepped into the PolyU campus with some trepidation, because I had read that that particular hall of education had been occupied by protesters over the past couple of days.

What I saw as I arrived at the campus caused my jaw to fall to the floor. Podium level glass walls of numerous buildings had been smashed. Most of the staff and students had fled. The place was deserted. There were fragments of glass everywhere.

I decided to go and see if anything had happened to my "office".

I caught my breath as I reached it.

The Block X coffee shop had been totally "renovated", to use the protester codeword. Hardliners had smashed all the plate glass windows and destroyed everything they could reach.

My chair and table had been burned to cinders or thrown outside, along with all the other furniture. The display of items for sale had been shattered. The glass cabinet in which the food was kept had been pummelled with something heavy.

The remaining food was exposed to the air and rotting. The cash register had been hammered open. There was no money left in the tray.

Someone had picked up the coffee shop's mascot, a teddy bear, and set him on fire, in a childish but rather creepy display of mean-spiritedness.

I was deeply dismayed. This was nothing to do with the fact that I used this café as my office. It was the fact that this action was a direct attack on free speech—there was no other way to see it. A family member of one of the shareholders of one of the companies that ran Starbucks had dared to refer to rioters as rioters, and because of that, all the firms under that holding company were considered legitimate targets.

But my heart's response was not political. I was feeling deep sadness for the community that grows up around any popular coffee shop.

It had been a happy place, packed by people of all nations and all ages, the biggest two groups of users being young Hong Kong people and young mainland Chinese people.

The coffee shop's hard-working young Hong Kong-born staff all made the effort to learn customers' names, even foreign ones like mine.

I hope none of them were hurt in the attack.

Thank you for literally ONE THOUSAND cups of coffee, and the hundreds of news reports, papers and book chapters I have written here.

I'll miss you guys! Love and peace, I hope you find new jobs and a new community somewhere.

* * *

The protesters' "renovation" policy looks bad, but when I speak to a division of my parent group which is monitoring Telegram, far worse things are on the horizon.

"They are now openly talking about killing police officers," says my source. "They want to move more into bombs."

I tell them that they have been using petrol bombs for weeks—are they talking about other sorts of bombs?

Yes. "One of the plans is to create chlorine bombs, because they can be manufactured at home quite easily," he says. "You can put gases such as hydrogen chloride into a container and then just add a reagent."

Others are looking into other forms of improvised explosive devices.

The Telegram discussions worry me. Things are not getting better.

Police have also been tipped off about people working to create bombs. Tracking them down is not easy—Telegram is an anonymous site that doesn't enable the contributors to be traced.

CHAPTER 36

Occupation Of The Universities

In Which We Cross A Bridge—

Chinese University Battle Continues—Mainlanders Flee

LATER ON, THIS same grim morning, Hong Kong independence campaigner Joshua Wong presses a button and puts a video clip onto Twitter.

Pow! The Internet lights up. His post is instantly retweeted by thousands of people.

It's picked up by the UK's Daily Mail and soon the whole world can see it.

The short video shows the latest shocking example of Hong Kong "police brutality": A short movie of the city's wildly out-of-control officers attacking a pregnant woman on a raised pedestrian walkway.

How much lower can they go? What more proof of Transmogrification Theory was needed? Hong Kong police are monsters, right?

That's what Joshua Wong and the Twittersphere said.

This is what Joshua Wong and the Twittersphere did NOT say. There was another story there. You see, I recognized that footbridge. It was just a few steps away from where I was standing.

As mentioned earlier, several of the radicals at PolyU had yesterday been following instructions from the committee to replicate the Tolo Highway "deadly hailstorm" here in Tsim Sha Tsui—throwing things off the bridge on to the road below.

They knew that if they blocked the Cross Harbour Tunnel, they could really take a big step towards shutting down the city.

So yesterday they took over this and several other footbridges. The main one, as mentioned, runs from Hong Kong Polytechnic University to the Hung Hom transport hub, and is almost certainly the busiest one in the city.

Foot traffic is so heavy during busy periods that you literally have to queue up to just walk along it.

On the Monday, the black-clads had flung huge numbers of objects (chairs, bins, other heavy items) over the edge. Some did so without looking.

Below were women, children, and men, in school buses, cars, motorbikes, double-deckers, minibuses, and trucks. School bus drivers and staff at the nearby cross harbor tunnel tolling booths had dialed 999.

Police arrived, thank God—and the individuals retreated into the university on one side. The shower of objects stopped.

So far, so reasonable.

But there was a problem.

By mid-morning today, Tuesday, members of the public who had legitimate reasons for being there and using that bridge, including me, found ourselves with an insurmountable difficulty.

That walkway was one of very few ways of getting across the road (an uncrossable eight-lane highway) to a key rail/bus transport hub. Trains and buses were arriving and leaving all the time.

What to do?

Officers had been told to keep the walkway clear and were doing so. But we the public were clustered on one side. We needed to use it—we had trains and buses to catch, jobs to get to, families to return to. This was where I worked, so I knew other ways to walk to the station, via ten-minute detours—but not everyone knew them, and some people would miss their trains if they took lengthy diversions.

How to solve the problem? Unfortunately, some people took the confrontational route, demanding that police get out of their way.

Shortly before I arrived on the scene, a woman had fought with police and been arrested. (She was the one who had been filmed, and the clip sent out by Joshua Wong.)

Soon after I got there, a young man was abusive to the police officers and things soon turned unpleasant for him, too. He wasn't arrested, but he was sprayed with that nasty pepper stuff they use and collapsed on one of the staircases leading up the walkway. He was tended by other members of the public, who splashed water on his face.

I felt sorry for both sides. It was a real problem. The public wanted to use the bridge, but the police had been told to secure the footbridge and were doing so.

Who was next in the queue to try to cross?

It was me, actually. Aieeyah. I found myself at the front of the queue on the bridge at roughly the same time as an elderly woman who approached from another direction and looked terrified—and we were now heading the cluster of puzzled people waiting to get through the impenetrable wall of riot police to reach the transport hub.

Nobody was moving.

"I have a train to catch," the old woman told me quietly.

"I need to catch a bus," I replied. My bus, the 108, was already approaching.

We looked at each other and then the two of us instinctively started marching, slowly and steadily, towards the cordon of armed officers.

Someone on the police lines repeated the command to stay back. The officers in front raised their aerosols at us. We ignored them and kept walking.

At that moment, I could totally see why protesters got the nickname "cockroaches". Hong Kong police rarely use guns. They use sprays that look like economy-sized cans of Raid, a type of cockroach spray. It makes you feel like a bug.

I felt faintly ludicrous. This was going to be unpleasant.

But I had survived my mother's extra-hot seeni sambol, I reminded myself. Pepper spray could not be more painful than that—indeed such weapons often used the exact same substances.

Officers again gestured at us to keep our distance, but the old lady and I kept walking towards them, trying to look as unthreatening as possible. The fact that the woman was elderly and I am built like Mr. Puniverse probably helped.

When we were within earshot of the officers, the woman wailed: "I need to catch my train!" and burst into tears. She pointed at the station.

"I'd like to catch my bus," I said. (I skipped the tears.)

There was a moment of tension as the lead riot officer thought about this.

Then he turned. "Let them through," he barked in Cantonese to his men.

The wall of officers opened like the red sea and we were ushered through.

I skipped down the stairs on the other side, towards the 108 bus stop. I passed the pepper-sprayed man, still lying on the floor, tended by others.

Ah. So this is how it works, I thought. Hostility triggers hostility; violence begets violence; trust creates trust; and a rational request gets a rational response.

I remembered Benjamin Franklin's wise logic. You can't destroy an enemy with a gun; you can only destroy an enemy by making him your friend.

Behind me, the scary-looking riot cops politely ushered the old lady to the train station entrance.

Later, I spent some minutes reviewing social media coverage of events on that bridge.

The proportion of stories that said police officers attacked innocent people including a pregnant woman on a walkway for no reason: 100 percent.

The proportion of stories that said police officers had removed a lethal threat to tens of thousands of children going to school and workers going to their jobs: 0 percent.

In other words, it was coverage as usual.

* * *

But this long, long day was far from over. In many ways, it was just beginning.

Over at Chinese University, it was becoming increasingly clear that many of the "students" causing the continuing mayhem at Bridge No. 2 were not actually students at all. No one at the university knew who they were or who they represented or who controlled them.

But they were hell-bent on causing trouble, and rather good at it.

From dawn this morning onwards, they had worked hard to block numerous roads in the area and disable the train system. They again showered the East Rail Line with objects, in a dangerous attempt to make it impassable.

Police continually attempted to clear road barriers, but were showered with bricks and petrol bombs.

After one particularly rough pitched battle, the police used tear gas and non-lethal weapons to thin the crowd holding the No. 2 Bridge and managed to get across it. They entered the campus and arrested some of the most violent of the occupiers.

One group of protesters, realizing that one of the sports taught at the university was archery, broke into a storage unit and retrieved bows and arrows. The radicals were already suffering from a Hunger Games complex, and now they had the same weapons as Katniss Everdeen. The battle continued on and off in various parts of the campus all day.

But trouble was brewing elsewhere in the campus—and at other locations in Hong Kong. As evening fell, the radicals at Chinese University and Polytechnic University sent out a message to their well-organized troops elsewhere: "Besiege Wei to rescue Zhao."

The reference was to a classic military ploy from mainland Chinese history. In the story, the people of Zhao were struggling to fight off troops from the land of Wei. They realized that the balance of power was against them, and unless they changed the situation, defeat was inevitable.

The obvious thing would be to send messages calling on associates away from the battle to come to their aid.

But instead, they sent out calls for them to go and start skirmishes on the outskirts of Wei, besieging the attackers' hometown. Part of the Wei army would have to leave the scene of battle, making a crucial change to the balance of power at the original battle site.

* * *

At 8 pm that evening, masked rioters stormed into Festival Walk, a massive shopping mall in Kowloon Tong.

They shattered glass balustrades, broke plate glass windows and set fire to the giant multi-storey Christmas tree that is always a centerpiece for the mall at this time of year. The tree, which is four stories tall, burned fiercely, causing staff to fear that the entire mall would go up in flames, with potentially massive loss of life.

It was a terrifying sight. If the whole mall went up, the number of casualties and the destruction of property would be staggering. The district, Kowloon Tong and Kowloon City, is densely packed with housing of all social classes.

Mall staff fought the fire bravely with fire hoses to put out pockets of flame, but radicals threw more lit petrol bombs at the giant Christmas tree to keep it burning.

Fire fighters arrived and eventually managed to control the blaze, but by that time, the protesters had fled. The tree was a cinder and the entire mall was shut down for the foreseeable future.

* * *

And in my home patch on the eastern side of Hong Kong Island?

Trouble as usual. A masked gang suddenly appeared on the streets of Causeway Bay and conducted an arson attack on a shop. The China Mobile ground floor premises were set on fire. Staff ran for safety.

What crime had the company committed? None. It was targeted because the company had mainland Chinese roots and the radicals don't like immigrants. (Ironically, the vast majority of retail shop staff in this city are local Hong Kong people.)

This was just one of a series of attacks in multiple areas of Hong Kong on this nightmare day.

In Sha Tin, rioters set fire to a police van.

In Tin Shui Wai, a large rowdy crowd besieged a police station and tried to burn it down.

In Mong Kok, the main roads were blocked and barricades and numerous traffic lights and electrical junction boxes were destroyed.

The police were stretched as thin as a wire, as they had been on July 21.

But by calling in more strength from other sectors, they managed to keep the pressure on the radicals at Chinese University—and even make headway against them.

By late evening, the battle of Chinese University was winding down. Police had spent much of the day under assault from firebombs, and when they advanced into radicals' territory, they found huge stocks of petrol bombs had been assembled, ready for use—literally thousands of them.

Police themselves had also used weapons, although they had limited themselves almost entirely to non-lethal gear: Rubber bullets and tear gas, plus bean bag and sponge projectiles.

The police force's company leaders felt they had achieved their aim, which was to quell the violence with no loss of life.

In total, they reported making 142 arrests.

But as particulars of the arrestees were being taken down, officers noticed something: This didn't seem to be a student rebellion of people from this university. Many of the individuals had no connection with it at all.

The majority were neither students nor teachers. The media stories of a university uprising were false. The students were innocent.

* * *

The following day, the wind dropped, the clouds disappeared and the sunshine came back.

Someone on the network pointed me to a post on Facebook which carried a news item.

On that day, Wednesday, November 13, Taiwanese president Tsai Ing-wen, now soaring in the polls, tried to give a different spin to the Hong Kong police arrests of the Tolo Highway "deadly hailstorm" vandals.

She referred to previous "invasions into universities campuses" by police in her country, describing them as attacks on "freedom of speech".

It was a ridiculous thing to say, completely nonsensical and in no way a description of what was happening in Hong Kong. But the obvious subtext gave me a wry smile. This was another in a long series of thank you notes from Tsai to the Hong Kong radicals and their shadowy American financers. Thumbs up to the committee!

Ironically, while she was reveling in her continually rising poll numbers, and applauding the people who had brought violence to Chinese University, she seemed to have forgotten her own community's youngsters, many of whom were hiding there.

A number of students of Taiwanese origin were enrolled at the university, and they were feeling scared and unsafe. They called on the police of Hong Kong for help. Some 85 of them asked to be evacuated from Chinese University.

They were eventually flown home. The Taiwanese taxpayers had to foot the bill. The irony gods surely smiled.

But the trouble at Chinese University was far from over.

One division of hold-out protesters was working on assembling a wide range of dangerous and sometimes lethal weaponry.

As well as incendiary devices and bow-and-arrow sets, some had collected javelins from the sports grounds. Others were working on designing catapults that could send lethal incendiary devices a long distance, like the trebuchets of medieval times.

It was actually impressively creative, if you set aside the thought that the devices were designed to hurt or kill other human beings.

Less attractively, there were reportedly whole teams of other radicals who were busy making some sort of spike traps, using diagrams obtained from an unknown source.

Several reporters on the scene noted that the radicals were creating a wide range of primitive, medieval weapons, to make up for the fact that guns were extremely difficult to obtain in Hong Kong.

The weapon-makers had been sent “plans” by “friends” overseas.

No surprise there.

* * *

The university’s president Rocky Tuan was horrified to be told that the remaining protesters had once more resumed throwing objects onto the Tolo Highway.

They were now throwing such large items that the police had had to close down the entire road to ensure the safety of the road users. This caused untold inconvenience to people in a huge chunk of the city.

“We condemn the irresponsible act and wish to apologise to the general public for the resultant traffic chaos that has seriously inconvenienced hundreds of thousands of commuters,” Tuen wrote.

University management cancelled the rest of the semester’s lectures—as did their counterparts at other tertiary education centers. The radicals had made our universities simply too dangerous to visit.

Now that was an important point that the media's commentators missed. The education strike in September had been a flop, with very few students skipping classes. The scholars of this city clearly wanted to keep learning.

But the radicals, working with student union leaders, had finally raised the level of violence so high that they had achieved their original aim: to shut down all the universities. The media was still in the main referring to the battles as outbreaks of "pro-democracy" violence by "Hong Kong's student population", but there were now a growing amount of evidence that this was false.

They were not pro-democracy activists, and less than half the ones caught so far were university students, police sources said. Instead, they were anti-Chinese campaigners for Hong Kong independence, co-ordinated tightly by persons unknown.

For me, one of the saddest moments of this entire week took place later on this day, Wednesday, November 13.

While the media focused on "students" battling police, in reality, the vast majority of Chinese University students of all cultural backgrounds were horrified by what the radicals were doing, and were not in the least hostile to China—many had come from that country.

Even among the Hong Kong students, almost all of them had friends and classmates from the mainland.

Hong Kong police sent one of their marine department vessels to rescue the university's mainland Chinese students, who had requested to be evacuated from the occupied campus.

Footage showed a large group of scared-looking, serious-faced young people getting onto a marine police vessel on a small jetty at the waterfront and speeding away cross the Tolo Harbour.

This writer felt a lump in his throat looking at the images.

These innocent young people had studied extremely hard to get into a university in Hong Kong, and now the campus had been taken over by an anti-China movement known for beating up mainlanders. It must have been honestly terrifying for these young people, so far from their families.

As I'd noticed before, the student union leaders of the various universities tended to side with the radicals, while the majority of rank-and-file students gave them a wide berth.

And so it was at Chinese University, with most students keeping their heads down and staying well away from the battle area—but with student union chiefs getting increasingly involved with the radicals.

Later that day, the student union officers worked with pandem lawyers to apply to the Hong Kong courts for an interim injunction to stop police stepping onto the campus without a warrant.

Judges considered the matter and dismissed it as being incorrect in law and contrary to justice.

You can't let violent lawbreakers onto university premises and then bar the people who had been specifically commissioned by society to arrest them. No law-respecting country in the world would allow that.

CHAPTER 37

A Bridge Too Far

In Which We Keep Taking Pictures—Battle At Chinese University—A Fissure Between Protest Teams

THE TEMPERATURE DROPPED the next morning, to everyone's relief. On Thursday, November 14, this old-school reporter was on foot, in Central, with a camera and notebook. Since the Stock Exchange coffee shop had been scared shut and my university one burned to a cinder, I was office-less, and doing more wandering around.

At lunchtime, as normal, a group of protesters in black was blocking roads in Central. As usual, I was taking a variety of pictures. And also as usual, the black shirts rushed up to me and shouted: "Stop taking pictures."

But this time I did an experiment.

"No," I replied. And I carried on.

Click. Click. Click.

These particular radical protesters were quite young and didn't know quite what to do. They notified their leaders. Older, larger supporters approached and shouted at me.

But some in the quiet watching crowd defended me.

An American woman in the crowd shouted at me, telling me that it was illegal for me to photograph anyone on the street who did not want to be photographed.

This was wrong in law, but the scene was tense, and this was no time for a rational discussion. Fortunately, I heard the young Chinese man accompanying her putting her straight, telling her that there was no law against taking pictures on the street.

It was a difficult moment—but eventually the protesters backed off, leaving me to quietly dismantle a small portion of the barriers by myself.

As I did so, I reflected that what some Hong Kong mothers and fathers had told me had been absolutely right. In most circumstances, the protesters did not want to get into physical battles with anyone except the police.

Fighting with triad members was too dangerous, and could get them killed or hurt. Fighting with members of the public was easier, but bad for the image. Fighting with police officers was the safest bet: Hong Kong police wouldn't kill you and the chances of creating a scene that could be edited to make you a hero and them into villains ("another shocking example of police brutality") was high.

The best comment at the scene came from an old Hong Konger who was sad at the needless vandalism: "To anyone who believes in the rule of law, photographing lawbreakers is not a crime; it's a public service."

In the end, nobody beat me up. There were just too many witnesses.

My boss at The Standard, Ivan Tong, sent me a note later. "You're a brave man," he said.

My wife kind of agreed, but not in a positive way.

She said she was seriously worried that I was that special kind of brave which is spelt s. t. u. p. i. d.

A reader named Mandy Mo agreed with her. "You entrusted your safety to rationality," she wrote. "But how much rationality is there around these days?"

* * *

That evening, a member of my network asks a question.

"Why are they so adamant in stopping people taking pictures?"

Good question.

I didn't have an answer. I asked the network.

"There seems to be a widely held conspiracy theory that Beijing can remotely access the iPhones of tourists and passers-by and grab the pictures to send to the Hong Kong police to add to the victims on their Secret Murdering List," said one source.

"Surely that's all ridiculous?" I responded.

Yes, he said. It was ridiculous. "Even the FBI struggles to break into the iPhones right there on their desks. And the Hong Kong police force doesn't have a Secret Murdering List anyway."

I imagined that a secondary reason was that the younger radicals want to be photographed as Noble Freedom Fighters, but if members of the public snapped them "renovating" cafes or beating up passers-by with mainland accents, they needed to be stopped.

The radicals were very image conscious.

Reader Jennifer Lo said that believing the things that are printed in the more extreme sources was idiotic. "You're better off believing in Santa," she said. "At least he is all about spreading love."

* * *

During this endless week, the tension at Chinese University has continued, but has mutated in an interesting direction: It has turned into infighting. This has given everybody (should they want to notice) an insight into the fact that the so-called leaderless movement does have leaders—and they are disagreeing on tactics.

The student leaders feel that they should be making the decisions—after all, it is their university, and the newspapers were reporting this as a student uprising.

But the secretive non-students were having none of that. They were the ones with the connections and they were far greater in number and much better equipped, with a bottomless source of cash and instant access to legal and strategic advice.

This part of the story starts with a press conference at the ungodly hour of 3 am on Friday, November 15.

Three thin young men, fully masked and covered head to toe in black, claiming to represent the protest movement, announced that they would generously allow the opening of one lane in each direction of the Tolo Highway in exchange for the release of ALL the people who had been arrested for violence, vandalism, and assault and so on.

They also called for the government to go ahead with a planned local district council election on November 24 and the establishment of a police-free independent inquiry body.

In fact, the government was fully intending to go ahead with the November 24 election and already had a police-free independent inquiry body at work. But freeing people, many of whom were caught in the act of violent criminality and reckless endangerment of innocent people's lives? In a community that prizes the rule of law above almost anything else? No chance.

Reporters assumed that they were listening to student protesters, but in fact the three men in black were transmitting orders from a different source.

The real story became clearer later.

After daybreak, reporters were surprised to receive a furious statement signed by the university's student union heads.

These young people angrily took issue with the black-clads' early announcement and disassociated themselves from the three men who had given the press conference earlier.

In an aggrieved tone, the students' letter said that none of the masked people at the earlier event was from their group—and further more, the students of Chinese University opposed the plan to open the highway.

Now no one could miss the fact that it wasn't Chinese University students' union leaders who had been calling the shots, but the pro-revolutionaries.

Despite the letter, the student union chiefs were ignored. The radicals were in charge for now.

The Tolo Highway was opened at 12 noon—but bickering continued behind the scenes.

By 7.30 pm, the students took action and blocked all lanes again. Within minutes, trucks, buses and cars were trapped on both sides of the highway with no way to move in any direction.

For Hong Kong's millions of commuters, it was misery time again.

* * *

Back in Kowloon and on Hong Kong Island, an apolitical clean-up movement was growing. Residents were increasingly going to protest sites and dismantling the blockages that prevented cars and buses moving.

Nick Wong of the Brick Removal Movement, a jokey spontaneous assemblage, said: "Yesterday when I started clearing there were only two or three people, then 10. Today there were 40 to 50."

Radicals and their supporters shouted abuse at him.

But he and other others ignored them and kept going.

Elsewhere, this was a dangerous thing to do. Tsim Sha Tsui residents clearing roads near Polytechnic University yesterday had bricks and other hard objects flung at them.

I put out a warning about it to readers of the newspaper and members of my social networks: Be careful, everyone.

At this time, I received a memorable note from father-of-one Mark Leung, who is a totally modern, pro-democracy, pro-freedom person, but is unfooled by the wildly misleading media narrative. He says he has dropped his opposition to the demand to retract the classification of rioters as rioters, as they have asked.

"Let's retract the term 'rioters'," he says. "And instead use 'terrorists'."

As rumors emerge of bomb factories working at both Chinese University and Polytechnic University, I realize that he was right on target. Under-reported police raids had identified a growing fascination with explosive devices.

Separately, a reader named Simon noticed that in one of the new slogans being spray-painted on various walls, black-shirts describe their own activities as "rioting".

This is despite the fact that the official policy is for anyone who uses the word *rioter* to be given severe punishment. He showed me photos of the slogan, which says: "Rioting is the language of the unheard."

Maybe the thing to do is to catch the black-shirt graffiti guy in the act of painting the slogan and then point out what he is doing to his black-shirt comrades.

"Hey. This guy is writing on the wall that you're rioters!"

Then stand well back.

My students agreed that Hong Kong youngsters don't use philosophical graffiti lines in English like that. They were being supplied by outsiders.

Meanwhile in Kowloon, protesters mixed cement to build extra walls at Polytechnic University. Oh well, that university is known for teaching courses on building and construction, so I guess it could count as a "practical" lesson.

On Friday evening, November 15, the fissures that had been visible earlier that day in the "occupying force" at Chinese University continued to grow.

The student union heads wanted to consolidate their presence at the university. All entrances were now blocked. It was their kingdom.

But the violent radicals representing the committee pointed out that it was their campaign and they had been advised that it was time to move on.

Their ultimate aim was to bring down Hong Kong, free it from China and create a revolution. The moment had come to return to the heart of the city, where more interesting action and high profile action was possible.

Observers saw clusters of individuals begin to leave the Chinese University campus as darkness fell on Friday night.

Most would not say where they were going.

But in fact, a plan had been given to their leaders. They were told to recreate their success in occupying Chinese University, but in a better location—one that would get better media coverage internationally.

New plan: Take over Polytechnic University, which was right in the heart of Kowloon, next to the Cross-Harbour Tunnel—the arterial vein that was the main traffic route from Hong Kong island to the rest of the city.

Their ambition: take over the Cross-Harbour Tunnel and block it completely — and then move to take control of Hong Kong's biggest transport hub, right next door.

And then they would really rule the city.

* * *

For the first time, the presidents of all nine of Hong Kong's universities issued a joint statement to make clear their position — and they stood together against the radicals.

Many people in the media were writing up the actions of the university staff and management as if they were supporting the protesters and approved of the occupation of the universities.

But this was not the case at all. While individual academics at a much lower level, like Benson Wong, were strongly in favor of the protests, all working university administrators wanted to be clear about their opposition.

"The past week has seen a rapid escalation of violence and confrontation throughout Hong Kong," it said. *"Several universities are now under protesters' control; on-campus hazardous materials have been taken; staff and students have left campus out of fear for their personal safety.*

"These events are challenging our universities in the most fundamental way. No political viewpoint gives a licence to damage property, employ physical threats or use violence against individuals."

* * *

Chinese University's Rocky Tuan, whose own academic community had been the location of much of the trouble of the past week, released an additional letter about the situation at his establishment.

He used it to make it absolutely clear that MOST of the masked protesters who occupied the campus "are not CUHK students".

They were outsiders, and their behavior was terrible. "The masked protesters set fires, removed bricks from pavements, stole vehicles and broke into our academic buildings and hostels, wrecking properties and damaging facilities. Our canteens and kitchens have also been taken over," he said.

But his letter raised eyebrows among the network for another reason.

It said that police and university staff had gone into the areas the radicals had occupied and made some shocking discoveries.

They had brought in materials and supplies from outside and created an assembly line to produce a very large number of fire bombs—quite literally thousands.

While one group had been doing that, another group had broken into university science departments' laboratories and storage rooms and stolen large amounts of highly flammable chemicals.

These were extremely dangerous, as they "may be turned into explosives, posing serious life threats", Tuan wrote.

The implication was clear: a bombing campaign was on the cards.

CHAPTER 38

Takeover Of A Campus

In Which Radicals Find A New Home—A Tour Of The Campus

WOOHOO! INDEPENDENCE AT LAST. By Saturday, November 16, the revolutionaries had taken over Polytechnic University and several other halls of education and turned them into tiny, fully autonomous kingdoms.

Entrances were blocked. Young men covered head to toe in ISIS-like black outfits patrolled the rooftops, keeping watch.

This writer was at Polytechnic University, eyes as wide as saucers.

The previous night, I had heard that the radicals were secretly leaving Chinese University in small clusters, but no one knew where they were heading.

Now I had the answer. They were coming here. They were arriving, in dribs and drabs, at Polytechnic University, where I had been teaching for 17 years. Scribbling in my notebook, I had five immediate observations.

1) There seemed to be surprisingly few of them. As I have mentioned before, this university had more than 16,000 enrolled students and more than 1,000 teachers, so was usually a busy place. And, according to the media,

we were being joined by thousands of students from Chinese University.

So shouldn't there be huge numbers here, ten thousand or twenty thousand or thirty thousand, or more?

No. The radicals arriving were tiny in number — arriving in twos and threes and adding up to just a few hundred so far. Almost all of them had joined the main radical base, which had been set up in the student dining hall, next to the Jockey Club Innovation Tower. The rest of the campus was completely deserted.

If they continued to arrive in such tiny groups all day, we may end up with a thousand or fifteen hundred, but that was all.

Most people didn't seem to know their way round the campus, and none of the faces was familiar to me. It was clear that most of the people being painted as students were not what they seemed to be.

2) Another observation: they were children. I mean, many of them were literally children, as police sources had told me in October.

Almost all of them looked like teenagers or people in their early 20s, and a good proportion of them, perhaps half, looked like they were 18 years old or younger: Secondary school children.

No wonder they knew nothing about the government's steps to introduce democracy in 2013, or that rumors of hundreds or thousands of mass murders were just ridiculous conspiracy theories, or that allegations that Hong Kong had lost all its freedoms were plainly wrong.

Many simply weren't equipped to make such judgments. They were too young.

3) Yet at the same time, they were very clear about their purpose, which seemed to have evolved again. It was not primarily to call for democracy or

even for independence now.

They were painting the word "revenge" in English and Chinese at multiple locations on the campus. That was now the main motivating story. They wanted vengeance for the six victims "murdered" at Prince Edward MTR Station, for the "murder" of Alex Chow Tsz-lok, thrown from a car park building, and for "murders" of more than 1,000 other people by the police.

They saw China as the Kingdom of Darkness and anyone who wasn't actively fighting it as betrayers, who had aided and abetted a group of active murderers.

It may sound ridiculous to say this, but the atmosphere was something like people preparing for one of the battles in The Lord of the Rings. The police had been painted as a violent subhuman group of murderers— like orcs. And Xi Jinping was Sauron, with Carrie Lam as Saruman.

It was interesting: If you were 15 years old and been told what these young people have been told, that the Hong Kong authorities were really a dangerous army from a different place, speaking a different language, and actively raping and murdering huge numbers of innocent people, then you'd also want to go to war against them.

I would. As I talked to them, I fully understood their position.

You could not blame them. These were children and youths—the problem was not with them, but with the older people feeding them this information.

4) Despite their youth, they had a very specific strategy all planned out. There were clear hierarchies, and cohorts with leaders. The children were fighting this war, but there were adults behind the scenes.

And they had a clear target for this weekend: Shut down the Cross-Harbour Tunnel to bring Hong Kong's main traffic channel to a complete halt, and then move on to close the Hung Hom transport hub.

5) At this time, and in recent weeks, there had been numerous sightings of people who appeared to be Caucasian activists involved with the local black-clad protesters during period. Of course, people of all ethnic backgrounds were free to participate in legal demonstrations, so they were never picked out by the police.

But some of them raised eyebrows among observers.

From the end of September until now (the middle of November), there had been numerous sightings at the protests of Witold Dobrowolski, a Polish man apparently here as a tourist. He was sometimes referred to in the media as a journalist or photographer, without mentioning that he was the former editor of Szturm, a neo-Nazi magazine.

Dobrowolski was regularly seen at violent uprisings around the world, and was in Ukraine in 2017.

Our network had no specific details about who he interacted with or in what ways he may have been involved.

* * *

By one o'clock in the afternoon of that Saturday, November 16, the Independent and Fully Autonomous State of Polytechnic University had been fully fortified.

All exits and entrances were blocked and controlled by masked youths in black.

The footbridge to Hung Hom station was now completely impassable, blocked with a meters-deep pile of barriers. Residents now had no way of using it to reach buses or trains and had to find other ways of getting to it, or simply abandon their journeys.

The streets outside the university were littered with thousands of spiked weapons that prevented cars from approaching and made it dangerous for humans or animals to even walk nearby.

I stepped on a small spiked device and it went straight through my shoe and sock into my foot. This reporter worked with a limp for the next few hours.

At the time, I didn't know what it was, so I posted a picture of it on the Internet.

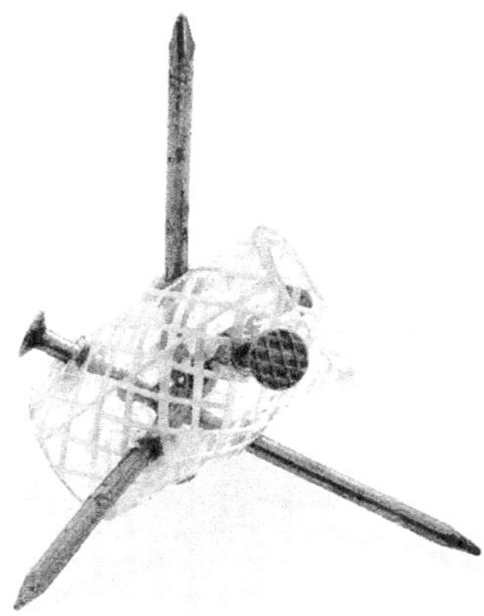

Ian Dubin said: "They're called caltrops: they re a medieval weapon."

Government critic Rob Ferguson was less sympathetic. "You need to get to the Lee Kee shoe repair shop," he joked.

A bit of research revealed that there were very nasty items, mass produced earlier this week after the committee distributed instructions obtained from friends in the West. You cut thick pieces of plastic into chunks, roll them up, and hammer nails through them at three different angles. You then scatter large numbers of them on the roads—and any unfortunate human being who steps on one will see the nail go straight through his shoe into his foot.

The caltrops also burst car tires or damage the feet of police dogs and other animals.

But they weren't the only danger. Any residents of the Tsim Sha Tsui East area who tried to approach the university to clear the roads so that their community's buses could get through, were attacked.

One group of youths stood at a raised podium on one side of the university firing arrows—and shot one through the leg of a man, a police media liaison officer, talking to people some distance from the university.

Inside the campus, the premises had been divided into segments for practicing different types of warfare.

The path between blocks C and F had been turned into an over-arm bomb-throwing practice area. The idea was to build up the strength of a throwing team, so that they could hurl firebombs a longer distance into the lines police officers defending public buildings.

I watched men train younger people how to do a long run-up and then release their missiles at "about 42 degrees" so that they flew in a graceful curving arc, smashing into a pillar in the distance.

In another area, masked archers were practicing the use of high-technology bow and arrow sets.

Over in the swimming pool area, men were experimenting with different substances for Molotov cocktails to see which spread the furthest and burned for the longest period. They'd been told that adding detergent to the petrol made it stickier, so that it would adhere to the skin and clothes of police officers, causing significantly more harm. The pool was empty of water, so provided a perfect enclosed area for trying out incendiary devices.

The student canteen was a bustling area of people eating snacks that had been provided in huge amounts by supporters. There were sacks of child-friendly food, such as instant noodles, chocolate and potato snacks, and a steady supply of rice boxes.

More worryingly, you could see that some glass-walled buildings had been broken into—people were clearly going into the laboratories to see what they could steal.

This was a significant worry. PolyU was an engineering university, which meant that it was full of dangerous chemicals, stuff that was explosive or flammable or which could kill you with fumes alone. I believe a store of cyanide was kept at the university for experiments, for example. I hoped there wasn't anything radioactive.

At the rear end of the campus, which is on a sort of raised podium covering an entire city block, I found a petrol bomb-making workshop. The "factory workers" were having a lunch break when I got there, but you could see the long lines of beer bottles and the supplies of petrol and thickening fluids.

Other students were attaching large numbers of nails with tape to the outside of a large gas canister. This was a genuinely horrific weapon. It would make a huge explosion and send large nails in all directions. There was not the slightest doubt that it was designed to kill or main a large number of people very quickly indeed.

They may be children, but make no mistake—a radicalized child with a nail bomb like this would cause immense harm.

Others seemed to be combining petrol bombs with propane gas cylinders.

But ultimately it was not the horror of the sheer number of weapons that stuck in my mind, but my dismay about the mindset that had been created.

These young people had been told that it was okay to kill or maim people who did not support their cause. It was okay to die to defend "facts" that you had read on websites like Telegram or LIHKG or Apple Daily. It was a good and noble thing to risk your life, your liberty, your future, to save your society from an active group of mass murderers that you had never actually seen killing anyone.

I felt the irony of my own role in the process. This was the university where I had taught the power of stories, day in and day out, year after year—and now I was finding out that false stories, if repeated often enough, could cause enormous harm to young people.

One of the young men took me on tour and pointed to the slogans that had been graffitied in large letters in English and Chinese around the university.

The new underlying theme of "Revenge" was augmented by other lines. One said: "Talking is not enough: you must act."

Another, which I thought was odd, was a denunciation of users of Taobao, the Chinese online shop (the local equivalent of Amazon) and very popular among Hong Kong people.

I asked the youth guiding me around to explain what the problem was. "Taobao is Chinese," came the answer. "Our people don't like anything from China."

None of them allowed me to film them directly, but one let me record his voice, and another his shadow.

There were quite a few individuals present who seemed to be not actively involved, but looked like "followers", simply doing what they were told.

I had been told that there was an undercover police officer in this group, and I tried to spot him, but I failed. Everyone looked united in their tasks. The undercover agent, if he was there, blended in perfectly. Given the number of violent weapons on the campus, I was glad that law enforcement knew what was happening here.

CHAPTER 39

The Battle of PolyU

In Which My Workplace Really Does Start To Look Like A War Zone

THAT NIGHT, AS DARKNESS FELL, the battle started. The youths slipped out of the cover of Polytechnic University and widened their field of occupation.They set fire to the footbridges, including both walkways which went over the Cross Harbour Tunnel road. They used potentially lethal weapons, hurling huge numbers of petrol bombs and shooting arrows at the police, while police responded with sponge rounds, tear gas and rubber bullets.

Numerous cars were set alight. At one point, there was smoke and flame over the whole area—it really did seem like a full-scale war.

A police van, with a driver inside, was engulfed in flames. I prayed that he would not be burned alive. (I later heard that he managed to get out.)

It all seemed like total chaos, but it was cleverly planned—and remarkably successful. Within hours, the radicals had used their massive store of weapons to achieve their aim.

The Cross Harbour Tunnel was closed. The main artery between Kowloon and Hong Kong Island was shut—and staff at the tunnel company told reporters they had no idea when it would be re-opened.

The committee's game plan was working.

Sunday dawned hot again, and Polytechnic University was quiet in the morning.

But the air was filled brick dust particles that made it hard to breathe, and tear gas residue that stung the eyes if you got too close.

Residents of Tsim Sha Tsui, upset to have their roads blocked by bricks, barriers, garbage and spike-traps, began clearing the area outside the Rosary Church at about 10 am.

One cleaner found a store of what seemed to be dangerous chemicals on the street and called police for help in taking it away.

But some protesters were already awake and active and quickly blocked the activities of local residents, scaring them away and re-assembling the barricades on Chatham Road South and Austin Road.

And then the protesters started throwing bricks at the local residents—who quickly fled and called the police for help.

By 11 am, a significant group of riot police had arrived to protect the Tsim Sha Tsui residents, and a now common scene unfolded, with local people running for cover, protesters throwing bricks and firebombs, and police using tear gas and rubber bullets.

Normally at this corner, the Rosary Church would be holding services at this time. Things had changed.

* * *

With their advantageous position, in control of an entire city block surrounded by major highways, it looked as if the radicalized youths were winning the game.

They had succeeded in closing the Cross Harbour Tunnel. They controlled all the walkways from the Polytechnic University area to the main transport hub of Hung Hom. And they were holding the entire university.

The attempted occupations of all the other universities in the city had fizzled to almost nothing by this time, but Polytechnic University was tightly held.

But police chiefs realized that whatever hidden committee was doing the planning for the radicals had made one small but strategically significant error.

They had stranded the youths on a single city block surrounded by main roads—all of which were now occupied by police officers.

The radical protesters were marooned. They had cornered themselves, and they knew it. They were well and truly trapped.

From one point of view, what they were doing was a successful occupation. From another, they had put themselves into a siege situation.

The police company commanders, discussing what their next moves should be, realized something.

They didn't even have to go in.

They didn't have to do anything. They could just take a seat.

Reporters remembered the 2015 words of Serbian professional revolution consultant Srda Popovic about how an arresting force can handle an occupation: "All it has to do is wait."

* * *

This has been a long Sunday. In the afternoon, I flee to a local *dai pai dong*, where I find people moaning about how radicals had disabled the main link between Kowloon and Hong Kong island.

But one man, who had a good grounding in business, as many Hong Kong people do, sat in the corner smirking. "Don't tell the protesters," he said. "But they've driven all Hong Kong's traffic to the other two tunnels, causing a massive boost in revenue. And you know who owns those two, don't you?"

Hmm? I had a think. Ah. Suddenly I knew why he was smiling.

The main owner of the other tunnels was CITIC Pacific. Or to put it another way, the international mainland Chinese elite that the committee hates more than anything. So ironic.

I thought about this. My newspaper (The Standard) had already reported that the Hong Kong restaurant trade was suffering horribly, as were some fast food shops such as Maxims and Yoshinoya.

But other fast food brands, such as branches of McDonald's, were reporting an increase in income, with the burger seller a protesters' favorite.

Again, the majority owner of McDonald's in Hong Kong was CITIC. In contrast, the restaurants that they were smashing up were mostly owned and operated by Hong Kong people.

The other people at the *dai pai dong* moan. "Why don't the black shirts just take ALL the money from Hong Kong's coffers and post the lot to Beijing?" one asks.

I finish my noodles and head back to the fray.

* * *

Following the model set by Chinese University's Rocky Tuan, his Polytechnic University counterpart Teng Jin-guang tells us he has decided that will personally take the lead in trying to sort out the problem.

He was on the outside and met with police on Sunday afternoon. Police suggested that he might not wish to go into the university, because they now believed that most of the young people were not his students at all.

They were radical youths, under the leadership of people not related to the university.

So instead, university president Teng retreated and made a video, designed for release the following morning.

Elsewhere in the city on that Sunday, November 17, the clean-up crew was in action. Large groups of Hong Kong residents, joined by people from six government departments, cleared blocked roads in Pok Fu Lam, Tai Po, Kowloon Tong, Tseung Kwan O and Sheung Shui.

Pandem politicians complained bitterly when People's Liberation Army soldiers joined in the clean up processes Members of the public did not complain about the help, but some saw the funny side.

"They're supposed to be the evil bad guys running over us in tanks", commented reader Kelvin Cheung, with his tongue in his cheek.

"How dare they be polite and helpful instead! This is an outrage."

Dear Commander Xi,

It has come to our attention that young men from the PLA in Hong Kong swept the roads, cleaned away rubble, fixed broken railings and acted in a polite and civilized manner.

This is an outrage.

Do you have any idea how much time, energy and money we have devoted to building up an image of them as faceless death machines who only skill is the massacre of innocents?

We sincerely hope that this will not be repeated.

Yours truly,

As evening fell on Sunday, November 17, police, as usual, were focused on a "least harm" strategy — the aim being to bring the occupation to an end with as little injury as possible to people on any side of the dispute.

But at the same time, there was no question of allowing violent radicals to commit acts that were clearly terroristic in nature, such as the creation of incendiary devices, chemical explosives, or nail bombs, and walk away free to use them on innocent people.

From their point of view, a group committed to violent law-breaking and moving towards terrorism had cornered themselves in a single city block. This was the perfect opportunity to round them up and prevent further harm.

In other places around the world, the army would simply march in to subdue the radicals, estimated at the time to be somewhere between 900 and 1,800 people.

But Hong Kong had no army, and the police were having to do the job, despite constant criticism.

Their decision had been to simply invite the people inside to come out peacefully. They would all have to come out some time. The police knew that the main campus of Polytechnic University did not include any kind of hotel or hostelry accommodation, which were in separate dormitories elsewhere in the district. In the main campus, there was nowhere to sleep.

The radicals had showed me on my earlier tour that they had set up mats on the floor of one of the podium level classrooms, and were using it as sleeping quarters or a sick bay. Yet those mats might be okay for a quick nap for 20 people, yet nobody would want to sleep there for more than a single night.

Large amounts of food had been sent in by supporters, but it was of the snack type: instant noodles and chocolate–not something you would want to live on, day after day.

To encourage a quick ending, the police used a pandem technique and talked to lawyers. Following those discussions, they made an announcement that was broadcast into the university and given to the media to share.

It was simple. There were huge amounts of unmistakable evidence that a major riot was taking place over this weekend, starting with the burning of footbridges and cars, and continuing on to this armed occupation of the campus.

There had also been attacks on people: Members of the public as well as members of the police, and the destruction of many facilities.

The law specified a riot as an affray by a group of three or more people. People are charged with rioting not individually but as a group.

So they gave people inside a simple choice.

This was it: If you do not wish to be identified as part of the group committing the crime of rioting, walk peacefully out of the university's Exit Y and tell us so.

If, on the other hand, you DO wish to be identified as part of that group, then don't join those walking peacefully out of Exit Y, and take responsibility for your decision. The choice was entirely your own.

Police said they would wait until 10 pm for people to make up their minds. Representatives of the people inside were given the message in detail and asked to take it to everyone inside, make sure everyone heard.

It was also on every radio station, and discussed on numerous websites. This was an opportunity for anyone who believed in peace and the rule of law to leave.

* * *

By 10 pm, many people had left the university, but there were still hundreds of people who had chosen to stay. The best guess, at that time, was 900, but no one knew for sure.

I'd already left the university by that time, but some other reporters chose to stay inside. At this time, there was quite a lot of information coming from the university, either from journalists, or from people filing material on social media.

I was upset to hear from one good source inside that the police message had been totally misreported to some of the youngsters on the inside. "Instead of saying that they had to leave by 10 pm if they wanted to avoid being declared to be a rioter, the older ones told the younger ones that police had given orders to everyone to stay inside," he said.

It was a shocking betrayal of responsibility—and one which could have harmful consequences for the futures of the children inside.

Yet some of the children and adults inside did receive and understand the real message, and had chosen to collect their bags and leave.

As mentioned, several journalists chose to stay inside to deliver information to the outside world, and there was also apparently the undercover agent too.

An additional source of information was people watching from the blocks around the university. One particular office block looked right onto the A block entrance.

* * *

Late that night, on the inside, the leaders of the radicals had realized what had happened: they really had trapped themselves. The entire city block was surrounded by police.

And what's more, having waited until past 10 pm, they had all technically and legally chosen to define themselves as the rioters taking responsibility for the horrendous mayhem of the weekend—and thus faced charges of up to 10 years in jail.

"We need to break out," one of the leaders said.

One source told me they discussed it as they sat in a messy circle, mostly in the open area behind block A on the main podium.

A strategy was broached, the source said: Anyone with a medic jerkin or press jacket would be asked to take it off and give it to a senior radical. These leaders, wearing the tunics, would then present themselves at Exit Y or Exit A as innocent non-participants, who should be allowed to leave without arrest or trouble of any kind.

They would make good their escape, and then double back with more comrades and make so much trouble using petrol bombs and bricks obtained from supporters on the outside that the police would be distracted, and everyone else could then escape en masse.

This unlikely plan was deemed good, and the radicals tried to get it organized.

But it was difficult. Some of the medics were reluctant to give up their tunics. The tunics were the only evidence they had that they were not among the most dangerous of the radicals: the bomb-throwers or nail-bomb builders who faced the longest prison sentences.

Yet some of the radical leaders were highly persuasive. Eventually, a group of about 50 people dressed in tunics were ready to peacefully walk out as "medics and press".

One source said that the undercover agent had slipped away from the group and called his contact outside. This was actually easier than you might think. The university was a mass of classrooms scattered across a dozen buildings on multiple levels — it was not difficult to find a quiet spot to make a phone call or use a walkie talkie.

The word quickly ran through the line of officers outside: a line of people wearing medic or press tunics is going to appear from Exit Y. They are NOT the real thing.

Watchers reported that a group of people in medic and press tunics appeared at the exit and walked towards the waiting police officers. Skeptical officers started questioning them. Each reporter was asked for a press card with a picture on it, and each "medic" was asked simple medical questions.

But in fact, this was barely necessary, at least on the medics' side. It was plain to everyone that some of these were definitely the sullen, wall-eyed male radicals at the front of the protests, not the rather mousy medics who lurked in the background.

After the questions were asked, several of the so-called medics seemed to have no knowledge of even the most basic principles of first aid.

But of course that was not the story the world heard.

Within minutes, social and other media outlets were telling the world that "doctors and nurses" had been arrested by police in a fresh outrage.

An eccentric Hong Kong doctor named Darren Mann contacted the press and criticized the police for treating medical personnel like terrorists: "The arrest of personnel is almost unheard of in civilised countries and is incompatible with the compact of humanitarianism."

But while the version of events by people like him dominated the news cycle around the world, people physically present at the scene could see that the allegation that doctors and nurses had been arrested was clearly wrong.

The nursing profession is now limited to graduate entry only, and the youngest fully qualified doctors tend to be between 26 and 30.

CHAPTER 40

"We've Trapped Ourselves"

In Which Sporadic Escapes Are Attempted—
Finally, The Best Outcome Is Achieved

INSIDE THE CITY block campus, many protesters stayed up most of Sunday night, realizing that they had got themselves into a terrible situation.

Many of them sat in clusters, formulating escape plans.

The odd thing was that since the campus was surprisingly large, it was easy to wander off and find yourself completely and frighteningly alone, as if everyone else had run off.

But eventually, everyone found themselves a cluster of friends, and each group had a different escape plan.

* * *

Early on Monday morning, a group of about 20 protesters tried to escape by running along the railway tracks that ran alongside the university on Hong Chong Road, behind university blocks U and Y.

Police managed to capture some of them—some sources say it was about half. Others made it to the Hung Hom residential area and disappeared.

Everyone else remained inside at that time.

As full daylight spread across the campus on the morning of Monday, November 18, the video made by Teng Jin-guang, president of Polytechnic University, was published onto YouTube, and reporters and radicals watched it on their phones. It was short, just over a minute long.

In it, he urged everyone to leave the university. He said that he had spoken to police and wanted calm to prevail: "If the protesters do not initiate the use of force, the police will not initiate the use of force."

He urged protesters to leave peacefully and added that he would personally "accompany any student to the police station and ensure their case will be fairly processed".

This was a sincere pledge. The police had told him that very few of the radicals were his students—and he may well have time to accompany all of those who were to the station.

But would anyone else surrender peacefully?

That morning, it seemed unlikely. As the hours continued, there were numerous escape attempts.

Groups tried to climb out over walls, or through delivery entrances, or through holes in the fencing. There were at least five break-out attempts between 8 am and 2 pm on that Monday, some of which were "covered" by people behind them throwing petrol bombs to distract police.

In all cases, police managed to avoid major harm and intercept the escapees. Sometimes, the radicals turned back and returned inside. In other cases, police caught and arrested them.

There was one furious battle in which a radical who was struggling violently was caught, and one angry officer dragged him along the ground and put his foot on the man's head. Predictably, that image was quickly appeared in the press around the world as "another" shocking example of "police brutality".

The actual modus operandi of the police force—a long game of patience—was not really covered at all. It was like being on a film set: long hours of waiting, and then a brief period of drama, and then another long period of waiting.

One big group, numbering 80 to 100 people, tried to escape onto Cheung Wan Road, at the Exit A main entrance of the university, at about 2 pm. But police arrested many of them, while others ran back inside.

* * *

By Monday evening, the scene had quietened, and was becoming surreal.

Police were broadcasting songs in an attempt to lighten the mood and break the deadlock. They had picked some surprisingly witty choices, including Hacken Lee Hak-kan's Farewell to Campus and a classic piece of Chinese music, Ambushed From All Sides.

It may have worked. About half an hour later, at about 7.30 pm, ten protesters, looking rather worse for wear, walked out and surrendered to police—where they were quickly sent for medical care.

Rather more bizarrely, a group of protesters from outside the siege appeared at the bus station area and unexpectedly tried to rush INTO the university — a few succeeded, while others were arrested.

At about 9 pm that night, one of the most visually dramatic attempts to escape took place. A few protesters lowered ropes down from the footbridge over Chatham Road and rappelled downwards.

Their comrades, on motorbikes, drove at high speed to the spot to pick them up. In the event, only about three and four managed to escape by this method, as police reacted quickly and stopped the operation—but still, that handful of people had made a dramatic escape that ensured them a place in the history books, and provided colorful images for the media.

From the outside, various Hong Kong grandees had asked to enter the university to try to affect a peaceful surrender. Most were refused permission, but others were taken more seriously.

One of the more successful forays in that direction took place on Monday evening. A team of three people entered: the university's council chairman Lam Tai-fai, a law professor named Eric Cheung Tat-ming, and a well-known politician named Jasper Tsang Yok-sing.

After discussions with this trio, many of the young people agreed to end the occupation.

Those who were 18 or over were formally arrested. But for the many minors who surrendered, legal processes were deliberately delayed for humanitarian reasons and they were allowed to leave with their school principals or parents.

My heart broke when watching one painful scene in the campus that was captured on camera. Adults (presumably parents or teachers) were gently drawing a teenage boy away from the crowd of radicals. Suddenly a larger young man, who is angry, tries to persuade him to stay, and physically grabs at him, clutching at his arm.

The child looks torn, but chooses to leave with the adults. Even in the fuzzy image, you can feel the misery on all sides.

* * *

Late on Monday night, instructions were received from the committee to the people remaining inside and university and all the supporters in various locations outside: "Besiege Wei to rescue Zhao".

Oh no. Police who intercepted the message knew what that meant: Big trouble elsewhere.

As mentioned earlier, this was a technique in which trouble is created at a different location to thin out a besieging force.

And so it started. From late that Monday evening until the early hours of Tuesday, November 19, battles broke out all over the nearby Yau Ma Tei and Jordan areas.

The plan was to create maximum mayhem close enough to the university so that police surrounding it would be called away to tackle it. This would weaken the force watching the university, allowing the remaining radicals to escape.

The attacking force, who appeared to be about 1,000 in number, were split into multiple small groups, and showered police officers with bricks and rods.

Almost 1,000 petrol bombs were thrown, with several causing premises to catch fire.

Police, ambulance and fire service staff were soon working flat out.

The Hung Hom branch of Standard Chartered Bank was set on fire by men dressed in black, despite the fact that it had no connection with mainland China.

"Excuse me, but we're a British bank, founded by a Scotsman in India," a customer told me via a message after the news spread. "Hands off."

By the early hours of Tuesday morning, 213 radicals had been arrested for violent crimes against people or property.

And the officers waiting patiently outside Polytechnic University? Enough of them remained in place to stop the plan from working.

Police were working multiple shifts and impossibly long hours, but this was too big an opportunity to miss.

The motherlode of violent radicals was right here—if they managed to arrest them, they were convinced that the violence level would fall dramatically.

That was the goal: to get everyone out of the university, with nobody hurt or killed — and bring peace back to our community.

* * *

And me? I was still on the outside, looking in, and musing on the problems. Not everyone was helping. Pandem supporters had been gathering supplies which they wanted to smuggle into the campus to extend the occupation — a move that would simply extend the misery of these unfortunate young people.

A politician and a bishop turned up at the scene. Fernando Cheung of the Labour Party and Joseph Ha, Auxiliary Bishop, asked the police to step back and let the remaining radicals go.

Police officers patiently explained that no law-abiding society allowed individuals to try to kill people, run a bomb factory and destroy major pieces of public infrastructure—and then walk away, free to try again another day. The law doesn't work that way.

Besides, the key point was that the police *were* ending the occupation peacefully. You could see that if you opened your eyes. The police were not attacking the radicals inside in any way. No one was being harmed. They were simply waiting for them to peacefully come out, and hundreds of people had done so. The right thing to do was encourage the rest to follow.

The bishop and the politician, gently schooled, backed off.

* * *

On my phone, I saw a message from reader TF Liang, who said: "A friend who lives in Paris said: 'Even the French, who are the kings of going on strike, cannot fathom the Hong Kong riots.' "

It did seem to be unfathomable, if you read the mainstream media. Many in the media and in politics were spinning the story to turn it upside down, making villains of the Hong Kong people's legitimate attempts to arrest violent radicals who had holed themselves up in their own bomb factory with children they had radicalized.

As I was writing this note, the media quoted a member of a group called Protest The Children speaking on behalf of the radicals inside, saying: "The reason we are staying here is that police are not letting us out."

This was, of course, the opposite of the truth. Police had been asking people to leave peacefully since the weekend.

"Hong Kong police are creating a humanitarian crisis inside PolyU," a student union leader told one newspaper, which dutifully printed the quote as if it made sense.

In truth, those of us who were there could see that the police had never stopped inviting the youngsters to come out. The ones who did emerge were checked by people who really were trained in medical care and the ones who needed further care were sent to hospitals. Younger ones who were put into the custody of their own families.

But of course, none of this was being reported by the media.

I stood at a distance, thinking about responsibility and the misuse of the power of stories.

These people—the bishop, the politicians, the media—are teaching our young that any action, however violent, illegal or harmful it is, is allowable if you have the right excuse.

In this case, the excuses started off as "the guy who owns this shop came from China" or "they told me that I needed to fight to separate Hong Kong from China". Now it had changed to wild allegations that "police murdered many people and we must all fight to the death as revenge".

The truth is that responsibility is one of the most important qualities any human being develops. Until the moment you start to take responsibility for your own actions, your life is not your own—it belongs to other people.

* * *

On that long Tuesday, November 19, more than 600 hold-outs at the university surrendered, mostly peacefully—and police were shocked to find that the majority of them were teenagers, with quite a few of them aged under 18.

About half of them were deemed to need medical care, and police sent about 280 to 12 public hospitals for check-ups.

The youngsters, who were clearly glad that the occupation was over, told the police that there were very few left inside—maybe 100 or so at the most.

Then my phone beeped and I got a call from one of my most knowledgeable financial sources.

"It's over. We just pulled the plug," he said.

"I know," I responded. "I'm outside PolyU right now. Hundreds are coming out peacefully. It seems to be over."

"No," he replied. "I'm not talking about that."

"So, what, then?"

"We found the huge stash of money financing the protests. Or one of them, anyway. HSBC just closed it down. There's going to be nothing left to pay the protesters' salaries. The committee is fucked. It's over."

Interesting. I headed to Central to hear more.

EPILOGUE

Regaining Our Equilibrium

In Which The World Continues To Change Gently, And Few People Notice

HONG KONG HAD BEEN holding its breath for two weeks but let out a sigh of relief that seemed to last for months.

The majority of the hold-outs at Polytechnic University ended their occupation peacefully on Tuesday, 19 November. Almost 700 had walked out by the end of the day, and police reunited most with their parents, who took them home. The ones who were sent for hospital check ups were found to need rest and decent food, but none of them were found to have been seriously harmed.

Out of about 1,600 occupiers, only 46 had any relation to the university itself.

On that day, while individuals trying to whip up anger reported that large scale atrocities were continuing, people at the scene could see that the whole thing was winding down peacefully, exactly as police and other witnesses at the scene had dared to hope.

Safety officers had then gone in to the university–staff and students were not allowed to enter–and reported back on what they found. Inside were more than 4,000 Molotov cocktails.

More worryingly, about 600 petrol bombs had been found tied to portable propane canisters, and could have caused many lives to be lost.

A week earlier, many journalists had commented on the impressive amounts of food at the university canteen in the Communal Building during the height of the occupation. But in those following days, it had become obvious that no had done any cleaning, and the place was crawling with flies and maggots. One particular sink was just a writhing mess of pupae. "They didn't manage to generate enough democracy to decide who should do the washing up," sighed Tom Guendert, looking at the images.

Most scarily, there were rumors that some radicals had tried to escape through the sewer systems and got lost or trapped there. Emergency workers had gone into the drains and search for a couple of hours to see if it was true—not one of the nicest jobs in town. Happily it turned out to be false.

Other dark rumors were true. Some of the buildings were badly damaged. Not only had the glass walls been smashed, but a huge conflagration had been lit, leaving many of the red brick walls scorched. It was a miracle that the whole university hadn't been burned to a cinder, security officers said.

Some of the scientists had been escorted to their labs—and reported that large amounts of chemicals had been stolen. Some were clearly dangerous, easy to use to make explosives or chemical bombs. Many were toxic or corrosive or highly flammable, and most could be used in lethal ways.

A stash of explosive material would be found in an abandoned school building the following year.

* * *

Elsewhere in the city from that Tuesday onwards, the "love Hong Kong" movement came out in force, giving a much needed bit of TLC to the city's streets. Everybody was doing it. Young and old, local and foreign, rich and poor—the adopt-a-brick movement was springing up everywhere.

A reader forwarded me a picture snapped on her smart phone. The slim, white-haired gentleman spotted dismantling brick barricades was none other than Robert Ng, billionaire chairman of Sino Group.

It wasn't just a publicity stunt—he and his children were already known for getting actively involved in rebuilding campaigns. And none of the images were professional ones arranged by PR people, but just random ones taken by someone with a phone standing nearby.

Financier Nick Wong said he had now become a regular street cleaner, up early every morning to clear the barricades near Jordan.

"I never thought I'd be a trash man," he said.

Reader Gin Leung later told me that Douglas Woo, chairman of Wheelock, was also seen doing the same thing.

He was spotted with his jacket off, lugging bricks and wooden pallets off the road.

I wonder if we can get ALL the tycoons to dress in overalls and sweep the streets.

I would pay to watch that.

* * *

And across the water on Hong Kong Island? On Friday, November 22, staff at the coffee shop in Exchange Square above the Stock Exchange were busy again.

At mid-morning, Ashley, the manager, came out from behind the counter and approached the tables. Instead of ushering us out as she had been doing in recent days, she smiled and said: "We're not going to close. We're going to stay open, see what happens."

Yay! We all went to the counter for another round of cappuccinos and cold brews and hibiscus teas (Oh, what hipsters we were).

At about 12.30 pm that day, a tiny group of die-hard protesters gathered outside to shout "Five demands! Not one less!"

But members of the public just walked past. People had had enough.

* * *

In the media, some international journalists had by now seen through the false narrative planted by the pro-revolutionary groups attempting to engineer a coup.

Australian journalist Hedley Thomas said he had phoned a lawyer friend in Hong Kong—and found himself being shouted at.

"You're a journalist and you guys are responsible for a lot of this now!" the lawyer yelled. "Every camera is pointed in one direction to paint this false narrative of the police as brutal bastards and the protesters as heroic democrats with a noble cause."

Hedley did some reading and decided the lawyer was right to complain.

Black-shirt members set one man on fire and killed another with a brick but bizarrely "the protesters have suffered little damage to their brand", he said, amazed.

US journalist Rania Khalek made a similar mental journey.

She made a map of protesters whom the international media presented positively—and then compared them with a map of the geo-political interests of the US and allies.

It was a perfect match.

Black-clad gangs in Hong Kong "are guaranteed the hero treatment in the US media," she concluded. And that was true "no matter how much violence you inflict".

Gradually, an increasing number of commentators started to mention the huge gulf between the superficial story in the media and the complexity of the real situation.

"If activists here in the US were to use methods that Hong Kong students have been using–shooting at cops with arrows and flaming arrows, and tossing hundreds of water bottle 'Molotov cocktails' and burning police vans–there'd be a massacre," wrote Dave Lindorff of CounterPunch.

My network was soon in a positive mood. Father of two Mark Steven Yong said he had thought pigs would fly before the Western media gave a balanced view. "But now I can see a pig gaily flying past my window. Hurrah!" he said.

Over in the courts, Hong Kong judge Russell Coleman scolded the international media for using words such as "protesters" and "pro-democracy activists" for people who were quite clearly vandals and arsonists. "Persons who commit such crimes are simply, and properly described as, 'criminals'," he said. Their political allegiance should be irrelevant. But that's only true if you genuinely care about presenting a fair and balanced view, of course. Many in the Western media didn't, the people of Hong Kong had discovered.

These journalists, and let's be honest, many of us in Hong Kong too, had become witting or unwitting participants in a grand deception. A reader named Siulan Law summed it up: "What happened in Hong Kong was a secret service orchestrated finale involving both conscious and unconscious assets of the CIA."

* * *

Gradually, details of the stories behind the stories began to leak out.

While we were all sad to hear that a number of people had been hurt by the firebombs thrown by protesters, we were surprised to learn who the victims were. "Most were the throwers themselves or their friends," said our source in a hospital.

Confirmation of this came from a video-collecting reader who said that were now more clips of protesters accidentally setting themselves or their friends alight than there were of petrol bombs hitting police officers.

In the violent days of November "at least six protesters had set themselves on fire," he added.

A reader from a military background, who did not want his name printed, said that what baffled him was the continual portrayal of tear gas as being far, far worse than firebombs. In fact, there was no comparison. Tear gas was used by police forces all over the world because it caused itchy eyes and a runny nose for about 30 minutes but no long-term harm. It had been developed and popularized in the West for precisely those reasons.

Petrol bombs, in contrast, were potentially deadly weapons, and use of them attracted life sentences in some Western countries. Similarly, large objects dropped from footbridges onto moving traffic and numerous cases of items placed on railway tracks: these could have caused horrendous accidents indeed. The perpetrators would have faced serious charges in Western countries, but the media considered these acts not worth mentioning.

Similarly, the use of laser pointers to burn people's retinas in Hong Kong was downplayed as nothing: The UK's Guardian newspaper gave their coverage a dismissive, sarcastic headline referring to "an offensive weapon, also known as a laser pointer".

But the following year, the same newspaper would report that a man was arrested in Seattle for shining a laser pointer into a police officer's eyes, and other media would add that more than 100 US police officers had been hurt by the devices.

In Hong Kong, the district board election went smoothly on Sunday, November 24. The pandems got more votes than the other side, and of course the international media reported it in a way that reinforced the Big Lie, that "Hong Kong" was a monolithic group of people who hate China and hate their own government.

"The silent majority have spoken," said "yellow camp" writer Anthony Dapiran, a lawyer.

In fact, they clearly hadn't. The results were not a huge surprise, and the actual results were somewhat disappointing for the pandems. Normally, during periods of unrest, they get a solid 60 percent of the vote, and this year, some of their members were saying it would jump to 70 percent. In the event, it was 57 percent, despite the almost total support for their side from the local and international media, and commentators like Dapiran.

And more importantly, the total number of voters was just 2.94 million—which meant that fewer than half the 6.5 million adults in Hong Kong voted. The apoliticals had clearly remained silent.

The news of the pandem group's win was carried by the Western media with undisguised glee. Awkward facts such as the news that the winning team's supporters had earlier smashed up 30 offices belonging to other political parties–well, no one found space to include that.

But Hong Kong's quiet majority cheered up at the thought of young rebels doing District Councillor duties. The job would be an excellent education.

"It's hard work," said Joyce Chan. "Chanting slogans won't satisfy the residents."

Peter Bentley agreed. "It's not about shouting 'liberation of our time' at meetings."

They'd have to get MTR stations back in shape, repair wrecked pavements, and protect their local restaurants from "renovation".

But that wouldn't be the toughest aspect of the job.

"District Board meetings are the worst," said reader Keith McNab, who had endured several. "The councilors have the most mind-numbingly boring job I can imagine. It won't be as exciting as rampaging through the streets."

In the event, some of the new district councilors from the pandem side openly announced that they would not be using their share of the public purse to serve the people of their districts, but only the individuals who had supported them. This neatly revealed that several of the people labeled "pro-democracy" for the past six months had not the slightest interest in it. They were in for the money and power, and didn't mind admitting it.

* * *

A week after the peaceful end of the PolyU occupation, the feeling that Hong Kong had emerged from a dark period of violence into a sunnier place spread further. The 108 bus driver in North Point was back in action — and he was smiling, happy to be back on the job.

The Cross Harbour Tunnel re-opened at 5 am that morning, a hugely symbolic act of recovery. I never thought I'd be so happy to see a huge traffic jam of double-decker buses.

On the LIHKG online black-shirt forum, a schedule of civil disobedience events was distributed.

MONDAY: Mass rescue of the "group of brave brothers" alleged to be still hidden at Polytechnic University;

WEDNESDAY: Hong Kong-wide general strike;

ALL WEEK: Preparation for massive operation to block Hong Kong airport on coming weekend.

But here's the key point: apart from lightly attended pandem lunch-time protests, none of the scheduled protests happened.

There were no gatherings. There was no arson. Nobody "renovated" restaurants or set fire to banks. The offices of democratically elected politicians were not trashed.

That morning, I took the 108 bus through Causeway Bay and into the harbor tunnel to reach Polytechnic University on the Kowloon peninsula.

The campus was a ghost town. A languid young man had been spotted on Tuesday morning, and a sleepy teenage girl was found in the student union, but there was no "group of brave brothers."

* * *

And of course people began to realize the truth about the money. Over the next few months, numerous groups were found to have set up accounts for the protests. The HSBC account, named Spark Alliance HK, was frozen in November. At the time, it contained more than HK$70 million (US$9 million). Police said the account was used to pay multiple protesters for participation, many of whom were young, just teenagers.

In one case, a young man of 18 years old, an employed youth accused by police of being a drug trafficker—the arrest had revealed stashes of ketamine, cocaine and cannabis—was found to have been paid several amounts of money from the account.

His "earnings" for being a radical protester for a period of a few weeks between October and November amounted to HK$48,000 (US$6,200).

This was good money. For purposes of camparison, the average monthly wage in Hong Kong at the time was HK$18,000.

They also found evidence of long-range planning. That account had been set up in 2016, after the Mong Kok riots. At least part of the money came from crowd-funding, but other sources were hard to trace.

During the arrests related to that particular case, police seized a total of HK$130,000 in cash. They also found a receipt for HK$165,000 spent on a variety of items, including helmets, gas masks, laser pointers and arrows.

One of the people behind the account, police said, was a 50-year-old man who had spent some of the cash on personal financial savings plans for his own benefit.

But there were other funds too—including, police would later reveal, a HK$10 million fund from "foreign sources" reportedly linked to Jimmy Lai, publisher of Apple Daily.

In addition to the NED money, there were numerous other secret cash streams from the United States, including a "rapid response fund" and a technology fund.

While it sounds innocent enough at the American end to say that the cash was being sent to Hong Kong to promote democracy, reality was very different. The protests were developing into a clear case of radicalized terrorism.

At first, reviews of what had happened left people stunned at the astounding amounts of needless harm done.

The damage to the MTR alone was estimated at HK$1.6 billion (US$206 million).

Engineers said the length of metal public safety railings ripped up to be turned into improvised weapons or barricades was more than 60 kilometers.

The repair bill for my university alone, PolyU, came to HK$700 million.

The total bill for setting the city back to rights was beyond calculation, with numerous shops burned, cars destroyed, businesses closed and offices trashed.

But that's just money.

Far worse was the damage to society, which lost its crown as one of the most peaceful places on earth, and was now riven by anger and hostility.

During the period covered by this book, there were at least 14 cases in which protesters were found to have been handling explosives, including tri-acetone tri-peroxide, an explosive used in tragic large-scale terrorism cases in Sri Lanka and London.

The behavior of the Hong Kong police was hardly flawless, but when put in context with other forces dealing with other riots around the world, it was actually impressive.

Facing similar mass riots elsewhere on the planet, police forces quickly stepped back to let the army take over, and numerous deaths resulted. But the Hong Kong police worked hard with two goals in mind–to minimize potential deaths or harm, and to bring the insurrection to an end without the need to call in the army. Against the odds, it succeeded in both cases.

But the attempts to blacken the name of the Hong Kong police were so comprehensive and successful that in the summer of 2020, Lord David Alton's staff were still working to try to create lawsuits against Hong Kong officers with British nationality.

Others, closer to the action, had a different reaction. Grenville Cross, one of Hong Kong's most respected lawyers, wrote: "The era of lawlessness which erupted on June 9 last year is coming to an end, and Hong Kong is again becoming a safe city in which to live and work. In good times and bad, the police force has heroically protected Hong Kong against those who wished to harm it, and its officers are owed a debt of gratitude, not only by the people of Hong Kong, but also by the nation as a whole."

Although the debate didn't end, that middle week of November was the end of the series of radical protests in a real sense. (I won my bet.) There were still spasmodic protests over the next few months, but they were small: rarely attracting more than 100 people, and often far fewer. One shopping mall protest had four individuals, another had a single individual.

Hong Kong was no longer a place of petrol bombs and tear gas. The violence was gone, as were, thank goodness, the "renovations".

There were terrifying leaked stories about future planned attacks, such as the preparation of IEDs (improvised explosive devices) from a Taiwan cell for later use, but these, if used, would be part of a later attempted revolution, not the one this book covers.

The rise of Covid-19 eventually ensured that nobody wanted large-scale gatherings of any kind, but by February of 2020, we'd already had two months of relative peace.

* * *

Nine thousand kilometers away, Benedict Rogers of Hong Kong Watch continued to paint nightmarish pictures of this city as an oppressed hellhole, but they were too extreme for anyone to believe except UK parliamentarians and the people who spend their time writing "news" on Twitter.

Just before Christmas, Rogers shared a picture of a little girl in a Santa Claus outfit facing Hong Kong police officers to remind the world of the horror faced here.

"Let's work for a world in which no child anywhere has to experience this at any time," he wrote.

Unfortunately for him, Hong Kong people shared the rest of the pictures from that set, showing that the child was not being menaced by the police, but quite the opposite—she and her family wanted to pose with the brave officers who had kept the peace.

So in truth, people *should* work for a world in which each and every child can experience what that child encountered in Hong Kong: a scene in which the police and the public work together to create a peaceful community.

* * *

Also in December, local Hong Kong people told me the shocking truth about Kong Tsung-gan, who presented himself as a local-born citizen and was quoted in numerous Western media outlets, including the Washington Post, the UK Guardian, France24, the New York Times, Deutsche Welle (a major German news station) and many others.

He was, they claimed, a fair-haired Caucasian former Amnesty International staff member from Louisiana in the United States. His real name was Brian P. Kern.

I put the truth into my column in The Standard, and the website which hosted him, Hong Kong Free Press, threatened to sue the newspaper and get us blacklisted from all the major journalistic organizations around the world. The newspaper's editor, Ivan Tong, declined to remove the story from the newspaper website or archives.

The threatened lawsuit never appeared.

As mentioned earlier, we found Kong Tsung-gan's name, books and columns highlighted in the website of Canvas, the Serbian group specializing in helping topple governments.

In the first week of December, a group of heavily tattoed young men known to have been involved with Azov, a far right neo-Nazi group in the Ukraine, arrived in Hong Kong.

The administrator of the Free Hong Kong Center, the Ukraine-Hong Kong group on Facebook, explained that they were no longer neo-Nazis and were just here for tourism.

Some local people welcomed them. "I mean, they are not associated with Azok now, why not accept them as fellow freedom fighters?" wrote Hui Ho Ching on the Facebook page.

Others were more skeptical: "Omg u ppl are gullible, there are Nazis with actual nazi symbols tattoed on their bodies. But of course since they support ur cause all is neatly forgotten or ignored," wrote John Huang.

The four visitors said they were no longer associated with Azov, and now belonged to Gonor, an organization which provided masterclasses in street protests.

However, the Hong Kong protests had largely dissolved by then, so there really was nothing for the visitors to do—except some actual tourism.

* * *

In the summer of 2020, after discussions involving 200 Hong Kong people, Beijing passed the National Security Law for our city, dropping it on our heads fully formed, with no chance of amendment.

The international press reported that it had killed freedom of the press and "has in effect ended the autonomy promised under the 'one country, two systems' arrangements that was supposed to pertain in Hong Kong until 2047", according to the Economist.

These reports were the opposite of the truth, and could be disproved in five seconds flat. Hong Kong websites were still full of energetic criticism of China, cartoons of Xi Jinping proliferated, and I continued to make jokes and memes about our leaders, just to see if I could. (I could.)

Anti-China papers like Apple Daily were still published every day, and, if anything, attacked the Beijing leadership more vehemently.

To people in Hong Kong, it was obvious that the law hadn't killed the free press, but was targeted at the underground subversives attempting to overthrow the government.

But the mainstream media did not and could not cover this angle, as it would expose the truth, which is that they had been fooled by a subversive committee of pro-US people and agents from the revolution industry from day one. So they simply didn't go near the real story.

* * *

The "yellow camp" continued to get all the positive attention from the international media, but was riven by internal disagreements. To take one example, there was continuous trouble at Hong Kong's Lung Mun Café chain, an important center for the radical protesters. The goings-on therein could inspire a whole mini-series.

At first, the cafe chain became famous for denouncing the police and attracting a huge clientele of anti-government protesters.

Then there were some mysterious attacks on the premises, followed by a series of furious arguments between the restaurant boss and other "yellow camp" fundraisers over the placement of large donations. Where had the cash gone? In the summer of 2020, the café's staff announced it was "leaving the yellow economic circle".

This was followed by an attack on a staff member at the Tsim Sha Tsui branch. After spending the best part of a year badmouthing law enforcers, what did the staff do? They called the police and demanded that officers protect them from their "enemies".

The silencing of voices telling the other side of the story has continued. Hong Kong independence campaigners set up a group on the Telegram app to remove from social media anyone who had criticized them or said anything positive about the government or revealed the existence of the Hong Kong subversives' relationship with America's revolution industry.

The group, called the Wumao Central Settlement Zone, listed names of people who have dared to depart from the media narrative. ("Wumao" is a term that implies "paid commentators" from the Communist Party of China.) Every day, zone members were required to file a certain number of complaints with social media administrators in a bid to get people silenced.

"It's basically a co-ordinated effort to de-platform people," said a reader who wanted his name printed only as Lok.

Zone members also acted as a propaganda unit, required to do daily duties of retweeting or upvoting positive references to the protesters.

Silencing of critics? Propaganda unit?

Funny how people at one extreme are EXACTLY like people at the opposite extreme.

* * *

In the 1990s, the Western media confidently predicted the death of Hong Kong numerous times. They got it wrong. Every. Single. Time. Those same headlines returned this year, and are going to be just as wrong again.

I'm going to finish with an anecdote from today's Standard newspaper.

Today, the apolitical Hong Kong business community is obediently siding with conservatives on the topic of law and order and stability.

Yet at the same time, it is ramping up advertising of overseas properties, to take full advantage of those who wish to flee.

Their attitude can be summed up like this: "Don't worry, everybody, there is not the slightest need for you to leave Hong Kong." [Pulls brochure out of inside jacket pocket.] "But if you feel you really want to, check out these cool condos in Malaysia."

It's a funny, practical, pragmatic approach to life – and perfectly illustrates the unique Hong Kong approach to politics: Instead of getting uptight, make the best of every situation.

Live. Thrive. Rise. Don't let negativity hold you back. Feed your children and carry on moving onwards and upwards.

This is the Hong Kong way.

Made in the USA
Coppell, TX
27 July 2021

59557975R00266